Islam and New Kinship

Fertility, Reproduction and Sexuality

GENERAL EDITORS:
David Parkin, Fellow of All Souls College, University of Oxford
Soraya Tremayne, Co-ordinating Director of the Fertility and Reproduction Studies Group and Research Associate at the Institute of Social and Cultural Anthropology, University of Oxford, and a Vice-President of the Royal Anthropological Institute
Marcia Inhorn, William K. Lanman Jr. Professor of Anthropology and International Affairs, and Chair of the Council on Middle East Studies, Yale University

ISLAM AND NEW KINSHIP
REPRODUCTIVE TECHNOLOGY AND THE SHARIAH IN LEBANON

Morgan Clarke

Berghahn Books
New York • Oxford

Published in 2009 by
Berghahn Books
www.berghahnbooks.com

©2009, 2011 Morgan Clarke
First paperback edition published in 2011

Library of Congress Cataloging-in-Publication Data

Clarke, Morgan, 1972-
  Islam and new kinship : reproductive technology and the shariah in
Lebanon/ Morgan Clarke.
    p. cm. -- (Fertility, reproduction and sexuality)
  Includes bibliographical references and index.
  ISBN 978-1-84545-432-6 (hbk) -- ISBN 978-0-85745-140-8 (pbk)
  1. Human reproduction (Islamic law)--Lebanon. 2. Reproductive rights--
Lebanon. I. Title.

  KBP2484.5.C53 2009
  344.569204'194--dc22

                          2008052935

British Library Cataloguing in Publication Data

A catalogue record for this book is available
from the British Library

ISBN 978-1-84545-432-6 (hardback)
ISBN 978-0-85745-140-8 (paperback)
ISBN 978-1-84545-923-9 (ebook)

To J., in apology for all the grumbling.

CONTENTS

ACKNOWLEDGEMENTS

The initial fieldwork on which this book is based took place in Lebanon in 2003–04. I have made many visits to Lebanon since, making new friends and incurring new debts in the course of new projects. Here I confine myself to thanking those who were instrumental in the writing of this book in particular. Another book will be needed to acknowledge what I owe to all those who have helped me since.

For their exceptionally generous efforts in helping my attempts to understand more of Islam in the course of what was my first major research project, I am very grateful to – in order of our acquaintance – Shaykh Muhsin ‘Atwi, Shaykh Muhammad Kana‘an, Shaykh Hasan Marmar and Shaykh Muhammad Dali Baltah. I had the privilege of an interview with Ayatollah Muhammad Husayn Fadlallah in 2004 and all the staff at his offices have been exceptionally helpful ever since: I must thank Hajj ‘Ali Sammour in particular here. I would also like to thank Shaykh Ahmad Darwish al-Kurdi for generous guidance that while not directly bearing on this work, has no doubt informed it and will inform others to come. I would also like to thank Shaykh Muhammad Tawfiq al-Muqdad, Archbishop George Khudr, Shaykh Amin al-Kurdi, Sayyid Haidar al-Hakim, Sayyid ‘Abd al-Karim Fadlallah, the offices of Ayatollah Sistani in Beirut and all the many other shaykhs and priests with whom I conversed in researching this book, too many to name in full here.

I am most deeply indebted to my friend and mentor Professor Talal Khodari of the Lebanese University for his inestimable assistance in helping me navigate the tricky waters of the Lebanese legal system and so much more besides. In this regard, Professor Ibrahim Traboulsi and Avocat à la

Cour Muhammad Jouhari were also most generous. Many medical specialists gave me invaluable assistance, as will be clear, but in the majority of cases I explicitly undertook at the time to preserve their anonymity. These debts are thus harder to acknowledge, but I owe much gratitude to all the doctors who talked to me. I can at least thank Dr Antoine Abu Musa for his comments on a version of the chapter on medical perspectives included here, and Dr Michel Abu 'Abdallah, who was kind enough to read a draft of the whole book, and who, along with Mrs Leena Sinno, most generously provided me with medical contacts. The Centre for Arab and Middle Eastern Studies at the American University of Beirut very kindly gave me a research associateship in 2003–04 and again in 2007–08. I must thank Dr Aliya Saidi for her efforts here. I am also grateful for the use of the library of al-Imam al-Ouzai College, Beirut. Many others contributed, including a number of lawyers and the staff of the religious institutions I visited, during my fieldwork proper, as well as during more recent visits; I must apologize for not naming them all individually. Any and all factual errors or poorly judged interpretations that may be found in this book are my own and are not to be attributed to any of those I have named here.

Turning closer to home, I would like to thank above all my doctoral supervisor at the University of Oxford, Paul Dresch, without whom none of this would have been possible. I am also heavily indebted to Judith Scheele for her patience in reading innumerable drafts of this work. I would also like to thank David Parkin and Soraya Tremayne for their support of the publication of this book, along with Robert Parkin and Geert van Gelder for their comments and suggestions at various points, as well as Janet Carsten and Marcia Inhorn for their critical contributions at different junctures and Peter Parkes, who has been an enthusiastic and generous correspondent over many years. My new colleagues at the Department of Social Anthropology at the University of Cambridge have been most welcoming, and I would like to thank especially my mentor James Laidlaw as well as Marilyn Strathern for their encouragement and assistance. Again, none of the above is in any way responsible for anything mistaken or ill judged that the reader might find here.

The research upon which this book is based was funded by an ESRC doctoral studentship; the final stages of the production of the book itself were undertaken during a British Academy postdoctoral fellowship: I am grateful to both organizations for their support. Finally, particular thanks are due to everyone at Berghahn Books for bringing the book to publication.

Many generous hosts have welcomed and helped me over the years, in Lebanon, Syria, Iran and elsewhere, too many to name individually here. But I would especially like to thank for their hospitality and friendship, again in order of acquaintance: Ghassan Youssef and his wife Fabienne, Saleh Youssef and all his family – and most especially, for many a feast, Muhammad and Munawwar – Feras Kotob and all his family, Dr Rashid Dihni, Shaykh Omar Jalloul, and last, but very far from least, Tom Perry. It is also a pleasure to make good a promise to thank Abu 'Ali for his tea, which is indeed delicious. Finally, I would like to remember here my late teacher of Arabic and friend Sayyid Nizar Fadlallah, whose patient, if vigorous instruction, I will miss very much. The most generous host of all has been my mother, Dr Joan Morgan. Thank you to you all.

My fieldwork (2003–04) started shortly after the American and allied invasion of Iraq. I left just before yet another traumatic period in Lebanese history: the assassination of Rafiq Hariri on Valentine's Day 2005, the Syrian withdrawal from Lebanon followed by a further wave of assassinations, a war with Israel in the summer of 2006 and a continuing struggle between Hezbollah and other local political actors fuelled by outside interests and powers. Another stay in 2007 came at a time of further bombings, assassinations and the prolonged fighting at the Nahr al-Barid Palestinian refugee camp; 2008 saw more killings and major political upheavals whose consequences are yet to be fully played out. On a more personal note, I made a short visit in 2006, just before the war with Israel, to find that someone who had been kind enough to assist me, and indeed become a friend, had since been killed for the sake of another's *amour propre*. If my research often seemed to me trivial by comparison at the time of my fieldwork, it does so still more now. If writing books does have any power to do good in the world, I profoundly regret that this one will do so little for those who helped so much in its writing.

NOTE ON TRANSLITERATION

I have followed standard conventions for transliterating Arabic, albeit in a simplified form. Long vowels are indicated by a macron (e.g. ā). *'ayn* is indicated by an opening quotation mark ('), *hamza* by a closing one ('). Emphatic consonants have not been indicated in the main text. They are, however, marked in the glossary of frequently employed Arabic terms, where they are indicated by subscript points (e.g. ḥ). *Tā' marbūtah* is indicated with a final *–h,* or *–t* in *idāfah*. Transliterations of Arabic words in citations have been altered to maintain consistency. Words in common usage in English are not italicized and are given largely standard spellings (e.g. 'shariah', 'Quran', 'hijab', 'fatwa', 'mufti', 'ayatollah'; I prefer 'shaykh' to 'sheikh'). Names of people, places and organizations are not given diacritical marks, and I have often used conventional spellings (e.g. 'Beirut', 'Hezbollah', 'Fadlallah' rather than 'Fadl Allah'). For the Quran, I have usually used Dawood's (1990) translation. Otherwise, all translations from Arabic and French are my own, except where indicated.

ABBREVIATIONS

AI   artificial insemination.

AID   artificial insemination by donor.

AIH   artificial insemination by husband.

ART   artificial reproductive technologies.

DI   donor insemination.

ET   embryo transfer.

FBD   father's brother's daughter, as in 'FBD marriage' (also 'patriparallel cousin marriage').

HFEA (British) Human Fertilisation and Embryology Authority.

HFEB (British) Human Fertilisation and Embryology Bill.

HLA   human leukocyte antigens [testing] (used to match potential organ donors and recipients and as a form of paternity testing).

ICSI   intracytoplasmic sperm injection (a variant of IVF treatment, where the sperm is injected into the egg through 'micro-manipulation' under a high-powered microscope).

IVF   in vitro fertilization.

NRT   new reproductive technologies.

OIC   Organisation of the Islamic Conference.

PGD   pre-implantation genetic diagnosis.

STD   sexually transmitted disease.

INTRODUCTION

In Spring 2007, I was sitting on a sofa in the lounge of the home of a distinguished Shiite religious scholar in the southern suburbs of Beirut. Books and papers, escaping from the over-flowing book-cases, lay piled on the table in front of me. The uppermost caught my eye: an Arabic translation of David Harvey's *The condition of post-modernity,* a photocopy of Foucault's *Power/knowledge* in English, an issue of an Arabic literary periodical devoted to deconstruction-ism, a book on *Muhammad, the prophet of peace.* But I had come to discuss the author's latest work, a slim volume dedicated to the Is-lamic legal problems raised by new reproductive technologies such as in vitro fertilization (IVF). We sat and chatted over tea, running through issues such as whether, as the husband of an infertile wife, one should marry an egg donor to ensure that a procedure using her egg was not adulterous, or whether a surrogate mother could be seen as analogous to a 'milk mother', the wet-nurse who is awarded, in Is-lamic law, some of the rights of a mother proper. These are not hy-pothetical questions: 'I get so many telephone calls about this', the shaykh told me. 'Can I use my wife's sister's egg? If I can't carry a child, could my mother carry it for me?'

This book is about many such conversations, about how Islamic legal scholars have dealt with the dilemmas posed by these new medical treatments and scientific understandings, and how they have reconciled traditional understandings of the family and kinship with the radical challenges such new techniques imply. These debates constitute a lively and rich case study as to how these religious specialists 'keep up with the times', as local rhetoric has it, one that gives special insight into the dialectic between these living traditions and those of liberal, Western moral thinking, within which these developments have been equally keenly debated. Of course, Islamic legal scholarship is neither produced nor consumed in a vacuum, and these discussions are firmly situated in the context where they were researched, Lebanon, whose religious diversity and legal pluralism added immeasurably to the breadth of the research. Both Sunni and Shiite Muslim debates, in themselves highly diverse, are explored here. The initial, core fieldwork was carried out in 2003–04, the 'ethnographic present' here, with further visits in 2006, 2007 and 2008, with the Islamic legal scholars themselves in their homes and offices, and in Lebanon's religious law courts. Other, different voices were also heard: most importantly, extensive interviews were conducted with Lebanese medical practitioners working in the field of assisted reproduction.

I am an anthropologist, and these themes are powerfully suggestive of wider, comparative issues: kinship has been more or less central to the discipline since its very beginnings, and the furore provoked by the advent of IVF itself led to a vigorous renaissance of kinship studies – 'new kinship'. This project originally grew out of an earlier interest in some of the more recondite areas of the anthropology of the Middle East, concerning kinship in particular, and it was the work of the French anthropologist Édouard Conte that provided illumination into how I might make my own contribution. In the course of a discussion of what he sees as a suppressed 'feminine part' to 'Arab kinship', Conte (2000b: 297–302) refers to the findings of a colloquium organized by the Jordanian Society for Islamic Medical Sciences on the theme of 'Contemporary medical affairs in the light of the Islamic shariah'. In the case of surrogate motherhood, it was ruled that it is the birth mother to whom maternity should be assigned rather than the egg donor: it is the nurturing role that is seen to be key, rather than shared genetic substance. It struck me that there was, crudely speaking, a 'new kinship'–sized hole in the study of the Middle East, and a Middle East–sized hole in the new kinship studies. I thus decided to follow Conte's lead, by examining Islamic Middle Eastern reactions to such new reproductive technologies, as a way to further anthropological understanding of kinship in the region, and as a way to contribute to and comment on the new kinship studies more generally.

The attempt to uncover deeper kinship assumptions was in some ways a failure. It is, no doubt unsurprisingly, simply impossible to read 'the Middle Eastern kinship system' off what Islamic legal scholars or Christian Lebanese medical practitioners, for instance, have to say about assisted reproduction. In fact a key issue proved to be the very diversity of positions taken, and the tensions between 'official' kinship ideology and individual practice. The latter issue is complicated in Lebanon by a colonially instituted legal system that grants the various religious communities their own religious courts with jurisdiction over Lebanese citizens in matters of personal status, in competition with a robust civil legal apparatus and liberal, secular tradition: the kinship precepts of religious law are thus very much contested.

Further, public reputation before local communities and social networks – 'the neighbours', for instance – is important; sexual propriety, to which reproduction (even if medically assisted) is assimilated, is a central value in this context. Where people employ unconventional or controversial methods to remedy infertility, then, such as the use of donor sperm or eggs, they may prefer not to advertise that fact, and indeed may maintain publicly that resulting children arrived in the conventional manner. This is hardly unique to Lebanon. But while I was keen to seize upon examples of the fluidity of relatedness and the rethinking of traditional categories that, for reasons I will describe, I took to be vital to my 'new kinship' project, I was forced to remark that such fluidity and challenges to reproductive mores are, ideologically speaking, deeply antithetical to much contemporary Middle Eastern, especially Muslim, thinking. That is not to say, however, that Islamic thought is simply hidebound and conservative in this regard. As we will see, Islamic legal thinkers, generally speaking, openly embrace the possibilities of such new technologies, and often surprise in their solutions to the problems such possibilities can pose. But in any case one would not want to privilege too much the clerical view: such 'Orientalism' has rightly been seen as deeply problematic; and as an account of 'kinship' it would be inadequate. And yet in trying to highlight examples of the creative strategies individuals employ to further their personal projects, which may involve subverting religious precepts and the institutions of state law, one then runs the risk of being accused of a negative depiction, one that focuses on 'wrong behaviour', as it were. But if one ignores such actions, one merely reproduces a moralizing rhetoric that terms such individual agency 'hypocrisy' or 'lying', rather than seeing it as the 'choice' of the new kinship discussions. And anthropological criticism has its own moralizing tendencies. There are no easy solutions here. The proper, anthropological path, it seems to me, is rather to step outside of a futile moralizing dialectic that sets, for instance, 'illiberal Islam' against 'immoral West', and take such moralizing, as well as notions of propriety, integrity and hypocrisy, as one's comparative subjects.

There is another conversation here, then, between these 'new kinship' studies and the Islamic legal discussions. Confronting the two, as this book is, to the best of my knowledge, the first to do, sheds critical light on this portion of the anthropological tradition itself as a creature of liberal modernity – which is but one possible vision of modernity among many, including, arguably, some of the strands of the contemporary Islamic legal thinking I investigate here: what Deeb (2006) calls the 'enchanted modern' of certain pious, politically committed sections of Muslim society, in this case among the Shiites of Beirut's southern suburbs, for instance.[1] It also illuminates a contemporary European and North American interest in the 'biogenetic' in kinship as not so much a consequence of scientific and technological advance, as is usually claimed, but as intimately bound up with changing conceptions of sexual morality, the core theme of the Islamic debates. While the new kinship studies have turned on the theme of nature versus culture, Islamic debates turn on legitimacy and illegitimacy.

These are intensely political themes: Middle Easterners might be forgiven for thinking themselves literally under assault by Western liberalism, of which the new wave of kinship studies and the social and sexual fluidity they are so interested in are, as I will argue, a characteristic product. Here I have a distinguished predecessor. I think it is fair to say that it was Marilyn Strathern's *After nature* (1992a) that truly launched and underpinned the wave of anthropological writing regarding assisted conception and kinship that I address here. It in large part inspired my own research. But rereading the book now, what I find most striking is Strathern's deep and explicit concern with the political climate of the day, the 'Enterprise Culture' of British Thatcherism (see also Strathern 1992b). My own work, which in many ways belongs to the tradition she inaugurated, heads in a rather different direction, but one equally linked to the politics of its time: the authoritarianism of Tony Blair's (now Gordon Brown's) Britain, with its unhappy conjunction of lip service to certain 'liberal' ideals, ruthless abandonment of other, rather more material ones and profound ambivalence towards 'Islam' and the various ways in which millions of Muslims would like to construe their religion. Political frustrations aside, the tension between 'Islamic' and 'liberal' conceptions of moral propriety also throws much anthropological prejudice (in analytical terms) into relief.

This political dimension to research in the region is inevitable in the present climate, even regarding what one might assume are relatively innocuous issues. Some extreme right-wing American conservatives, for instance, seeking the reasons for Arab and Muslim intransigence towards American foreign policy objectives, even look to the region's notional fondness for 'clannish' 'cousin marriage', a stock, if dated, theme of the anthropological literature (Clarke 2007b: 389). Further, the U.S.-led invasion of Iraq and its aftermath have led to an inflammation of sectarian sentiment. After a talk I gave in London detailing some of the surprisingly unrestrictive positions I had found amongst the views of leading Shiite authorities on IVF, an audience member asked for a quiet word: 'You must be careful', he told me, 'this is dangerous stuff. If the Wahhabis get hold of it...' I took his point, although 'the Wahhabis' are hardly a category to be conjured with as crudely as that. It is true that Islamic legal opinions can be taken as emblematic and used as ammunition for the sectarian rhetoric in which much political antagonism is cast at this historical moment. But I have not censored my account in this regard: these opinions are matters of public record, globally disseminated, and none of my Lebanese Shiite clerical colleagues held such fears.

One might also note here regarding the dialectic between, roughly put, 'progressive' and 'conservative' Islamic legal opinion, a theme I pick up at various points in the book, that the boundaries most certainly do not fall neatly along sectarian lines, even if some would like to think they do. Indeed many of the most progressive authorities, Sunni and Shiite, frequently argue for an end to the perception of a difference between 'Sunni' and 'Shiite' itself, a 'difference' that is, they might argue, a tool of Western imperialism. Further, with regard to 'sectarianism' in Lebanon, I should stress right away that categories like 'Sunni', 'Shiite' or 'Maronite' cannot simply be taken as given (Deeb 2006: 10ff.; Norton 2007: 163). Religion may play a greater or lesser role in individual projects of self-fashioning: many in Lebanon very consciously reject it entirely; some indeed see in religion and confessionalism the source of all their country's woes –

liberal secularism has a distinguished tradition in Lebanon, and a considerable and important contemporary constituency. Lebanese Muslims and Christians may find more in common with each other than with co-religionists elsewhere. Others take their distinctive religious affiliation deeply seriously. Others may exploit it for their own purposes. But whatever the case, as a result of the course the French Mandate over Lebanon took after the First World War, religious affiliation is a portion of bureaucratic identity in Lebanon, one that one cannot opt out of, a fact of some moment in the matters of kinship with which we are concerned, as we will see.[2] We are, furthermore, interested here in religious reactions to new medical technologies, and to avoid employing the categories people in Lebanon themselves use to classify such matters would be perverse. I keep to them. But it would be as well to remember throughout that issues of confessional identity and its political implications are sensitive and contentious in Lebanon and the wider region, as well as analytically complex. Equally, both the Sunni and Shiite Islamic legal traditions are heavily contested, and the diversity of perspectives to be found within them in Lebanon, let alone in the wider Islamic world, needs to be recognized.

If I may return briefly to my more old-fashioned anthropological themes, at a more abstract level anthropologists have found the 'endogamous' rhetoric of kinship in the region somewhat paradoxical and, as in Europe, one struggles to isolate neat and coherent patterns as one might as a kinship specialist in other regions, such as those of cross-cousin alliance, for instance (Dresch 1998). But, as Mundy (1995: 89, 167–71), who is something of a sceptic in this regard, observes, an anthropologist of a structuralist, generalizing bent can pick out some core, shared notions, notably those of protection, especially of womenfolk, and the male public standing that depends upon discharge of that duty. While I do often wonder whether my Lebanese friends would recognize themselves in some of this high anthropology, these notions will indeed prove useful for setting out the analysis here. While the region has often been seen as individualistic (Lindholm 1996), in this sense we will find a decidedly social vision, one opposed to the rhetoric of individual rights in terms of which much Western discourse surrounding assisted reproduction is couched. This notion of the protection of what is intimate and of one's own public standing allows us to understand not only much regarding the rhetoric and practice of kinship, but also the interest in camouflaging unorthodox solutions to the problems that infertility poses. It also allows us to see the particularity of the contemporary, liberal West, with its compulsions towards an uncovering of the intimate and a celebration of the unorthodox.

In sum, if I may be permitted a simplistic sketch here, both contemporary, liberal Western thinking and Islamic legal thinking, at least in some of its most recent, politically committed refractions, strive to free their followers from the tyranny of 'what the neighbours say', but in very different ways: roughly, 'Islam' says 'this is what is right, do that', and 'the liberal West' says 'do what you do, that's right'. Faced with much the same problems – infertility, for example – different concerns and strategies may be in play. We start with kinship, then, but we finish by looking to these wider patterns of freedom and constraint and the alternative visions of modernity that they may entail.

Sources, methods and issues

There is a vast amount of Islamic legal material available in Arabic and English, the limits of my competence, let alone Farsi, Urdu or Bahasa Malaysia/Indonesia, to pick just a few. Online fatwa services, providing answers to the questions of Muslims (and non-Muslim researchers), have proliferated, a great mass of material has been published in books and journals, and one can contact famous authorities direct, in person, by telephone, fax or email. My own investigations took a variety of turns, just as might those of potential customers of assisted reproduction seeking religious advice. I asked knowledgeable Muslim acquaintances, trawled the Internet, and bought whatever books and magazines I could find covering the topic. I also interviewed religious specialists (shaykhs) great and small, mostly in Lebanon but also in Syria and Britain – minor shaykhs, one might note, were sometimes interestingly 'off message', although would certainly not presume to know better than the leading authorities. Beyond the fatwa literature, there has also been a rash of popular books in Arabic concerned with assisted reproduction, and to a much greater extent cloning, which has gripped the Islamic imagination and which I also explored. There is further, valuable secondary literature in English, including material by Muslim medical specialists with a strong interest in the Islamic perspective on their work,[3] as well as a certain amount of non-Muslim academic commentary.[4] In my account here I mostly focus on the primary and most authoritative opinions, rather than commentary or little-known scholars, unless of particular interest. Given the volume of material and number of ulama with an opinion on such matters, this account cannot and does not aspire to be comprehensive, and it is heavily influenced by the interests and preferences of my Lebanese informants, although most of the authorities cited are of global stature and not, indeed, resident in Lebanon. It is representative of the terms of the debate in Lebanon as I found it in 2003–04 at least.

While the shariah is eternal and universal, the production and consumption of Islamic jurisprudential literature (*fiqh*) are very much local and contextual, and fieldwork was an attempt to come to terms with that. This field research was, as already stated, mainly undertaken in Lebanon, where I lived, based in Beirut, for ten months in 2004 and to which I made many visits from neighbouring Syria for several months before that (starting in 2003). I studied Arabic in Damascus, where I lived for a year prior to this project in 1999–2000, and did so again for eight months before my fieldwork, beginning in late April 2003. I did interview some religious and medical specialists in Syria, and I open the book with an example of adoption taken from my time there. But Lebanon, unlike Syria at that time, had a very vibrant and advanced fertility treatment sector, and free access to a wide variety of religious opinion, Muslim and Christian. Lebanon's complex religious constitution (legally and demographically speaking) had a major bearing on my findings, and I recognize this throughout. Most importantly for my purposes, both Sunni and Shiite Muslims, who have distinct legal traditions, are substantially represented. Subsequent trips to Lebanon, one for one week and another for two months, made in 2006 and 2007 respectively, clarified some points. In 2008 I undertook a further six months fieldwork in Lebanon, but for a new and distinct project. In 2004, I also made one brief trip to Jordan and another, more fruitful, to Iran, where I visited one of the country's foremost fertility centres and gained some valuable comparative insights. I have subsequently also had the opportunity to talk to Shiite authorities in Britain, where interviews with several fertility specialists were helpful as well.

My very first visit was to the office of a representative in Lebanon of Ayatollah Khamene'i, Supreme Leader of the Islamic Revolution in Iran, in Harat Hrayk, deep (as it seemed to me then) in the Dahiyah, the Shiite suburbs of Beirut, since devastated by Israeli bombardment.[5] The offices seemed dark and intimidating, decorated with serried ranks of portraits of Khamene'i and Khomeini, but the darkness was, as it turned out, due to a temporary power cut. Seated beneath a portrait of the Supreme Leader, the shaykh initially lectured me in fearsome manner on the evils of America and Israel, a common enough pattern to my interviews. But he was, I think, pleasantly surprised by my genuine interest in the abstruse and warmed to me, presenting me with some manuscript copies of articles he had written on cloning: 'It is so much easier nowadays, with the Quran and *riwāyāt* [traditions concerning the Prophet and the Imams] searchable on CD-Rom.' The telephones kept ringing with questions: one from Nigeria – 'With which foot does one enter the toilet?' – another from London – 'I have an international reputation!' he told me proudly.

As for an interview with Lebanon's own ayatollah, Sayyid Muhammad Husayn Fadlallah, I at first only managed to arrange an appointment with a functionary in the sayyid's offices. After wandering lost through the streets of the Hezbollah-controlled southern suburbs, I eventually found the office complex (since destroyed in the 2006 war with Israel), tucked away up a side street near the sayyid's grand mosque, also in Harat Hrayk. Passing roadblocks and armed sentries, evidence of the very real dangers of life for a politically active religious personality in this part of the world, I was led to a small office to meet my liaison. He quickly realized that my questions were beyond his competence and popped out. A few minutes later, he returned: 'Oh you are very lucky, the sayyid has some spare time today.' I was led upstairs to the sayyid's reception rooms and having waited awhile in a rather grand antechamber, fussed over by various attendants bearing tea, I was ushered into the presence of the ayatollah himself, sitting in one corner of a hall lined with chairs, kindly, of a certain age, as befits his station, but with the sharp eye of a renowned legal mind. I was seated at his side, and he spoke gently and patiently throughout. A tape recorder was set up, for it was necessary that our interview be recorded; I was to have one copy, made for me subsequently, and the sayyid would keep the other, 'in case you misunderstood him'.

For further elucidation, I was referred to the head of the sayyid's fatwa-issuing department, Shaykh Muhsin 'Atwi, who was on the occasion of our first meeting extremely busy with Hajj (the pilgrimage to Mecca) affairs: before going on the Hajj, people come to make a will, including bequeathing missed prayers for their sons to make up. However, we managed to talk in moments snatched between these sessions and the constant calls from a veritable bank of telephones, the shaykh clasping phones to both ears while hearing out a Hajj petitioner. Shaykh 'Atwi dispenses advice and fatwas by phone, as well as answering emails and faxes, consulting the many volumes of the sayyid's published works of *fiqh*. I was to return to his offices many a time, and I owe a great deal to his knowledge, generosity and hospitality. I was also fortunate enough to see the ayatollah himself once more on a return visit to Lebanon subsequent to my fieldwork, when I presented him with a copy of my doctoral dissertation – 'On kinship? Very good: too many people are passing themselves off as descendants of the Prophet these days', he murmured – which no doubt has since been lost to the Israeli bombardments of 2006 that destroyed his home, offices and much of his charitable network.

Some shaykhs were to be found at home, where we might converse in more relaxed fashion. Shaykh Muhammad Kana'an, then head of the Sunni courts in Lebanon, received me at work, but was also kind enough to arrange a more extended meeting at his Beirut flat. Shaykh Kana'an first asked if I wished to record our session and then launched into a detailed exposition of the Sunni position on assisted reproduction and related issues. He finished by giving me a long lecture on my responsibilities as a Westerner who had lived in Islamic society and knew Arabic. I must tell people back home the truth; 'we don't ask for more than that!' I did not restrict myself to Sunni and Shiite figures, although my meetings with the 'big men' of other confessions followed similar patterns. Shaykh al-'Aql Bahjat Ghayth, highest Druze authority in Lebanon, although a somewhat controversial figure, resided at a grand neoclassical edifice, the House of the Druze in Beirut.[6] Suitably garbed in long white beard, white hat and blue cape, with piercing blue eyes, he spoke with bewildering speed of man's place in nature and Pythagoras's legacy to human wisdom. When I asked for an appropriate Christian thinker, Greek Orthodox Archbishop George Khudr was the first name put forward. His offices are in an alpine eyrie, suspended between snow-capped mountains and the glittering sea with Beirut spreading out below – picture-postcard Lebanon. I was ushered in through a reception room to a more intimate study looking out over the vista. There the archbishop sat in a deep armchair, by the constantly ringing telephone bringing the requests of the faithful, smoking a sizeable cigar through his white beard. Vastly cosmopolitan, he discoursed in English and reminisced fondly about his time in Oxford, where he had once stayed as a guest at Christchurch College. He spoke approvingly of the Anglican Church, and especially of their allowing their priests to marry. 'Such was the case in the Orthodox Church until a thousand years ago...'

I spoke, then, to as many religious specialists as I could, of all confessions, although the vast majority were Sunni and Shiite Muslims. But for rare exceptions, we spoke in Arabic, mostly of a 'high', literary variety (*fushā*). The total number can only be estimated, as a visit to a court or an office would invariably result in meeting and chatting with many new shaykhly contacts. Certainly I have spoken to dozens over the years, but a more restricted number have become friends and trusted sources, to whom I had frequent recourse. A formal interview with a leading authority, such as Ayatollah Fadlallah, might be recorded, but I worked mostly with pen and paper. As part of my efforts to understand how Islamic law worked in practice, and its relationship with the state, I spent as much time as I could in the offices of those issuing fatwas and in the religious courts: of the latter, there were three that I visited on a weekly basis through much of my fieldwork (in 2004), two Sunni (one the court of appeal) and one Shiite. Much of what I learned there does not belong in this book and must wait for another. Here I restrict myself to the questions of kinship and reproductive technology that were my initial focus. Still, this contextualization of 'Islamic law' is important for our purposes here, and I expand upon this theme in due course. I have named most of the important personalities, as is wholly appropriate: an opinion as to religious law has little value without knowing the identity and standing of its source. But I have also frequently had recourse to anonymous references to 'shaykhs' and 'judges', where the identity of the source is immaterial and I felt that they would not necessarily wish to be identified personally with a piece of information or opinion.

A further rich vein of material came from interviews with medical practitioners. In Lebanon, I visited eighteen fertility treatment clinics, of varying sizes and capabilities, and conducted in-depth interviews, several times in some cases, with thirty-three doctors, four of whom were women: twenty-one Christian (of various denominations), two Sunni Muslim, seven Shiite, three Druze. While I spoke to many of the 'big' names, I also learnt a great deal from less famous figures, and indeed non-specialists. Some doctors were self-confessed 'mere' gynaecologists who would have to refer patients for infertility treatment; some were doctors claiming to practise IVF but without any obvious resources for doing so; others were doctors working in or indeed running centres, either independent or within private hospitals; others were doctors who owned and ran their own centres, or 'had a laboratory'. A centre, or the doctor's office, would commonly have some unobtrusive religious decoration, such as an icon of the Madonna, or a pertinent Quranic verse – 'it relaxes the patients' – but more obvious would be posters of babies in appealing positions – sitting in flowerpots being a particular favourite – and collections of kitsch porcelain figures of babies, baby animals and the like, that would leaven the world-standard 'clinical' look of white walls, white coats and minimal clutter. A couple of the newest, best appointed centres had opted for something rather more luxurious, perhaps leather furniture or even some somewhat risqué pictures and statuary. The interviews were, for the most part, conducted in English, and were, again, recorded on paper rather than on cassette. Indeed, they were almost all off the record; much of what doctors had to say was controversial, and almost all wished to be cited anonymously.

Some may find my portrait of the Lebanese fertility scene somewhat unflattering. Many of the doctors I spoke to were deeply concerned at the lack of regulation of fertility treatment in Lebanon, and I have reported those concerns, along with some associated gossip, where others might have preferred a discreet silence, given that Lebanon's image in the wider world has much to contend with already. Some of what was said may have been due to the intense competition in this portion of the medical sector; it appears in retrospect that I may have been drawn into local professional rivalries. That makes these voices no less interesting for the anthropologist, of course, although questionable as a factual account no doubt, and I have not reproduced everything I was told. The reader should know that I owe a great deal to those who helped me: I hope my reproduction of their candour does more good than harm. I have not cited any of the doctors' names, and I have tried very hard not to include any material that might point to any doctor's identity. I also circulated drafts of my work to a number of doctors, as I did also to my closest religious contacts. Interviews with a number of lawyers specializing in personal status law and the staff of several orphanages were also illuminating and much appreciated. Again, given the sensitive nature of much of what was discussed, I have not named my sources here. I further draw on research undertaken in several newspaper archives in Beirut.

The bulk of my ethnographic material thus comes from professionals: religious, medical and legal. Some may think this inadequate, or overly 'intellectualist'; in particular, the lack of evidence from patients undergoing infertility treatment is regrettable. I did make some attempt to arrange interviews with patients, but I have to admit that I myself found the prospect a deeply uncomfortable one and did not pursue it as zealously as I should have. My sex (male) seemed an obstacle, to me at least, to probing deeply sensitive matters with female patients, especially religiously committed Muslims. However, Marcia Inhorn, the leading medical anthropological expert on assisted reproduction in the Middle East, had just spent a year interviewing hundreds of patients in two of the most important centres in Lebanon, and her findings constitute an important parallel resource, to which I refer. This book is not for the reader looking for a clinic-based, medical anthropological study of infertility treatment in Lebanon. It is about religious responses to these new technologies. My material on doctors' perspectives, though relatively limited, helps us to put the religious responses into context.

Here we need to turn to another, allied issue. The interesting cases, the ones that open up conceptual fault lines for the analyst, are most often the controversial, even the exceptional ones. Islamic debate centres on the propriety of the use of donor sperm and donor eggs, and of surrogacy arrangements. Unsurprisingly, then, my conversations with religious and medical specialists concentrated on these issues, even if they constitute a minority of procedures actually undertaken. So too in my conversations with judges and lawyers, especially regarding adoption – nominally forbidden under Islamic precepts – I was interested in cases that highlighted the tensions in Lebanon's peculiar legal system, and in instances of people challenging and resisting that system as well as the often suffocating demands of public conformity. Some might suggest that my account thus presents the exceptional and the recalcitrant as normal, normative even. That is very far from my intention. I do at points discuss the unusual and the rebellious, and indeed the rhetorical and the hypothetical, but I do not pretend they are otherwise. All study of assisted reproduction is in any case study of the relatively exotic (Simpson 1994: 834). And my account reflects not only my own intellectual interests, which were shared in enthusiastically by my Lebanese informants, but also the concerns of the Lebanese doctors I spoke with, and the deep dissatisfaction of many others with a legal and political system that, as one lawyer put it to me, forces them

to wrap their arm around the back of their head in order to touch
their earlobe, rather than reaching up directly.

Plan of the book

The first part of the book presents the theoretical and historical context of the study: the anthropological debates that the book seeks to
contribute to, and the Lebanese context in which field research took
place. Before plunging into the argument proper, I first present as a
prologue a story of adoption taken from early in my research. It
dates from my time in Syria and is thus distinct from the rest of the
material, but it should serve as a comparative example and give an
idea of the issues we will be faced with. Chapter 1 then provides a
brief account of the new kinship studies, anthropological studies of
new reproductive technologies and those of kinship in the Middle
East; this section is very much aimed at the anthropological audience, and non-specialists could no doubt skip through it. Regarding
the new kinship studies and those of new reproductive technologies,
I argue that despite their avowed novelty these anthropological
trends are part of a wider and long-standing liberal tradition interested in questioning received moral categories, a tradition controversial in the Islamic Middle East, in an argument that I have broached
elsewhere (Clarke 2008) and here explore in fuller fashion. Regarding the Middle East, I deal briefly with the issue of father's brother's
daughter marriage and the notions of honour and 'closeness' that allow this 'problem' of anthropological analysis to be dissolved. I then
turn to the theme of substance, in particular the Islamic legal institution of milk kinship. Despite the valiant attempts of some analysts,
a coherent 'logic of substance' proves hard to isolate: this indeterminacy is mirrored in the diversity of Islamic legal opinion we will encounter regarding assisted reproduction. My account here is no
doubt scandalously brief for the specialist, but I have dealt with various aspects of these issues at greater length elsewhere (Clarke 2005,
2007b, 2007c, 2007d). Chapter 2 discusses the production and consumption of Islamic legal texts, generally and also with special reference to Lebanon, where Muslim and Christian communities are
formally integrated into a complex, multi-confessional political and
legal environment. 'Islamic law', it is stressed, is often better seen as
a domain of open-ended opinion and debate rather than one of codified 'law'. We take up the examples of adoption and the status of

foundlings in Lebanon, issues parallel to those of fertility treatment
that will serve to introduce important ideas of family and propriety,
as well as the themes of resistance to and manipulation of state bureaucracy.

In Part 2, we move to the ethnography of Islamic legal discourse
and then Lebanese medical discourse. Chapters 3 and 4 are devoted
to Islamic legal reactions to the new reproductive technologies, first
Sunni and then Shiite. Sunni and Shiite authorities share basic legal
principles and notions of society and kinship, and their discussions
of assisted reproduction turn on the same issues: most importantly,
where third parties beyond a husband and wife are involved, as in
donor procedures and surrogacy arrangements, is this in some sense
analogous to *zinā* ('fornication' or 'adultery')? We find a diversity of
opinion here. While Sunnis, broadly speaking, rule out such possibilities, the opinions of some Shiite authorities in this regard are surprisingly unrestrictive and seemingly raise the prospect of new
patterns of relatedness. Again, this is a point I have made in previous
publications (e.g. Clarke 2006a, 2006b, 2007a) but here explore
much more fully. The material is complex, but I have tried to keep
the narrative flowing: much detail, especially regarding the opinions
of numerous authorities and on more technical aspects of the debate,
has been confined to the notes, which the specialist should find useful; I have thus sought to ensure that the index helps navigation in
this regard.

In Chapter 5, I present the voices of medical practitioners in
Lebanon. The key points here are that advanced fertility treatment is
readily available in Lebanon, and that it has proved hard to establish
regulation of it that is satisfactory to all. This leads to a relative freedom of practice, on the one hand in comparison with the extensive
controls imposed in the West, where many of these doctors previously practiced, and on the other hand – and especially – in comparison with many other countries in the region. This freedom can
potentially be used by doctors and clients to perform a variety of ethically challenging procedures, such as donor procedures and surrogacy arrangements, and is thus the focus of keen debate, which
ultimately turns on the stances adopted by Lebanon's various religious communities. A key trope of the medical discourse is the cen-
trality of confidentiality, even secrecy, and the tyranny of the wider
society's demand for conformity to notions of propriety largely
shared by people of all religious communities.

In Part 3, the final chapter ties this material together, first setting

the liberal anthropological tradition, of which the new kinship studies are a part, against an intense public focus in Islamic Middle Eastern discourse on 'morals', especially sexual morality. We can
undoubtedly take examples from the ethnography of 'elective', 'non-
biogenetic' relations or the 'rethinking' of traditional categories that
are, in my reading, the focus of the new kinship studies, which hope
to problematize certain British and American ideas of kinship. But
that would be to ignore a Middle Eastern reluctance to embrace such
an 'immoral', Western project. Where certain strands of Islamic legal opinion do surprise, then, in their lack of restriction of controversial procedures, we need to understand that lack of restriction in
terms of a very different intellectual tradition and situate it within
broader political projects that seek to render 'Islam' relevant to, indeed constitutive of, modern social life, as I describe.

We have moved from the realm of kinship theory to that of politicized sexual morality, but, I argue, attention to the latter helps illuminate some of the preoccupations of the former: the Islamic focus
on legitimacy, on being born in wedlock, throws into relief the extent to which this element of kinship has diminished in importance
in 'the West', and thus perhaps helps explain the relative prominence
of kinship's 'biogenetic' element in Western discourse, one of the
new kinship studies' core interests. In further exploration of the issues, I discuss paternity testing in Lebanon, which highlights the disruption of assumptions of privacy and 'not knowing' that such
geneticization of kinship might entail. In the Lebanese cases,
broadly speaking, both conventional rhetoric and its accommodation
to practice need to be taken together. The space between them is acknowledged and valued, rather than collapsed, as might be the ultimate conclusion of both politically committed Islamic and liberal
rhetoric.

Notes

1. Literature on 'alternative modernities' has burgeoned of late (see e.g.
Gaonkar 2001; Knauft 2002). Of particular inspiration to me here has
been the work of Deeb (2006) and Abisaab (2006) on Lebanon's Shiite
community. Deeb (2006: 14–15 n. 29, 30, 32) provides a very full list
of pertinent references.

2. In a public lecture, Ayatollah Muhammad Husayn Fadlallah, perhaps
Lebanon's most distinguished Islamic personality and a notable opponent
of confessionalism, was asked ironically whether cloning could become

established in a sectarian country such as Lebanon. 'Each clone', he replied with equal irony, 'would choose his sect, because in Lebanon they tie every aspect of human affairs, regarding one's rights and services, to one's sect. There are many secularists now who curse confessionalism, but blithely have recourse to their sect, because he who wants work goes to his sect for it. So don't you worry about cloning so far as confessionalism in Lebanon is concerned' (Fadlallah 2002b: 15).

3. Such as Dr Gamal Serour (e.g. 1993, 1998), director of the International Islamic Centre for Population Studies and Research at al-Azhar University, Cairo, and Dr Hassan Hathout (e.g. 1991), linked with the Islamic Organisation of Medical Sciences in Kuwait. Dr Ahmed Yacoub's (2001) published doctoral dissertation in law on Islamic responses to medical developments is useful. Muslim intellectual Munawar Anees (1984, 1989) has written on the ethical challenges of assisted reproduction from an Islamic perspective, in work I refer to later.

4. Vardit Rispler-Chaim's (1993) book on Islamic medical ethics proved an especially useful resource in the early stages of this project. My German is, lamentably, not good enough to do full justice to Thomas Eich's (2005) recent monograph here. Marcia Inhorn (e.g. 2003, 2006b) has discussed some of the fatwas in some detail.

5. See Deeb (2006: 42–66) for an admirable description and demystification of the Dahiyah.

6. I interviewed several Druze authorities as to their position on assisted conception. That position is not perhaps as fully articulated as the Sunni and Shiite positions, and I do not analyse it here in the same depth. In any case, where the Druze have no particular ruling of their own, they follow Hanafi Sunni law. My discussions with Druze authorities turned around two principles: the first, a great respect for rational knowledge, which would incline one to trust medical science; the second a disinclination to contravene 'natural' principles, which might lead one to disapprove of human intervention in reproduction. I would like to take the opportunity here to thank, in order of our acquaintance, President of the Druze Courts Mursil Nasr, Professor Sami Makarem of the American University, Shaykh al-'Aql Bahjat Ghayth, Shaykh Ghassan Halabi (with whom I shared a lively conversation concerning western bioethics and a fondness for *The Matrix*) and Shaykh Sami Abu-l-Muna and Shaykh Malik of the 'Irfan Schools, Simkanieh.

Part I

CONTEXTS

It was He who created humankind from water
and gave it kinship and alliance.

(Quran 25:54)

Prologue

AHMED'S STORY

Before reaching Beirut I spent some months in neighbouring Damascus, where I was privileged to hear one family's story, whose themes resonated throughout my subsequent research. I recount it to the reader here to serve, as it did for me then, as a prologue to what was to follow in the rather different settings I explored in Lebanon.[1]

I visited Ahmed[2] with a mutual friend at his shop in an area of Damascus well known for stores specializing in Islamic literature. I had been told that Ahmed had adopted a child, which surprised me: adoption is nominally forbidden in Islam. My friend had briefed Ahmed, and he had obviously prepared his remarks. He started by showing me some photos of his adopted daughter, from when she was very young through to the present, including photos with his family. He and his wife had not been able to have children. The problems lay on his side: they had gone to the doctor and the doctor had told him he did not have any sperm. There was absolutely no possibility of him having children, not even with fertility treatment such as artificial insemination ('Not with donor sperm?' I wondered to my friend later. '*Harām 'alayk* [shame on you]!' he replied). His wife said she would stay with him – they would just have to go without children. But Ahmed was not prepared to leave it at that. After much thought, and inspired by a doctor of his acquaintance, he suggested that they adopt a child. They went to an institution for orphaned chil-

dren in another area of Damascus, where among the many children
there, one particular girl kept on staring at them. Ahmed's wife was
much taken with the girl, and they ended up choosing her.

Then, Ahmed continued, they had to get through the paperwork:
the first step was to register at the Ministry of Social Affairs. He
showed me the paper, a very large and impressive document, covered in stamps and seals, as is usual. As far as I could make out as
we sat huddled behind the counter of the tiny shop, this was an au-
thorization to foster the child rather than adopt her, for in accordance
with the Islamic precepts of the majority of its citizens, adoption per
se is illegal in Syria. After registration, Ahmed had to go to a great
deal more trouble to overcome various other bureaucratic obstacles.
For the purposes of state bureaucracy the girl was registered in
Hama, another city in Syria, where she had been born. It would have
been an enormous inconvenience, Ahmed told me, for him to go to
Hama, several hours away, every time some paperwork needed doing. So he tried to get this changed, this time at the Ministry of the
Interior. This should have been impossible: the government insists
on knowing the place where someone is born, and the local sheriff
(*mukhtār*) keeps the records there. But Ahmed wanted her registered
as being born in his quarter of Damascus. As this is usually impossible, it took, in Ahmed's words, 'very, very big *wasta* [connec-
tions]'. But he managed: '*al-hamdu lillāh* [thank God] – God must
have been watching over things because He made it easier.'

Next he wanted to change her name. Her name was originally registered as Zaynab Muhammad. That is, besides her personal name,
Zaynab, the name of the father entered on her records was Muhammad, though this was made up (*khiyālī*): actually the father's name
was unknown. The first matter, then, was changing her personal
name, Zaynab, to Fatimah – the name Ahmed and his wife wanted –
and then came changing the family name (*kunyah*) to that of
Ahmed's family. This is also not, generally speaking, allowed. Indeed, it should, before anything else, require a visit to the courts to
change the person's status from one of lack of parentage (for her father was unknown) to having parentage (*min 'adam al-nasab ilā wu-
jūd al-nasab*). The relevant official refused at first, deeming it
'absolutely impossible'. But again, through powerful *wasta* in the interior minister's office, it was arranged that the minister himself ring
the man up, whereupon all was well. I was somewhat confused by
Ahmed's narrative, but our mutual friend explained to me later that
Ahmed's plan had at first been to tell the girl when she grew up that

her father had been his brother, and that he and her mother had been killed in the fighting in Hama, when the regime had crushed an uprising by the Muslim Brotherhood there in 1982.[3]

I asked about the religious standpoint. 'Of course', Ahmed told me, 'adoption [tabannī] in the fullest sense is not allowed, but taking in an orphan[4] is a very good deed – there are verses in the Quran all about it.' I went further, asking if veiling (hijab) might not subsequently prove a complicating issue: once girls come of age, according to Islamic precepts, they have to veil before unrelated men; if she were not considered his daughter, in the terms of religious law, then she would have to veil before him, a problematic commonly raised in Islamic discussions of adoption. He mistook me: 'Yes, of course there could be problems. With others do you mean? Outside the house? Of course I wouldn't let her out without being properly dressed, it would be like taking in a lamb, raising it and then releasing it into the jungle!' 'No, inside the house', I clarified. 'Well, I feel like, whatever one might say, I am the father. I don't have any feeling like that [i.e. sexual] because I raised her, I am her *rabb* [guardian], I bathed her on my knee.' Still, he and his wife had attempted to persuade his brother's wife, breastfeeding at the time, to breastfeed the girl: this would, according to Islamic law, have created 'milk kinship' (*ridāʿ*) between the girl and Ahmed's brother through his brother's wife. Ahmed would then have been her 'uncle' (*ʿamm*); he would have had 'kinship' (*qarābah*) with her, would have been 'close', 'a relative' (*qarīb*) – which would have been better. But their efforts were in vain. From what my friend told me subsequently, it seemed that Ahmed had won his brother over, but his brother's wife had adamantly refused the proposal, perhaps simply through an aversion to suckling an unknown other's child, likely illegitimate, or through reluctance to facilitate the incorporation of this outsider into the family's social and economic relations.[5]

Now, Ahmed told me, his adopted daughter 'knows everything'. The advice of a psychologist he consulted on the matter was that it would be better to tell her about her adoption, rather than let her find out later and lose her respect for her parents because they had lied to her all her life. At any rate, one day she just asked Ahmed's wife straight out: 'Are you my real mother [*umm haqīqīyah*], and is daddy my real father [*ab haqīqī*]?' His wife rang him at work, and he came home and took the child to a restaurant. He told her the story of 'The chalk circle' – known in English as the Judgement of Solomon. He told her then and tells her now anything she wants to know. He is clearly extremely proud of her – she is good at school – and told me of her plans to become an oncologist. I asked if he would like another child. 'Material considerations don't allow it', he replied. 'I give her all she needs and wants. Better that, than have more than one and not look after them properly. If I had more money ... Then I would.' I asked if the adoption had been a problem for the rest of the family. He said that his wife's family had not objected at all, and although his own parents and siblings rejected it at first, his parents have totally come round. Indeed, the last photo I saw was of all the family together.

After our talk with Ahmed, my friend and I discussed the conversation. I had found Ahmed's story moving and impressive, but my friend was keen to explain the rationale, as he saw it, for the Islamic prohibition of adoption. In his opinion, it was banned in order to discourage sex without marriage (*zinā*). If children could be adopted, then there would be nothing to stop people practising *zinā* in profusion and then giving the resulting children away. Further, Islam entails a particular organization of society, in particular as regards inheritance. 'What if somebody really loves some boy', my friend asked rhetorically, 'like an adopted one, and gives them the real son's inheritance – there's no justice in that!' Bureaucracy had been such a problem for Ahmed because in these matters the government tries to follow Islamic principles: there are worries that people will adopt girls in order to sell them into slavery, use them as prostitutes or even to obtain children from them for sale in turn. 'They might set up a brothel: there's the whole question of the white slave trade.' I asked my friend – and should have asked Ahmed – why he had adopted a girl and not a boy, as I had perhaps expected, as an heir. 'People are much more comfortable with the idea of a strange girl visiting, being in the house, than a strange boy. That's the way people think here.'[6]

Where I had been keen to see the elements of choice and constructedness in kinship, then, my friend was keen to point to its 'moral' dimension, specifically the concerns of sexual morality. This dialectic of interests was one that would be played out through much of my subsequent research into assisted reproduction in Lebanon, if in various ways and with varying emphases, as we will see.

Notes

1. And not, that is, to be seen as of a piece with it.

2. All names have been changed.

3. Perhaps thus incorporating pious resistance against the government into her origin story.

4. Here he used the word *yatīm*, properly referring to a child whose father has died, rather than using *laqīt*, meaning 'foundling', which would have been more exact but bears a weighty stigma: it is assumed that such a child is a bastard, the abandoned issue of an illicit union.

5. We will consider 'milk kinship' further in the next chapter. This strategy for creating kinship with the adopted child is not an isolated example. Compare this account given to me by a Sunni judge in Lebanon: 'I know a family who didn't have kids; there was a *laqītah* [foundling girl], they took her in. Then the wife got pregnant! Then they breastfed the *laqītah*.' A Shiite shaykh gave me a similar account. Bargach (2002: 281 n. 1), writing on Morocco, envisages a single woman adopting and taking hormonal drugs in order to lactate, breastfeed the child and institute this form of kinship. Islamic legal scholar Shaykh Wahbah al-Zuhayli (2003: 199) records being asked by a petitioner about the legality of such arrangements; he notes that were the child to be suckled by the wife's sister, it would still not be considered kin to the husband (see below, Chapter 1).

6. A doctor in Lebanon subsequently told me that '[m]en prefer to adopt girls rather than have donor sperm, because the girl is at home and grows up with you – you can enjoy bringing up a child – but in the end she'll get married and have a different name'. Bargach (2002: 97–98) suggests some different motivations for a similar pattern in the context of Morocco.

'NEW KINSHIP', NEW REPRODUCTIVE TECHNOLOGIES AND IDEAS OF KINSHIP IN THE MIDDLE EAST

New kinship

The themes in Ahmed's story of kinship created and identity transformed, through choice as well as substance – in this case, breast milk – resonate with the preoccupations of what have become known, among proponents and critics alike, as 'new kinship studies'.[1] 'Old kinship' was concerned with typologizing and classifying, with 'theory'. Studies multiplied, most of them, it seems in retrospect, concerned with fitting 'kinship systems' into place within generalizing analytical frameworks such as 'alliance' and 'descent'. As such work accumulated, it became apparent that violence was being done to ethnographic data by attempting to force them into a restricted range of types. Indeed, by undertaking research with such types as a methodological tool, anthropologists could be missing much by failing to deal with societies and cultures on and in their own terms (Leach 1961; Barnes 1962). By implication, even the higher-order concept of 'kinship' could be seen as problematic: it was itself a type of social category and means of organization that had been erected a priori. This scepticism regarding kinship reached its apogee in the early 1970s. Needham expressed the point forcefully in his introduction to the edited volume *Rethinking kinship and marriage:* 'There is no such thing as kinship, and it follows that there can be no such thing as kinship theory' (Needham 1971: 5).

Another iconoclastic figure was David Schneider, who proposed that '"kinship", like totemism, the matrilineal complex and matriarchy, is a non-subject since it does not exist in any culture known to man' (Schneider 1972: 59).

While Needham anticipated Schneider here,[2] it is Schneider who has come to be regarded as the talismanic figure in the genealogy of the 'new kinship', Strathern indeed describing him as 'intellectual father' to her own influential study of English kinship (1992a: xviii). Two of his works have been seen as especially inspirational. The earlier of these was his examination of *American kinship* (1980 [1968]). Here Schneider presents an avowedly 'cultural' account of American kinship, dealing with its terminology and key institutions 'in very much the same way in which I would describe the kinship system of any society, anywhere' (1980 [1968]: 31). Schneider suggests that '[t]he American reader may find this particularly disconcerting, for at times what he may take as a self-evident fact of life I take as a tenet of his culture'. Thus anthropologists, trained by their experience in 'other places', are able to bring out the supposedly self-evident and given, but actually cultural and constructed in 'their own' culture. Schneider identified at the heart of American ideas of kinship a distinction between the 'order of nature' (sometimes also 'the natural order' or 'the facts of life') and the 'order of law', or 'substance' (an influential introduction, to which we will return) and 'code', which easily elide with another familiar anthropological dichotomy, that between nature and culture.

The later *Critique of the study of kinship* (1984) expands and justifies Schneider's earlier polemic against 'kinship' as an ethnocentric imposition on the rich variety of indigenous categories. Schneider compares two accounts of the institutions of the people of the West Caroline island Yap, where he had done his doctoral fieldwork. The first, to be seen as symptomatic of his own early approach, starts from the theoretical assumptions that a trained anthropologist takes, or took, with him or her to the field, theoretical concepts such as lineages and descent. The second, based on the later work of Labby, starts from the ideas of Yapese culture itself and proves analytically superior.[3] Schneider progresses to the idea that 'kinship' itself might be one of the pieces of misleading theoretical baggage with which the anthropologist is needlessly encumbered, commenting that rarely have anthropologists even bothered to address the question of the 'content of kinship' (1984: 53). His earlier work on *American kinship* (1980 [1968]) had 'only affirmed that American kinship (not

kinship in general) has the special content of shared biogenetic substance and a code for conduct enjoining diffuse, enduring solidarity'
(1984: 53). But now Schneider moves to observing that in anthropological thinking in general, since its very beginnings in the nineteenth century, the underlying concept of kinship had remained
stable, as 'a purely biological relationship deriving from the facts of
human sexual reproduction' (1984: 53). Cultures were seen to
'recognise' these facts to greater or lesser extent, and make use of
them as an 'idiom' in which to express social relationships, more or
less approximating to the 'true' relationships. Euro-American notions had thus been erected into universal ones. Further, 'kinship'
then was given an analytical priority derived from its central place in
Euro-American culture in particular, where it is assumed that 'Blood
is Thicker Than Water' (1984: 165). Schneider concludes that:

> It might turn out that European culture does provide a nice model,
> but that that model does not prove to be very generally applicable.
> Kinship might then become a special custom distinctive of European
> culture, an interesting oddity at worst, like the Toda bow ceremony.
> (1984: 201)

This critique and its predecessor (Schneider 1972) are widely
seen to have killed off kinship studies in the old style, before stimulating new directions. Schneider was to return Strathern's compli-
ment, commenting shortly before his death that kinship had risen
Phoenix-like from the ashes to which he had consigned it due to
'feminist work, to studies of gay and lesbian kinship, and to Marilyn
Strathern's *After nature*' (Handler 1995: 193). This 'narrative of kinship's death and resurrection' (Patterson 2005: 1) has become com-
monplace.[4] According to Janet Carsten, whose monograph *After
kinship* (2004) is avowedly 'a book about "the new kinship"' (2004:
xi), interest in kinship within anthropology declined during the
1970s and 1980s in the face of the assaults of Schneider in particular, but 'by the late 1980s ... one could discern that kinship was beginning to undergo something of a renaissance' (2004: 20), a
renaissance driven by two key factors. One was an impetus given by
studies of gender and personhood, especially within feminist anthropology, which 'began to feed back into kinship, revitalizing it and
contributing to a reformulation of what kinship was all about and
how it should be studied' (2004: 21). Accounts of gender found reproduction an inevitable focus, and led to attempts to bring analyses
of gender and kinship together, such as the collection edited by Col-

lier and Yanagisako (1987a). The other factor was the impact of new reproductive technologies such as in vitro fertilization, following the widely publicized birth of the world's first 'test-tube baby', Louise Brown, in 1978.[5] The possibility of 'artificial' reproduction, and a manipulation or even alteration of previously fixed modes of reproduction and hence 'kinship', led to public debate – such as the 1982–84 Warnock Committee and Report in Britain – wide public interest and in turn anthropological interest.

'Defamiliarizing the "natural"'

The very idea of kinship, and its status as 'natural', had been called into question by writers such as Schneider – an attractive strategy from the point of view of feminist anthropologists, as the gender roles they wanted to question were seen, in the Euro-American culture within which most were writing, as 'given' by the biological 'facts' of human reproduction. Further, 'nature' itself was treated as an item of culture, which paved the way for an assault on its supposedly given, fixed and distinct quality. Thus too the notion of 'biological kinship' as an ineluctable fact instituted by shared biogenetic substance would be ethnocentric, part of a distinctively Euro-American cultural repertoire that could itself be analysed as any other. Indeed, for those so minded, one could argue 'biology' itself to be a cultural construct and the very privileging of 'scientific facts' culturally specific. Some writers have felt that Schneider could and should have gone further. According to Carsten (2004: 22), Schneider 'rather curiously failed to resolve the contradiction that he so neatly demonstrated. He himself never quite abandoned the dichotomy between biological and social aspects of kinship, or suggested how this dichotomy might be opened up or reformulated.' This line of argument is rather seen by Carsten to have been developed in studies of gender and new reproductive technologies, both of which 'rest on a single project of defamiliarizing the "natural" and that which is taken for granted' (2004: 23).

So, for instance, Collier and Yanagisako (1987b: 7) argued that 'the next phase in the feminist reanalysis of gender and kinship should be to question the assumption that "male" and "female" are two natural categories of human beings whose relations are everywhere structured by their biological difference'.[6] And Yanagisako and Delaney's (1995) subsequent collection of essays saw the 'natural facts' of science as social constructs serving the power interests of male hegemony. Thus, it is worth noting at this point, feminist

studies of kinship would have a vested interest in providing ethnographic examples that would help in this project of questioning
Euro-American assumptions. As for new reproductive technology,
Marilyn Strathern, in her influential work *After nature* (1992a), argued that before the advent of highly potent modern knowledge of,
and technological intervention in, human reproduction, kinship had
been the paradigmatic area for 'the English' (and by extension 'the
West') to think through the relationship between the 'given facts' of
'nature' and what humans made of them. Social institutions such as
the family were seen to take after nature, but then the given status of
nature was destroyed by the possibility of altering what had previously been seen as unalterable.

Carsten, in the programmatic statement on the new kinship studies that introduces her collection of essays on *Cultures of relatedness*,[7] declares that '[o]ne of the purposes of this volume is precisely
to interrogate the role of biology in local statements and practices of
relatedness' beyond the West as well (2000a: 2). Thus the ethnographic essays in the volume are to be seen as demonstrating that societies form and think about 'relatedness' in many ways other than
sexual reproduction, and that one should be wary of simplistic distinctions between relations 'real' and 'fictive' or 'biological' and 'social'. So, for example, in Bodenhorn's (2000) account, the Iñupiat of
Alaska do not accord ties resulting from procreation any privileged
moral force. Lambert (2000) identifies in rural Rajasthan a complex
of relations grounded to a greater or lesser degree in sentiment, substance (breast milk, for instance) and nurturance. Kinship ties deriving from procreation are but one subset of this larger complex, seen
as distinct but are not privileged. 'New kinship', then, in this reading, has as its avowedly central theme a project closely linked to one
of feminist anthropology: 'defamiliarizing the "natural"'.[8] This is to
be a cross-cultural project (Carsten 2000a, 2004). Schneider's work
had helped usher in a new era of scepticism regarding the category
of kinship as a tool for cross-cultural comparison. Studies following
his questioning of the given status of kinship categories have tended
to focus on the West: assisted reproduction has been important, as
we shall see, but there have also been studies of other 'non-standard'
forms of kinship, such as adoption (Modell 1994; Carsten 2000b)
and between homosexuals (Weston 1991). Traditional anthropological studies of kinship, on the other hand, have, according to Carsten,
very much remained focused on the rural, undeveloped zones of the
world. By looking at reactions to assisted reproduction outside the

West, in this case in the Middle East, I intend to contribute to that continuing comparative endeavour. As we have already noted, however, the production of ethnographic examples suitable for 'defamiliarizing the "natural"' is neither epistemologically nor ethically uncomplicated in the case of the Islamic Middle East, where the advent of unfamiliar and 'unnatural' forms of relatedness may be seen as an unwelcome manifestation of imperialistic Western immorality.

New reproductive technologies

The advent of the new reproductive technologies (NRT, also ART, 'assisted reproductive technologies') looms large among the progenitors of the new kinship studies. 'Technologies such as AID (artificial insemination by donor) and IVF (in vitro fertilization) raised new questions about the nature of motherhood, of fatherhood, and of connections between children and their parents' (Carsten 2004: 21). This is an idea that comes up again and again: by expanding the possibilities of human reproduction, NRT force people to think about kinship. This process would then be valuable anthropologically. New lenses of the imagination appear through which to focus on old problems: 'the topic of NRT acts as an ethnographic window through which kinship ideas and assumptions can be discerned' (Edwards 1999 [1993]: 61). When people think about the issues such techniques raise, 'they model new possibilities on old facts. In so doing, they make explicit those "facts", and render visible to themselves what used to be taken for granted' (Edwards 1999 [1993]: 64). Holy (1996: 25) agrees – 'The new reproductive technologies and their discussion among specialists and the general public have significant consequences for the anthropological study of kinship. The reason is that they bring clearly into relief ... culturally specific Western [and non-Western?] assumptions about kinship' – as does Ragoné (1998: 118, reference omitted):

> With the introduction of assisted reproductive technologies (ARTs), seemingly simple yet nonetheless culturally bound assessments of what constitutes family, motherhood, and fatherhood ... can no longer be taken for granted. ARTs have served to defamiliarize what was once understood to be the 'natural' basis of human procreation and relatedness. In essence, ARTs have served, as the Comaroffs so eloquently said of ethnography, 'to make the familiar strange and the strange familiar, all the better to understand them both'.

In other words, NRT make anthropologists of all, by throwing into relief what was previously too obvious to see: to carry out anthropological studies of that process of popular reassessment would seem almost anthropology squared. And aside from any anthropological utility, NRT seem intrinsically exciting: they have something of the stimulating charge of supermodernity and controversy about them. Small wonder, then, that a considerable body of such work has emerged, including that at hand.[9] It is, however, worth standing back and considering a few of the propositions about NRT that circulate within the literature.

A wide variety of techniques can be found subsumed under the heading of 'NRT' or 'ART', including the use of ultrasound scanning of the foetus, for example, but it is those that impinge on conception that have inspired most anthropological interest. While a key element of the attraction of the topic is the very novelty of the 'new reproductive technologies', one might note that many of the techniques usually included under 'NRT' are not that novel (and indeed 'NRT' seems lately to have been replaced by 'ART' as nomenclature of choice).[10] There is nothing new in insemination by donor, nor indeed artificial insemination, by donor or otherwise. Artificial insemination of humans is documented in England as early as 1776 (Rivière 1985: 3), and there are classical Islamic legal rulings as to the status of such a child (see Chapter 4); the Church of England called a commission to report on artificial insemination by donor in 1948: it had been clinical practice in England since the late 1930s (Pfeffer 1987: 92). Nor indeed is it necessarily highly technological, which holds for surrogate motherhood as well (McNeil 1990: 1). It was the advent of in vitro fertilization (IVF), where fertilization takes place outside the body, that held out the prospect of unprecedented intervention in human reproduction:

> Fertilization outside the body ... has not only made it possible to monitor the process, it has encouraged the development of techniques using donor egg or sperm without the complications of sexual intercourse with a third party ... IVF thus stands (as a metonym) for all the possibilities that now exist for assisting conception. When people talk of the technologies in general, then, they usually mean fertilization taking place outside the body ... or ... gametes (eggs and sperm) being donated by third parties or ... women bringing to term children formed in part or whole from the genetic material of others. (Strathern 1999a [1993]: 25)

Even the 'reproductive' tag might seem erroneous if we consider some of the low rates of success reported for fertility treatments involving in vitro fertilization (see e.g. Franklin 1997). While the num-

ber of IVF babies born worldwide has passed the million mark, that
still represents a tiny proportion of the total number of births. NRT
still loom larger in the imagination than in reality.

It is the attendant controversy and keen public debate that really
lend NRT their charge, and that controversy actually arose somewhat
later than the 'new technologies' themselves, as Yoxen (1990) shows.
The key area of 'moral concern', in the 1980s at least, was embryo
research.[11] While there had been relatively little interest in techniques such as IVF before then, even though Steptoe and Edwards
had announced the first successful IVF embryo in 1968 (with a prior
claim by Rock and Menkin in 1944), and a commission into embryo
research was chaired in 1972, the Warnock Committee was not con-
vened until 1984, which leaves a long delay between the birth of
Louise Brown in 1978 and the emergence of related legislation. The
impetus to the atmosphere of 'moral panic' surrounding embryo research, and hence IVF treatment, was rather 'the influence of the
loose coalition of traditionalist and neo-conservative groups on the
Right in British politics', a 'moral Right' bringing with it a change
in the political atmosphere. This was manifested especially within
the Conservative Party, which started advocating a 'return to Victorian values', thus facilitating 'recurrent attempts by groups opposed
to abortion to exploit new issues in reproductive medicine and to re-
new their campaign in a less liberal and pluralist political culture'
(Yoxen 1990: 183–84)[12] and culminating, in this case, with Enoch
Powell's 1984 Private Member's Bill proposing a complete ban on
human embryo research. Thus the vagaries of British politics, and
especially the growing influence of pressure groups advocating a re-
treat from 'permissive' liberal values and legislation, led to the high
media profile of issues concerning fertility treatment, albeit indi-
rectly.

It is also worth noting that public and parliamentary debate regarding changing patterns of kinship in the U.K. is nothing new, as
Wolfram (1987) illustrates. The Deceased Wife's Sister's Marriage
Act of 1907, permitting the previously forbidden marriage to the
eponymous deceased wife's sister, had a prolonged gestation – sixty-
five years – and provoked huge public controversy. It was the first in
a series of acts[13] that further eroded the prohibition on marriage to
affinal relatives, who had previously been viewed as equivalent to
'blood relatives' in this regard, as a consequence of spouses being
'one flesh'. The 1908 Punishment of Incest Act made incest a crime
for the first time in England, but under a restricted definition: it ap-

plied to blood relatives in the second degree or less; previously sexual relations with affines had also been regarded as 'incestuous'.
This reflected and promoted a new, 'scientific' idea of incest, at odds
with the legislation of the time regarding marriage prohibitions: as
Wolfram (1987: 44) notes, the 'Incest Taboo' that rapidly achieved
prominence in anthropological writings was actually the newly limited prohibitions of the 1908 act. The Church of England was moved
to appoint a commission to investigate the matter in 1937, which, on
the express wishes of the Archbishop of Canterbury, drew on the expertise of anthropologists, Malinowski and Westermarck, whose testimony indeed precedes that of biblical criticism in the eventual
report (Church of England 1940; cf. Wolfram 1987: 7 n. 9). Again, a
new round of parliamentary debate in 1978 and onwards concerning
marriage to stepchildren provoked another Church of England commission, which again drew on the evidence of anthropologists: Jean
La Fontaine, Esther Goody and Wolfram herself (Church of England
1980). Thus, *pace* Rivière (1985), who noted the lack of anthropological involvement in the Warnock Report, anthropologists had very
much been involved in what were extensive public debates concerning ideas of kinship.[14]

Indeed, anthropology, and especially its exotic ethnographic examples, had a key role to play not only in these debates but also in
wider transformations of social and moral thinking in the West. Rel-
ativistic arguments concerning the conventional nature of social relations have drawn on anthropology since its Victorian beginnings:
'Via that argument anthropology has been a major contributor to liberal humanism' (Scheffler 1991: 365). The work of Malinowski and
Mead in the 1920s and 1930s was seized upon by writers such as
Bertrand Russell (1976 [1929] for example), proponents of a 'new
morality' to replace Victorian mores, as we will see later (Chapter 6).
Anthropology has merely been a rather self-conscious part of a
whole intellectual trend of reevaluation and 'relativization' of traditional 'moral' categories in the West, into which the 'new' area of
NRT fits comfortably. The 'moral panic' and kinship debates associated with NRT are not new at all.

Furthermore, one has to question whether the studies of NRT have
succeeded, where their aim is precisely to document exciting and re-
vealing cultural debate. On the contrary, it seems that people utilize
these new techniques to reproduce what is 'normal'. Carsten (2004:
168) identifies a tension in the literature between analyses portray-
ing 'a very radical shift in knowledge practices and in the way we

think about kinship in the West, and those depictions that suggest that medical advances have really left most things unchanged or merely illuminate old certainties in new ways'. We might consider, for instance, Franklin's (1997: 209–10) ethnographic account of IVF treatment in England, where, broadly speaking, people see themselves as reproducing normally, just 'giving nature a helping hand'. That is, kinship relations do not seem to have been problematized, underlying assumptions do not seem to have suddenly been thrown sharply into relief and new modes of relatedness do not seem suddenly to have emerged, although Franklin (1997: 6) gamely asserts that NRT 'add a significant set of new relationships into the kinship equation, and these are the relationships to science and technology'. Carsten (2004: 186) finds 'startling' 'the obviousness of the manoeuvres involved' in much English discourse concerning assisted reproduction, but argues that it is the very insistence on the recognition of the 'biological facts' that 'is what is most different about contemporary Western kinship', a point that will be interesting to debate when we come to discuss Islamic views.

Again, no sudden revolution in Western kinship thinking has been induced by the advent of in vitro fertilization, nor, *pace* Carsten, are we entering a world 'after kinship'. On the contrary, it is clear from the ethnographies that Westerners are striving to realize their very recognizable kinship fantasies, whether by downplaying the importance of the gestational carrier to families realized through surrogacy arrangements (Ragoné 1994), or by having one lesbian co-mother undertake the insemination of the other (Hayden 1995). These cultural manoeuvres are the latest episodes in a long history of continuity and change, as the best writing on the topic makes clear (e.g. Strathern 1992a). Stone (2004a: 332) argues that '[w]hile new constructions of kinship are occurring in European and American society and in this process choice is playing a larger role, there is at the same time a counter-current [the new genetics] drawing Americans, at least, back to biogenetic conceptions of kinship ... What we may be seeing, then, along with a destabilization of nature and the emergence of choice in kinship is a tension between kinship as choice and social construction and the older cultural conception of kinship as rooted in biological reproduction'.[15]

But this is perhaps to impose a false chronology: as Strathern (1993: 196) has said, 'there was always a choice as to whether or not biology was made the foundation of relationships', and, as Wolfram (1987) illustrated, the supposedly fundamental determining role of 'biology' (and certainly 'biogenetics') is of relatively recent origin. What about marriage, the oldest form of elective kinship of all, which has ever presented the opportunities and dilemmas of choosing one's relatives? What is new, if anything, is the fetishization of choice, equally bound up in the rhetoric of the right of individuals to receive infertility treatment at the expense of the state.[16] Anthropological narratives of disjuncture and emergence here tend to obliterate the theoretical and ethnographic continuities that are there alongside the changes.

On a related point, the student of assisted reproduction can follow a number of possible paths: one might consider the point of view of the practitioners, for example, or the patients, the general public, religious and other ethical opinion makers. The 'field site' might then comprise a clinic, a kitchen table, or a library. Edwards, Franklin, Hirsch, Price and Strathern's (1999 [1993]) project, for instance, was to cover as many as of the above as possible, to give a complete snapshot of assisted conception in British life at the time: Price talked to clinicians; Edwards examined the reactions of people in the north of England, Hirsch those in the south; Franklin dealt with parliamentary debate; Strathern presented her own reflections. Franklin has covered a great deal of ground over a number of published studies, from analyses of the culture of 'desperation' attributed to infertile women as depicted in various media (1990), to the parliamentary debates concerning legislation to regulate infertility treatment in Britain (1999 [1993]), to ethnographic accounts of women's experiences in undergoing IVF treatment (1997).

But for me, much of the most interesting work on assisted reproduction in general has been the analysis of legislation, both governmental and religious. This may just be a matter of taste, although I think it is also connected with the issue that I just touched on, namely that people actually undergoing such treatments – and the doctors administering them – are, understandably, keen to portray what they are doing as 'normal'. It is in the wider debate, on the part of those perhaps not so intimately involved with the issue, that the conceptual revelations an anthropologist might be interested in, as a student of kinship at least, arise. As Franklin (1999: 130) says in the course of her study of the British parliamentary debates concerning the proposed Human Fertilisation and Embryology Bill (HFEB) in 1989–90: 'the parliamentary debate was a unique instance of formal, public kinship negotiation'. The claim to uniqueness is extravagant: she continues, '[t]o the anthropologist familiar with kinship theory, the parliamentary debate of the HFEB could be seen as sharing much in common with debates in other cultures, in previous histori-cal periods in this culture, and indeed within the discipline of anthro-pology itself'; '[a]nthropologists and parliamentarians can indeed be seen to have something in common in the effort to elucidate the foundations of kinship' (1999: 131). So too the Islamic legal special-ists that are our subject here, who have to plumb the depths of their source texts and ethnographic knowledge, where relevant, to arrive at some coherent notion of how 'Islamic society' is to be constituted, and of how kinship is supposed to work, that will allow them to think through and accommodate such new developments.[17]

Given the perceived benefit of studying these new possibilities, from the perspective of anthropology, one would expect work to have been done outside 'the West', so far as such techniques are available. Such studies have started to appear, although they are still comparatively rare.[18] It is perhaps debatable, and interestingly so for my argument here, whether Kahn's (2000) depiction of assisted con-ception in Israel could be regarded as of a 'non-Western' milieu; Carsten clearly thinks not (2004: 178), although she admits to find-ing the nature of rabbinical debate strange and surprising. Not only is Israel politically, socially and economically isolated from the wider Middle East, it is religiously distinct, and has a very different relationship with modernity and Western morality, a key point as we shall see. But there has also been interest in fertility treatment in the wider Middle East, most notably in the case of medical anthropolo-gist Marcia Inhorn, who has produced a considerable body of work that largely focuses on gender, first concerning Egypt (1994, 1996, 2003), but now also Lebanon (2004a, 2006a) and the Arab Gulf. An-thropologist Soraya Tremayne (2006, n.d.) has recently been en-gaged in similar research in Iran. Her work does take an interest in kinship, and provides a stimulating point of comparison to my own.

Certainly, techniques such as artificial insemination and IVF are available in the Middle East and are being taken up with enthusiasm, their religious and social implications debated. Dr Gamal Serour, di-rector of the International Islamic Centre for Population Studies and Research at al-Azhar University, Cairo, notes that infertility rates among Muslims in developing countries are relatively high (10–15 per cent) and that '[t]he prevention and treatment of infertility are of particular significance in the Muslim World. The social status of the Muslim woman, her dignity and self-esteem are closely related to her procreation potential in the family and in the society as a whole'

(Serour 1993: 211).[19] The first IVF centre in the Arab world was established in Saudi Arabia and closely followed by centres in Jordan and Egypt, in 1986. After the first Egyptian IVF baby was born in 1987 the technique became more widely accepted: the first Sudanese IVF baby was born in 1989, followed by births in Saudi Arabia and Jordan, stimulating the establishment of clinics in Morocco, Iraq, Kuwait and Tunisia (Serour, El Ghar and Mansour 1991). Lebanon's own first IVF baby was also born in 1989, at the Sarhal Hospital ('First test-tube baby born in Lebanon' 1989). Thus, as Inhorn (2003: 1) points out, there are IVF centres not just in oil-rich countries such as Bahrain and Qatar, but also in larger, poorer countries such as Egypt and Morocco. She refers to a 'globalization' of assisted reproduction, and '[p]erhaps nowhere is this globalization process more evident than in the nearly twenty nations of the Muslim Middle East'. Let us note further that the world's first attempt at a uterus transplant took place in Saudi Arabia (Kandela 2000; Fageeh et al. 2002).

Ideas of kinship in the Middle East

Anthropological studies of kinship in the Middle East have reflected the rising and falling fortunes of kinship within anthropology as a whole. Kinship was a key focus in studies of the region: first in the late nineteenth century through the work of William Robertson Smith;[20] and later due to intense interest in the supposed prevalence of patrilateral parallel cousin marriage, with the father's brother's child (usually 'FBD', father's brother's daughter, in the literature) seen as a 'problem' from the perspective of wider anthropological theory, but then found to be a problem of the anthropologists' own devising by Bourdieu (1977) among others, although more recent medical research has confirmed that such marriages are statistically significant.[21] From the 1950s on, there was an explosion of interest in the topic due to its inconsistency with the major general kinship theories of the time, and especially that of Lévi-Strauss's *Les structures élémentaires de la parenté* (1949), founded on the nominally universal principle that kin groups exchange women in marriage. In this context, patriparallel cousin marriage, where marriage takes place within the agnatic group, appears as 'a sort of quasi-incest ... a sort of scandal' (Bourdieu 1977: 30). But as a positive marriage rule, in Lévi-Strauss's sense, FBD marriage simply does not work, as Copet-Rougier (1994) has demonstrated: in order to perpetuate FBD marriage, an element from outside will have to be brought in every other generation.[22] Taken on its own, then, 'FBD marriage' is insufficient and incoherent as a 'marriage system', and many anthropologists came to dismiss the debate as fundamentally misguided.

The key to understanding the rhetorical interest in parallel cousin marriage in the region, an interest that does translate into practice to a greater or lesser degree, lies in turning away from analyses rooted in 'kinship theory' and coming to terms with 'the cultural and social reality' of which such notions and actions are a part (Holy 1989: 15). FBD marriage is only one among a number of common marriage strategies. Marriages can be either 'close' or 'distant', but it is close marriage that is ideologically privileged, and given the precedence of agnatic relations over uterine, it is the patriparallel cousin who is the closest marriageable relative of all (Holy 1989). This marrying 'close' has resonance: the nearest to a word for 'kinship' in Arabic, *qarābah,* means, at root, 'closeness' (Eickelman 1976; Conte 1991, 1994b; Clarke 2007b);[23] a relative is one 'close' (*qarīb*).[24] Here we see the contrast with, for instance, nineteenth-century bourgeois Britain, where cousin marriage certainly occurred (Kuper 2002), but within a very different ideology: Wolfram (1987: 38–39) notes 'the close tie conceived to exist between being related to someone and being forbidden to marry them, as if by allowing marriage between two people, it followed, *ipso facto,* that they would no longer really be relations'. The rhetoric in the Middle East is quite the opposite: they are the ideal marriage partners because they are close relations. Certainly medical surveys of genetically transmitted diseases in the Middle East confirm an enthusiasm for 'consanguineous marriage' beyond FBD marriage alone; that includes Lebanon, although rates there are relatively low.[25]

This preference for 'closeness' is also an aversion to distance, to entrusting a 'stranger' with one's own. As one Lebanese doctor explained to me, '[t]he reason for marrying the cousin is that the girl's parents will know his mother and father, how they're living. Morals are the most important thing: faithfulness, dignity, character. With *bint al-'amm* [the FBD] you know everything'. This is a rhetoric of protection (Bourdieu 1966: 227): from a male perspective, protection of one's womenfolk and one's own public standing, or 'honour', which is intimately tied to them. That is to say that a man's duty of protection, on which his honour depends, paradigmatically applies to his womenfolk. Further, their sexual conduct redounds upon

him.[26] They are *harām,* 'sacred', and 'forbidden' to others. From
here derives the motif of 'covering' and 'veiling' of women that has
become so important to contemporary Islamist thought and such a
source of Western fascination. In this reading, then, an emphasis on
FBD marriage is congruent with a concern to protect one's own – a
male duty – and a concomitant ideology of the hierarchical superiority of man over woman (Bourdieu 1977: 44), and thus agnatic relations over uterine (Holy 1989: 119, 126–27; Bonte and Conte
1991).[27] For our purposes here, it is the interest in 'closeness' and
protecting one's own, as well as the ideology of gender that goes
with it, that it will be important to keep in mind.

Substance

But this hardly exhausts the issues to hand, and some have sought to
pursue the fundamentals of kinship in the region further, most notably through the device of 'substance'. This brings us to the second
'problem', or phenomenon needing explanation, that has occupied
students of kinship in the region, that of 'milk kinship', broached by
Soraya Altorki (1980), a theme to which we will have cause to return
in our discussions of assisted reproduction. Islamic law divides 'kinship', *qarābah* ('closeness', as above), into three parts: *nasab* (relations of filiation, 'consanguinity' in anthropological terms),[28]
musāharah (relations through marriage, 'alliance') and *ridā'* (relations through breastfeeding, 'milk kinship' in the anthropological literature).[29] Regarding *ridā'*, kinship-type relations are instituted by
suckling at the same breast, relations that include a prohibition on
marriage (but not inheritance rights, an important point not mentioned by Altorki). So an otherwise unrelated boy and girl, suckled
by the same nurse, become milk brother and milk sister and cannot
marry. Nor can the nurseling marry his or her nurse.

'Milk kinship' is not merely a legal nicety, but has a social reality,
as Altorki (1980: 240–43) describes for the Saudi Arabia of living
memory (as of the 1970s). In the past, large households with many
women living together promoted the breastfeeding of other women's
babies, for example when one mother was ill, or left to rejoin her
parents in the case of a dispute with her husband. More recently, the
availability of milk powder and a change from the traditional patrilo-
cal extended family household to neolocal nuclear family residence
has led to the decline of the practice.[30] Previously, milk kinship was
established for 'strategic purposes'.[31] It helped 'to make domestic
life more convenient' (1980: 240). In Islamic law, women should veil

before non-kinsmen.[32] 'Frequently, therefore, a man would ask a slave woman who had children herself to nurse his daughters, so that they would not have to veil to her son(s)' (1980: 240).[33] Also, were a marriage between a nursing woman's child and that of a relative envisaged, and unwanted by the woman or her husband, she might nurse the two children together, instituting a marriage prohibition and forestalling the unwelcome union (1980: 240–41). Dresch (2005: 266 n. 19) reports that in the Arab Gulf, milk kinship 'appeared almost a dead issue for a generation, but suddenly reappeared as a means to annul inconvenient marriages or avoid adultery charges': spouses might claim to have been, unwittingly, milk kin all along; couples found together in circumstances more intimate than those required of marriageable persons might claim that they were in fact milk kin, and hence intimates after all.[34]

We might note straight away that while 'substance' (*māddah*) does not, by and large, feature in Islamic discussions of kinship, a particular substance – breast milk – does seem to be playing a key role, and has proved an attractive theme for kinship analysts of a systematic bent. In particular, French anthropologist Françoise Héritier (1994; 1999) has incorporated her ideas of 'Arab kinship', including milk kinship, into a bold, universal theory of kinship and incest founded on the theme of substance, construed literally: for her, '[t]he fundamental criterion of incest is the contact between identical bodily fluids' (1999: 11). This has led her to identify a widespread prohibition against 'incest of the second type',[35] where such substances are brought into contact via a third party, as when a man has sexual relations with two sisters, or mother and daughter. Such marriage prohibitions are seen as being a manifestation of a universal 'underlying logic' (1999: 15), which can be found in every culture if one digs deep enough. Héritier takes as her starting point Islamic marriage prohibitions. Firstly, the Quran (seventh century AD) explicitly prohibits the following:

> You shall not marry the women whom your fathers married: all previous such marriages excepted. That was an evil practice, indecent and abominable. Forbidden to you are your mothers, your daughters, your sisters, your paternal and maternal aunts, the daughters of your brothers and sisters, your milk mothers, your milk sisters, the mothers of your wives, your stepdaughters who are in your charge, born of the wives with whom you have lain (it is no offence for you to marry your stepdaughters if you have not consummated your marriage with their mothers), and the wives of your own begotten sons.

You are also forbidden to take in marriage two sisters at one and the same time: all previous marriages excepted. Surely God is forgiving and merciful. Also married women, except those whom you own as slaves. Such is the decree of God. All other women than these are lawful for you, provided you court them with your wealth in modest conduct, not in fornication. (4:22–27)[36]

Héritier notes the prohibition of marriage with the stepdaughter (*rabībah*), if the marriage with her mother has been consummated: 'Can it be said any more clearly that bodily contact and the passage of fluids from one to another is the basis for the taboo?' (1999: 12–13).3

To turn to the prohibitions on marriage between milk kin, Héritier takes up an example of Altorki's from the Saudi Arabia of the 1970s, which shows the grave effects of contracting a marriage between milk kin:[38] such an arrangement, even if unintentional, incurs divine sanction as *zinā* (illicit sex), which Héritier (1994: 157) glosses as 'incest'. A married couple were found to be milk kin, unbeknownst to them. They had had four children: two were mute, one lame and one disfigured by smallpox. 'Informants regarded the children's misery as divine punishment of their parents' violation of the *radā'ah* taboo' (Altorki 1980: 243). Here we must note that *zinā* refers to the sin of having sex outside a legally recognized union: fornication before marriage and adultery after it are also *zinā*, indeed would be the most obvious translations of the term. 'Incestuous' sex is perforce *zinā*, because it is sex with relatives whom one cannot marry: it will be sex outside a legally recognized union. Thus 'incest' here is Héritier's interpretation, and not a translation of the indigenous category. Indeed, as van Gelder (2005: 4–5) points out, there is no word in Arabic for what English (or French) terms 'incest'.[39] *Zinā* will prove a key concept for us, as discussions of the use of donor gametes in artificial reproduction turn around whether they are analogous to *zinā*, so it is important to note it well here. This is not a trivial matter: *zinā* is a heinous crime in Islamic thought, one of the very few crimes against God for which He demands a set punishment (*hadd*), death by stoning for the married and lashes for those not.

Héritier further adduces other ethnographic and jurisprudential items, most especially the extension of the milk prohibition by classical Islamic jurisprudence (ninth/tenth century AD) by analogy with the prohibitions of consanguinity and affinity, themselves extended to include ascendants and descendants (grandmothers, granddaughters etc.) beyond the core prohibitions of the Quran. Milk nieces, milk aunts, milk daughters, milk grandmothers and milk grand-daughters are all forbidden in marriage, as are the milk mother of one's wife, and simultaneous marriage to two women who are milk sisters (Giladi 1999: 24–25);[40] further, the breastfeeding woman's husband and his consanguines are also prohibited, a stipulation that has led to considerable debate. Altorki builds upon her contemporary Saudi Arabian informants' 'folk theory' that 'the milk is from the man' (1980: 243 n. 3) to find a 'doctrine that the "fluids" of both the lactating woman and her husband [as 'copulation partner'] generate the milk' (1980: 233).[41] Héritier (1994: 158) incorporates the contemporary folk theory into a 'somatic scheme' (Parkes 2005): 'milk is transformed sperm'.

Héritier's theory is not without its critics:[42] its strengths and weaknesses both lie in its ambition, the scale of the universal project of which it is a part. An exciting comparative paradigm, it does not always have room for historical and ethnographic particularity. What is important for our purposes here is rather the very diversity of legal positions and physiological theories. As Dresch (1998: 131 n. 37) has it, Héritier's account wants a historical perspective: the rulings of classical Islamic jurisprudence, themselves controversial (Giladi 1999: 79–80), are different from those of the Quran; and the Quran itself changed what had gone before. We might further note that Shiite Islamic law has its own peculiarities (Khatib-Chahidi 1992; Conte 2000a; Benkheira 2001a). Milk kinship is juridically a controversial and highly complex area whose complexity will be equally apparent when we turn to Islamic legal reactions to the new reproductive technologies. And of course 'folk' notions do not necessarily map exactly onto juridical ones, nor are they themselves consistent (Altorki 1980: 238).

That diversity of opinion extends to other substances. For the European or American reader, the substance most naturally associated with the idea of kinship is blood, and Arabic and Islamic concepts are often so translated: *nasab* as 'blood relationship', for example. However, as Benkheira (2001b: 43) says, 'the Islamic scholars of the classical epoch are strangers to this way of seeing things' (see also Conte 1994a; Bonte, Conte and Dresch 2001). As for popular notions, Delaney notes that in the modern Turkish village context, for instance, 'since the identity of the person comes from the seed, not blood, villagers are relatively unconcerned about blood' (1991: 154). On the other hand, I myself found in the course of my fieldwork in Lebanon that blood was commonly used as a symbol of kinship in an immediately familiar fashion. Dresch (2005: 266 n. 18) notes similar references in discussions of nationality in the Arab Gulf, but finds them an 'import'. Whatever the case, 'blood' is not, it seems, the long-standing symbolic substance of kinship that one finds elsewhere.[43]

If we turn to sperm, a key substance as regards assisted reproduction, then it is clear for the Middle East that it was ever understood that the production of babies requires sexual intercourse and that the semen of the man plays an indispensable role in the process. What has been more obscure is the extent of that role, and that of the woman. This question was extensively debated in the classical period of Islam, as Musallam describes: after all, '[b]etween Galen in the early centuries of Christianity, and Malpighi and Harvey in early modern times, there are about fifteen centuries during which the basic contributions to biology were made in Arabic' (1983: 42). The majority of scholars followed Hippocrates and Galen in thinking that both the male and the female contributed 'seed'; indeed, Musallam argues that 'the remarkable consensus among all Muslim jurists from the tenth to the nineteenth century that contraception is licit' (1983: 52) can only be understood in the light of this theory of equal contribution – that is, to 'waste' the male seed is not in itself destructive.[44] Nevertheless, the rival position, that of Aristotle, that it was the man's semen that contributed the form and indeed soul of the child, while the woman contributed the physical material from which the child was formed, also had its adherents.

Contemporary Islamic scholars have, for the most part, digested the evidence of modern science, which has confirmed the 'duogenetic' position, as we will see when we come to consider their reactions to the new reproductive technologies. However, even when one has indisputable evidence of the female 'semen', the ovum, that hardly ends the debate, as the disputes over the maternal relation in surrogacy arrangements and donor egg procedures show, both in Western and in Islamic thinking. If the scholars were not agreed, still less must the rest of the population have had a single view (Gran 1979). In modern times, despite the influence of the duogenetic 'scientific' position, universally known in my experiences of highly educated Lebanon, there is evidence from elsewhere that some 'folk' opinions might be, or might have been, otherwise. Delaney (1991) founds an entire study of a Turkish village on the premise that their view of procreation is fundamentally 'monogenetic', the man being the origin of the child and the woman merely its receptacle, in an id-

iom of 'the seed and the soil'.[45] Inhorn (1994: 67–76) found a mixture of monogenetic and duogenetic opinion in her work on infertility among lower-class Egyptian women: some see women as mere
'catchers and carriers', others as 'suppliers of menstrual blood' and
thus playing a more active role in forming the baby, others as 'egg
producers'. Nevertheless, even where duogenetic opinion has taken
hold, it has not changed the 'patriarchal' assumptions that supposedly
underpin the monogenetic theory. Although, then, there clearly are
and have been a large number of ideas of substances associated with
kinship in the Middle East, we will struggle to find one, single, consistent account, and certainly not a logic of substance such as Héritier
conceives it, as the fundamental structure from whose axioms all else
flows. As Dresch (1998: 132 n. 37) puts it: 'The rhetoric of substance
needs a history. That of relations seems to need far less.'

Fluidity and fixity

In Janet Carsten's (1995) account of kinship in a Muslim Malay
fishing community, an important text in the new kinship tradition,
Carsten draws on ideas of substance and commensality to demonstrate how relations of kinship are here not given by birth, but
formed through co-residence and consubstantiality: acquiring kinship is a process. She discusses the Islamic marriage prohibition on
milk relations, very salient in the case of her community, and aspects
of indigenous ideas of physiology that also sound familiar from
other Islamic contexts: breast milk is believed to derive from the
woman's blood;[46] the man's seed is said to come from fluid in the
backbone.[47] But here, substances do seem involved in a logic or 'somatic scheme' such as Héritier's, with the emphasis placed on blood,
which Carsten sees as the key substance. Food is transformed into
blood, which is then further translated into breast milk. 'Through the
day-to-day sharing of meals cooked in the same hearth, those who
live together in one house come to have substance in common'; 'relatedness is derived both from acts of procreation and from living
and eating together' (1995: 234, 236).[48] Again, kinship relations are
not given but formed over time, part of a wider 'fluidity of identity'
(1995: 224).

Compare this account of Arabia in a bygone age:

> Closeness of kinship resulted as much from individual and collective
> choice as from physiological or hereditary determinants. The sym-

bolic exchange of blood or of milk generated an elective kinship, capable of annulling a biological relation. A free man could disown the son 'of his kidneys' and adopt, by conferring on him his name, the heir of his choice, let live or die his new-born daughters, renounce his agnatic identity, be 'reborn' as a member of a new group and recognise a second father there, trace his descent from several ancestors, elect his brothers, make an 'outsider' a neighbour, a neighbour an ally, a stranger a kinsman, cross the generations by marriage to his aunts, nieces, etc., take new wives, buy concubines, accord others sexual access to women under his control with an eye to increasing his progeny, exchange these with others, in short just about determine the number and quality of his kin. (Conte 2000b: 296)

Such fluidity and choice is the very stuff of the new kinship studies. But Conte is describing pre-Islamic Arabia.[49] With Islam, these practices were formally ended.[50] The Quran speaks clearly here:

He [God] does not regard ... your adopted sons as your own sons. These are mere words which you utter with your mouths: but God declares the truth and gives guidance to the right path. Name your adopted sons after their fathers; that is more just in the sight of God. (33:4–5)

Adoption, under the Islamic legal precepts that are our subject here, is a 'lie', a perversion of the 'truth', as leading contemporary Islamic scholar Yusuf al-Qaradawi (1994: 223–24) makes clear:

Islam rightly views ... adoption as a falsification of the natural order and of reality. Taking a stranger into the family as one of its members and allowing privacy with women who are not his *mahārim*,[51] nor he theirs, is a deception, for the man's wife is not the adopted son's mother, nor is his daughter the boy's sister nor is his sister his aunt, since all of them are non-*mahram* [non-prohibited] to him. Moreover, the adopted son acquires a claim on the inheritance of the man and his wife, depriving the rightful, deserving relatives of their inheritance. Such a situation arouses the anger of the real relatives against the intruder who encroaches upon them and usurps their rights, depriving them of their full inheritance. Frequently such anger leads to quarrels and to the breaking of relations among relatives.

Kinship, it seems, will not dissolve into protection or commensality so easily in these cases. That is not to deny the importance of shared food and residence in the Middle East, or the place of substance in notions of kinship: indeed, elsewhere I have attempted to analyse milk kinship in those very terms, as part of the wider ethic of hospitality that, in some contexts, explicitly links the right and duty of protection to the host's provision of food – 'bread and salt' – to his guest (Clarke 2005: 72–78). But such relations, subsequent to the Revelation, are not so easily transformed formally into those of kinship proper.

According to the vision of the Islamic legal establishment, relations of filiation (*nasab*), are not mutable or fluid, but are given, paradigmatically – but not exclusively – through procreation. Relation through procreation is not, however, a sufficient condition for the establishment of *nasab* in Islamic law. *Nasab* accrues to those conceived within a union of marriage. All children born to a married woman, subsequent to a minimum period after the marriage contract and prior to a maximum period after its dissolution through death or divorce, are related to that woman and her husband. 'The child to the [marriage] bed, and to the adulterer the stone' (*al-walad li-l-firāsh wa-li-l-'āhir al-hajar*), as a famous saying of the Prophet states, theoretically raising the possibility of a man being father to children not biologically his, although hardly condoning it.[52] However, if a husband is convinced of his wife's infidelity, he can and should repudiate her and her bastard within a set period after the birth of the child. The illegitimate child, the child of *zinā,* has no father under Sunni Islamic law, and neither father nor mother under Shiite law. There is no classical Islamic concept of a 'natural' child, although their existence is acknowledged and the problem of whether one can marry one's own bastard is debated – the majority of legal opinion prohibits it (Kohlberg 1985: 245–46; Salamah 1998: 170ff.).

In Islamic thought, society is a system of rights and obligations, based fundamentally on such relations between kin. As proper *nasab* is what gives one full membership in society, it is a right: it is a common theme, in discussions of illegitimate sex, that a child has a right to legitimacy.[53] Without it, he or she will be severely disadvantaged, deprived of the support, financial and otherwise, due from their relatives, and also of their inheritance.[54] As *nasab* is the principle on which this whole system of social rights and obligations is founded, and is acquired through sex within marriage, illicit sex (*zinā*) threatens the very framework of Islamic society, hence its severe nominal punishment – death by stoning or numerous lashes, as noted above (Coulson 1979). This is a vision, admittedly an ideal one, but one familiar from the Middle Eastern contexts I have worked in, at odds with the fluidity of kinship identity in Carsten's account of her Malay community. As in the European and North American models scholars such as Carsten seek to problematize, kinship is 'real', and nominally follows procreation: under Islam, adoption is formally forbidden, even if it may occur informally, or in contexts where Islamic law is not what is at issue, as we will see in the next chapter (and see Conte 2003). 'Relatedness' will not cover the Islamic Middle Eastern model: kinship relations are singled out as particular. Despite attempts to analyse those relations in terms of honour, 'closeness' or substance, filiation remains an indispensable principle.[55]

Notes

1. I have not been able to establish who first used the term, but Carsten (2004: passim), for instance, clearly views it as conventionally established (as do Patterson 2005 and Strathern 2005: vii). Stone (2001) talks of 'new directions' in kinship studies; Franklin and McKinnon (2001a: 1) of '[t]he new uses of kinship theory, and the novel sites and locations where kinship theory is being pursued'. Dousset (2005) prefers to distinguish 'classic' and 'modern' approaches. 'New kinship' offers the useful, if ambiguous, possibility of referring to both the new approaches to kinship within anthropology, and to the new forms kinship is supposedly taking in the modern West (for the latter see Carsten 2004: xi, 180).

2. Schneider saw his position as distinct from that of Needham, who had, according to Schneider (1984: vii–viii), retained 'kinship' as a useful word for the purposes of anthropological analysis. Schneider feels that he himself went further, claiming that it is positively misleading. This was not the first time that Needham and Schneider had clashed (see e.g. Needham 1962; Schneider 1965).

3. Again, not an original thought, Hocart for one having made the same point half a century earlier (Hocart 1937). As Patterson (2005: 8) wryly notes, it took some cheek for Schneider to declare 'his own inability to grasp the indigenous subtleties of Yapese kinship … a clear demonstration that all "kinship" was bunk'.

4. Patterson challenges this as 'perhaps more a reflection of Anglocentrism than anything else' (2005: 2), pointing to a continued interest in kinship studies in the traditional mould in France in particular. Lamphere (2001) sees more of a continuum than a disjunction, particularly in the case of feminist analyses. Franklin and McKinnon (2001a) point to several areas where Schneider was anticipated by others. The general pattern of a move away from formalistic kinship studies towards 'cultural' accounts focusing on gender, the person and the body nevertheless seems commonly accepted (besides Carsten's account cited below see Parkin

1997; Stone 2001; Parkin and Stone 2004).

5. Brown was the first baby to be born from an egg fertilised in vitro, 'in glass', i.e. outside the body, after many years of attempts on the part of the British pioneers Patrick Steptoe, an obstetrician and gynaecologist, and Robert Edwards, a physiologist. In such procedures, women are first given doses of hormones to stimulate 'superovulation'. Eggs that develop are then removed: initially this was by means of 'laparoscopy', a surgical procedure where an optical tool, the laparoscope, was inserted to view the ovaries and control the collection of the eggs, removed by passing a hollow needle through the woman's abdomen; this has now been superseded by the safer 'vaginal ultrasound guided aspiration', where a vaginal ultrasound probe with a fine hollow needle attached to it is inserted into the vagina. Under ultrasound guidance, the needle is then advanced from the vaginal wall into the ovary and eggs are removed through the needle by a suction device. The eggs are then placed together with processed sperm in a laboratory: some will be fertilized and thus become 'embryos' (see the note below on terminological confusion here). The final stage is 'embryo transfer' (ET), where the embryos are transferred to the woman's body by guiding a catheter through her cervix and then flushing them into her uterus.

6. Their approach has not gone unchallenged (see e.g. Scheffler 1991; Stone 1997).

7. Carsten proposed the adoption of the term 'relatedness' in an earlier attempt 'to rescue kinship from its post-Schneiderian demise' (1995: 224), although concedes (2000a: 5) that it could be seen as defined in a way that restricted it to genetic relatedness, and thus no improvement on 'kinship', or else as having such a broad application that it becomes 'analytically vacuous' (Holy cited in Carsten 2000a: 5).

8. Patterson (2005: 4) notes that the division between 'old' and 'new' kinship is itself gendered, 'old' kinship remaining a 'man's game', while studies in the new style are 'dominated by women, many of whom have specifically feminist agendas for demolishing what is seen by them as the masculinist citadel of "kinship"'. Scheffler (1991: 361) refers to 'the strange alliance of some feminists (anthropologists and others) with the antikinship school in symbolic anthropology': not so strange, in this reading.

9. For example, to cite but a few, the works of Strathern (1992a, 1992b), Ragoné (1994), Franklin (1997), Franklin and Ragoné (1998), Edwards et al. (1999 [1993]), Edwards (2000), Ragoné and Twine (2000), Franklin and McKinnon (2001b) and Konrad (2005).

10. This is symptomatic of a wider neophilism that embraces the delineation of a 'new kinship' that supersedes the old. 'Technology' points to

the same outlook (McNeil 1990: 1–2). Alternative terms such as 'assisted reproduction' and 'assisted conception' avoid the accusation, and 'ART' (assisted reproductive technologies) is perhaps now superseding 'NRT' in the anthropological literature (French usage perhaps favours the motif of assistance, as in *procréation médicalement assistée,* as does Arabic). But 'NRT' has been current enough for my point to stand. Strathern (1999a [1993]: 25) makes clear that she and her collaborators adopted 'new reproductive technologies' and 'the barbaric shorthand' 'NRT' as 'the colloquial designation': anthropological neophilism only reflects that of wider Euro-American society. On the point that there is nothing new in artificial insemination by donor or otherwise, see Strathern (1999b [1993]: 182) for a rejoinder.

11. There has been confusion as to the nature of the 'embryo'. As Crowe (1990: 45ff.) describes, the scientific community moved to describing the fertilized egg up to fourteen days after fertilization, i.e. before the formation, within the growing group of cells, of the 'primitive streak' of cells that will form the genetically distinct embryo rather than the placenta, as the 'pre-embryo'. The Warnock Committee, and subsequent public debate, took the embryonic stage as starting at the meeting of the egg and sperm.

12. These attempts were renewed in the 2005 general election campaign, where various parties (among them *Cosmopolitan* magazine and the Catholic Church) tried to make abortion an election issue. As Yoxen notes, the wellspring of the 'New Right' has been the United States.

13. These include the 1921 Deceased Brother's Widow's Marriage Act, the 1931 Marriage (Prohibited Degrees of Relationship) Act legalizing marriage with the deceased wife's aunts and nieces, and nephews' and uncles' widows, and the Marriage Enabling Act of 1960 allowing all relatives of the divorced couple to marry. The process continues (Simpson 2006).

14. Indeed, those previous debates were, so to speak, anthropologically literate. So, for example, the 1940 Church of England report cites theories of a move from matriarchy to patriarchy at some time in human history, and cites India and China for comparative purposes. The Levitical table of marriage prohibitions is analysed in anthropological terms, being found to show a patriarchal and patrilineal society: 'Thus the table can in general be explained by principles well known to anthropologists, and is comparable with many similar codes in other lands' (Church of England 1940: 26).

15. Stone (2004b) argues at length for individual choice as a third order of American kinship to be placed alongside Schneider's nature and law, in an analysis of contemporary American kinship through the lens of soap opera.

16. See McNeil (1990) on the language of individual choice and rights

in the matter of NRT. Franklin (1990) deconstructs the associated discourse of desperateness. Strathern (1992a, 1992b) has written powerfully on NRT, consumer choice and the enterprise culture.

17. Cf. Kahn (2000: 88) on the rabbinical debates in Israel. One thinks in particular of an anthropologist such as Édouard Conte, whose examination of Islamic legal reactions to the assisted reproductive technologies (2000b) is part of a larger project steeped in textual analysis. Islamic legal scholars, like anthropologists, deploy ethnographic example, usually in order to bring out what 'Islamic society' is not like. Van Gelder (2005) presents many examples of this in classical polemic against Jews, Zoroastrians and others. In more recent polemic the West comes to feature heavily. Pre-Islamic Arabia, the so-called 'time of ignorance' (*jāhilīyah*), is also important here: kinship practices were very different then. An appropriate example might be *nikāh al-istibdā'*, 'trade marriage', where a husband would allow a fine specimen of a man to sleep with his wife in order to procure high-quality offspring, an 'early version of procuring a sperm donor', as van Gelder (2005: 20) puts it.

18. See, for instance, Simpson's (2004a, 2004b, 2004c) work on Sri Lanka.

19. Contrast this rhetoric of social relations with that of individual rights in the West.

20. Smith's *Kinship and marriage in early Arabia* (1885) remains a seminal work, if flawed, however, by his determination to demonstrate the validity of his friend J. F. McLennan's theories of the evolution of society from matrilineality to patrilineality and 'totemism'. The first anthropological analysis of kinship in the Middle East was twisted to fit theories created outside the study of the region, a pattern we will see again.

21. See Clarke (2007b, 2007c). Dresch (2005: 264 n. 4) cites the medical research into genetically transmitted diseases by Al-Gazali et al. (1997), who give a rate for FBD marriage in the United Arab Emirates of 17.0 per cent. Medical statistics rarely pick out FBD marriages in particular, dealing rather with 'consanguineous' marriage, i.e. with second cousins or closer, also significant here (see below). Bonte's compilation of ethnographers' statistics from across the region (1994: 375, Table 1) has an average rate of FBD marriage of 12 per cent. Figures for Lebanon would commonly lie at the lower end of the spectrum (see below).

22. Thus, as Dresch (1998: 132 n. 44) highlights, 'parallel cousin marriage implies sister-exchange in the next generation but...no-one sees it that way'.

23. And, for Lebanon, compare Suad Joseph's (e.g. 1994) idea of 'connectivity'.

24. The opposite is not so much 'distant' (*ba'īd*) as a 'stranger' (*gharīb*, or *ajnabī*), a term that will recur here as it is also used for a gamete provider other than the spouse in fertility treatments.

25. The figures are impressive, with averages around 50 per cent for 'consanguineous' marriages, i.e. with the second cousin or closer, in the Gulf and Saudi Arabia, for instance (see e.g. Al-Gazali et al. 1997). For Lebanon, Khlat (1988) has 25 per cent for consanguineous marriages in Beirut. I have gathered some such statistics with full references elsewhere (Clarke 2005, 2007b, 2007c).

26. Whence the vast anthropological literature on 'honour and shame'.

27. Dresch (1998) reads it in terms of a wider interest in autonomy: again, dealing with others is problematic.

28. *Nasab* is a difficult term to translate, and not common in everyday speech, but refers to agnatic and uterine relations of filiation in legal discourse (see Conte 1991, 1994b on its ambiguities). It is also commonly used of 'genealogy', i.e. purely agnatic descent, projected backwards in time, seen, in Lebanon at least, as of interest to 'tribesmen' or elites. 'Blood relations', a common translation, is highly misleading in the present context.

29. The various terminologies employed in the anthropological literature can be confusing. I follow Hans Wehr's *Dictionary of modern written Arabic,* which has *radā'ah* as 'suckling'; thus one's *akh fī-l-radā'ah* is one's 'brother through suckling'; the legal relationship so created is *ridā'*, 'milk kinship'.

30. Examples of 'milk kinship' proved hard to find during my fieldwork: doctors confirmed the decline in incidences of colactation in Lebanon. That is not to say that these issues are not pertinent for our purposes here: they form an important part of the legal debate over the relations ensuing from the use of donor eggs and surrogacy arrangements (Clarke 2007d).

31. See Clarke (2007d). Parkes (see 2005 for full references), building on the suggestions of Khatib-Chahidi (1992), has traced out a historical complex of 'cliental allegiance fosterage', where milk kinship was used to institute relations of clientship that he finds extended through the ancient Mediterranean, Islamic Asia and even into some eastern Christian Churches.

32. Strictly speaking, women veil before all men save their husband and those relatives who are forbidden to them in marriage (*mahram*, pl. *mahārim*).

33. This issue and its solution should be remembered: exactly the same problems arise where some Islamic authorities allow the use of donor ga-

metes, but trace relatedness biologically. Someone's 'social' child would be forced to veil before them, or vice-versa, rendering domestic life intolerably inconvenient. Recall also Ahmed's attempts to render more satisfactory his adoption of a baby girl through instituting milk kinship with her (in the Prologue).

34. Such was the popularity of such ruses that the courts were proposing not to recognize milk kinship any more (Dresch, personal comment). One does not want to take milk kinship too seriously, then.

35. The first type being 'the usual but overly narrow definition of incest', as being between 'opposite-sex partners who are close blood relations or relatives by marriage' (Héritier 1999: 10).

36. The translation is Dawood's (1990), with the modification of 'milk mother' and 'milk sister' for his 'foster-mother' and 'foster-sister'. Note again that one can marry 'close' – all cousins are marriageable.

37. Yes, it can be: many jurists ruled that even looking at a woman in an inappropriate manner might constitute sexual relations entailing marriage prohibitions; were a man inadvertently to touch his daughter lustfully then his wife would be forbidden to him, for example (van Gelder 2005: 101–2).

38. Delaney (1991: 155) describes how, when the Turkish government launched a campaign to discourage marriages between close kin on hygienic grounds, the villagers countered: 'The doctors don't understand. We've been trying to tell them for years, but they don't listen. Blood has nothing to do with it. We always marry relatives and nothing happens. It is only when we inadvertently marry [milk siblings] that [deformed] children develop.'

39. The English meaning has itself varied historically (Wolfram 1987). As van Gelder also points out, there was no word for 'incest' in Ancient Greek either, although that hardly prevented the theme's prominence in Greek literature. Van Gelder does find, however, in his extensive survey of incest and inbreeding in classical Arabic literature, less interest in the topic than in European literature (2005: 181–85). Having said that, there is evidence that jurists considered incestuous, in the English sense, relations as more reprehensible than other forms of *zinā* (2005: 103–9).

40. An expansion founded on the Prophet's saying that breastfeeding prohibits that which birth (or consanguinity [*nasab*]) prohibits (Giladi 1999: 24; Benkheira 2001a: 13).

41. We might note that the milk relation with the nurse's 'copulation partner' is only instituted if he and the nurse are married (Benkheira 2001a: 27): the relation is thus legal as much as it is substantial. The juridical counterpart to the folk theory is the idea of *laban al-fahl,* 'the

milk of the man [lit. "stallion", "sire"]', that is, that the milk in some sense is that of the nurse's husband, he is the "'owner" of the milk' (Giladi 1999: 26). This phrasing, 'owner of the milk', is echoed in Islamic legal discussions of 'sperm and egg owners', i.e. donors, where *sāhib*, 'owner', might be better translated 'producer' or 'originator'. It is not supposed that by buying another man's sperm one can thereby acquire legitimate paternity through its use. Benkheira (2001a: 19–20; 2001b: 417) makes a similar point regarding milk.

42. Myself included, I should admit (Clarke 2005: 56–72). See also Parkes (2005).

43. In Europe, certainly, and in Southeast Asia as well, for example (Carsten, personal comment).

44. Thus masturbation, while forbidden by many jurists, was not prohibited on the grounds of being a homicidal 'spilling of seed' as in Christian and Jewish thought. Masturbation at the hand of one's wife or concubine was and is admissible. It is masturbating oneself that is seen as dubious, as a sexual act not taking place within a legal union. This of course has ramifications for fertility treatment, as many procedures require the procurement of semen. Contraception has remained permissible in modern Islam, although birth control as a means of population control has sometimes been regarded with suspicion, as a Western or Zionist plot against Islam (Fargues 2000: 91–97).

45. This image also occurs in Islamic discourse, being found in the Quran (e.g. 2:223, 'women are your fields'). It comes into play in some Islamic discussions of assisted reproduction, as we will see.

46. Although there is no sign here of the idea that 'the milk is from the man': 'Shared blood is shared female substance; it is never paternal blood' (Carsten 1995: 228).

47. This is a notion common to many Islamic settings (see Fortier's [2001] ethnography of Mauritania and the classical Islamic literature) and often seen as attested in the Quran: '[Man] is created from a gushing fluid, issuing from between the backbone and the ribs' (86:6–7).

48. As she notes (1995: 234), this would imply that husband and wife would come to share substance, in accordance with the logic of marriage, which is modelled on siblingship. Malay marriage turns 'strangers', affines, into kin. In the Middle East, by contrast, where marriage is modelled on hospitality (Dresch 1998: 123), one ideally pretends they were kin all along.

49. See Conte (1987, 1991, 1994a, 2003). Landau-Tasseron (2003) questions this common notion that adoption was widespread in pre-Islamic Arabia. However, while the 'fluidity' of pre-Islamic Arabia may

have assumed mythical proportions, it is a myth that is widespread in contemporary Islamic thought.

50. Prior to this particular part of the Revelation, Muhammad had himself adopted a son, one Zayd bin Harithah. The subsequent revelation that this was to be prohibited and annulled allowed Muhammad to marry Zayd's wife, whom Zayd divorced, and who would previously have been forbidden to Muhammad as his son's wife (Conte 1987). This has been the subject of much Christian polemic and Muslim apologetics.

51. Female relatives he is forbidden to marry, and can therefore interact with on more intimate terms. Interactions with women one could marry have to be controlled through veiling and other practices, a theme we have already encountered in our examination of milk kinship, and one we will return to again. For consistency's sake, I have modified the transliteration of Arabic terms employed in the published translation I am quoting here, following my reading of the Arabic original (Qaradawi 1993: 434).

52. A theme we will return to in our discussion of assisted reproduction. The principle may facilitate simpler, if covert, means of remedying male infertility, such as adulterous liaisons (see e.g. Peters 1990: 193).

53. As is stressed, for example, in an article on 'Children's rights in Islam' (Sa'id 1984: 220–21).

54. Islamic inheritance law is elaborate: rights are due in fixed proportions subject to the number and type of other entitled relatives. Such calculations can be complex, and Muslims will often seek expert advice. This system is much vaunted, and continues to be widely applied (Coulson 1971).

55. Nevertheless, even if we take the formal Islamic prohibition of adoption as read, it is in fact precisely the 'fluidity' of 'Arab' kinship reckoning that Murphy and Kasdan (1959: 21), for instance, in a classic social structuralist account, pick out as distinctive. Given the multiplicity of cross-cutting ties that 'close' marriage entails, genealogies can be read and constructed in any number of different ways (Peters 1990: 220–21); tightly defined lineages require, on the contrary, prescriptive exogamy. Fluidity, flexibility and indeterminacy are all there, but at a different structural level from the one Carsten is discussing for her Malaysian cases.

Chapter 2

ISLAMIC LAW AND THE RELIGION OF LEBANON: THE EXAMPLE OF ADOPTION

Religion, law and politics in Lebanon

Lebanon was created as a separate state by the Great Powers after the First World War to be a Christian dominated enclave within the wider Muslim Middle East, largely under the auspices of France, which had had a long history of involvement with the Maronite Christians of Mount Lebanon and was awarded the Mandate to supervise the new nation by the League of Nations.[1] The initial Christian demographic majority has, however, subsequently evolved into a relative minority, due to the relative increase of the Muslim population. The topic is a sensitive one: no official census has been carried out since 1932. But religious diversity goes further than a simple Christian/Muslim dichotomy. The area has long hosted a number of religious minorities: Maronite Christianity itself emerged as heresy through the Monothelite controversy of the seventh century AD but joined the Catholic Church in the sixteenth century, and many other 'unorthodox' religious movements, such as Twelver Shiism and Druzism, are represented by substantial communities. There was also a Jewish community, though by now it has all but disappeared.

This diversity was enshrined in the Lebanese constitution of 1926, drafted under French control. Article 9 states that:

> Freedom of conscience is absolute. In rendering homage to the All-High, the State respects all confessions and guarantees and protects their free exercise as long as it does not attack the public order. It guarantees equally to the populations, whatever rite they belong to,

the respect of their personal status and their religious interests. (Cited in Rabbath 1986: 99)

Article 95 states that 'the communities will be equally represented in public offices and the composition of the ministry', a principle that paved the way for the confessional power-sharing arrangements that have dominated Lebanon's modern political history, most notably the post-independence (1943) 'National Pact' between the Maronite president Bishara al-Khuri and the Sunni Muslim prime minister Riyad al-Sulh, and the sectarian conflicts that have disfigured it, in particular during the devastating 1975–90 civil war. The new state of Lebanon was thus organized along communitarian lines, a continuation and entrenching of the 'culture of sectarianism' that Ussama Makdisi (2000) has compellingly narrated not as primordial difference but as an expression of modernity, whose origins lie at the intersection of nineteenth-century European Orientalism and colonialism and Ottoman modernization.

That culture endures, albeit challenged, resisted and debated: 'religion is politics' was a maxim frequently put to me; 'It's a matter of who holds the reins of power – the bearded men', as one doctor had it. Certainly religious personalities have played a prominent role in modern Lebanese politics, from the Maronite patriarchs, including the deeply engaged current Patriarch Nasrallah Sfeir, through Sunni muftis such as Mufti Hasan Khaled, killed by a car bomb in 1989, to Shiite clerics such as the Iranian Musa al-Sadr, the 'vanished Imam', who brought the Lebanese Shiite community to historical consciousness and institutional independence before mysteriously disappearing during a diplomatic mission to Libya (Ajami 1986), and Hezbollah's leader Sayyid Hasan Nasrallah, who has a huge popular following inside and outside Lebanon and a clerical identity and style, if not the jurisprudential substance of, say, Lebanon's resident ayatollah, Sayyid Muhammad Husayn Fadlallah.[2]

Decree 60 L.R., 13 March 1936, issuing from the French high commissioner (Rabbath 1986: 102ff.), formally recognized seventeen 'historic communities' or 'sects' (*tā'ifah*, pl. *tawā'if*): eleven Christian, five Muslim and one Jewish, later to become eighteen with the addition of the Coptic Orthodox community.[3] Of these, the three demographically most considerable have come by convention to hold the principal offices within the regime, albeit in inverse proportion to their current demographic standings: the Maronite Catholics, who usually hold the presidency, the Sunni Muslims, who provide the prime minister, and the Twelver Shiites, who furnish the

speaker of parliament. Their respective powers were subsequently
rendered more equitable by the Ta'if accord of 1989 that was the beginning of the end of the 1975–90 civil war. Each of the 'historic
communities' is constitutionally granted the right to govern its own
affairs as far as electing its religious authorities, councils and tri-
bunals, and in matters of personal status: marriage, divorce, filiation
and inheritance – in short, kinship. Separate religious courts govern
matters of personal status for members of each community, whether
they primarily see themselves in terms of their nominal religious
identity or not. Thus, in such matters, Maronites – religious or not –
are subject to their own courts applying the 'laws' of the Catholic
Church – their final court of appeal is the Vatican; Sunnis, in their
courts, follow an Ottoman codification of Hanafi law, one of the major schools of Sunni Islamic law;[4] Shiites apply their own, Ja'farite,
law,[5] with final appeal made to 'the supreme authority [*marja'*, see
below] of the community in the world' (Law 72/67, 19 December
1967, cited in Rabbath 1986: 128). Personal status law in Lebanon
has then a nominally closer relation to its religious origins than in
much (if not all) of the Middle East, where 'Islamic' family law
courts commonly apply personal status laws codified in the modern
era, whose content may often be inspired by or couched in the terms
of the shariah, but also often reflects attempts to institute radical reforms (Anderson 1976). Further, again in contrast with much of the
rest of the region, Lebanon's religious courts are expressions and
emblems of the (here, confessional) political system, rather than
mere concessions to nostalgia for a pre-secular regime.[6]

But over and above the religious courts of each of the communities there is a civil legal apparatus. Each side is jealous of its own
powers and jurisdiction, and conflicts often result: personal status
law, precisely our area of interest, is a complex and contentious issue. As El-Gemayel (1985: 375), a partisan of the civil law, has it:

> It is unfortunate that a modern state like Lebanon, which had distin-
> guished itself prior to the war as a prosperous Switzerland-like haven
> in the tumultuous Middle East setting, should still be subject to so
> many different rules and adjudications in the name of the respective
> religious communities, while asking that the State's political author-
> ities enforce and subscribe to their communal regulations ... Thus the
> nation is burdened by a dualism that makes Lebanon a contradictory
> legal entity: one part is locked into rules that time has hardly
> touched, while the other struggles to keep pace with an increasingly
> transnational, intellectual, economic, and technological world.

This depiction neglects to note that time certainly has touched religious law, which equally 'struggles to keep pace with an increasingly transnational, intellectual, economic, and technological world', as we will see, even if the application in the courts of progressive thinking in this regard is a matter of debate in Lebanon's clerical circles.

The legal standing of each of the communities emerged gradually and separately due to extended controversy (see Rabbath 1986). They have, then, different legal statuses, further complicating matters. While the Catholic courts exist independently of the state, the Muslim courts are part of it by dint of the prior history of Lebanon: as part of the Ottoman Empire, (Sunni) Muslim courts were part of the state apparatus; their functionaries' salaries remain paid by the state. The Sunnis qua religious community are led by their officially designated mufti, who is titled Mufti of the Republic (currently Shaykh Muhammad Rashid Qabbani). As head of the Sunni religious community, given the political weight given to confessional identity, his role can be as much political as religious. The Shiites, a minority within Islam in global terms, if not within Lebanon, developed a separate and equivalent administrative and juridical body only comparatively recently, through the leadership of the Iranian cleric Musa al-Sadr in the 1960s and 1970s (Ajami 1986), and its weight in Shiite society is offset by that of other powerful actors, such as Hezbollah, accused by its critics of being a 'state within a state', and Ayatollah Fadlallah, of whom more will be said presently. It is to these religious bodies that, in many circumstances, a Lebanese citizen most naturally turns rather than the state: as one doctor put it to me, again rather overstating the case: 'You have to go to the *tā'ifah* for everything in your life, not the state. There is no law here: it has to be a matter of "God doesn't let you do that."'

However, that situation is not universally accepted: there has been a continuous history of movements that have attempted to break the stranglehold of sectarian organization. Proposals for voluntary civil personal status laws have been brought before parliament on several occasions, most recently in 1998, in order to put an end to the fact that one can only contract a civil marriage outside Lebanon (most conveniently and commonly in Cyprus): in case of a subsequent dispute, a Lebanese civil court will rule according to the law of the country where the marriage was contracted, an affront to Lebanese sovereignty in the opinion of many within the Lebanese legal establishment.[7] Until now every such project for reform has failed.

As things stand, then, matters of personal status are subject to religious law, and even self-confessed atheists will find themselves in
a religious court from time to time, to sign marriage papers, register
their children, settle an estate or attempt a divorce. Some may find
the process bewildering. I frequently did, in my own experiences of
Islamic courts:[8] besides the actual cases being decided, people con-
tinually come in and out, greeting the shaykh, asking his opinion of
a legal matter or some seemingly unrelated affair. The telephones are
ringing, the judge is swearing in a witness with a receiver on each
ear, papers are being thrust in front of him by the army of clerks.
Notes must be taken and records made in 'high' Arabic, in this case
a particularly legalistic variety. The judge dictates to his assistant, a
shaykhly apprentice: an unusually learned lawyer might be allowed
to dictate himself. Sometimes a matter of linguistic erudition, of
spelling or the use of the correct grammatical inflections, might arise
and allow the judge to display his command of Arabic, perhaps at the
expense of the lawyers present. The messiness of real life and personal testimony gets converted into crisp legalese. 'He's a monster,
a tyrant! He beats me, abuses me, my life is unbearable ...' enters the
record as 'it emerged that the plaintiff stated that there was strife between her and the defendant, her husband'.

A couple, members of the Lebanese diaspora in West Africa,
came to register their marriage at a Shiite court I frequented. 'But
you are Sunnis, not Shiites', the judge observed. 'Oh, our local
shaykh out there must be a Shiite then. We didn't think it mattered.'
It did. Others are forced to manipulate the system: a Christian man
wishing to marry a Muslim woman will have to 'convert' to Islam,
bureaucratically at least;[9] Christians whose 'sect' was reluctant to
grant divorce sometimes found it convenient to change to another, or
even to Islam, more liberal in this regard, before this particular loophole was closed (El-Gemayel 1985: 272). Daughters can be disinher-
ited by male agnates under Sunni law, and several notable Sunni
personalities without sons, such as the former premier Salim al-
Hoss, for instance, have 'converted' to Shiism to profit from the Shiites' different legal position (Norton 2007: 40).

Trained in civil law, in the French tradition, lawyers can then spe-
cialize in 'family law', i.e. religious law appertaining to personal status, and there are lawyers deeply versed in the shariah (one lawyer I
spoke to had two doctorates, one in civil law and one in Islamic law).
When asked about matters of personal status, such lawyers speak to
the full Islamic tradition, rather as a shaykh would. But it is clear that

in their legal proceedings they move freely between the civil and religious spheres. Sometimes they may try to draw on the putative totality of Islamic law. One (Sunni) lawyer told me he had dredged up a medieval opinion that one witness was sufficient for a sound marriage contract (two are normally required), but the judge was unsympathetic. Another Sunni judge complained to me that 'One time Dr X [he mentioned the name of a distinguished lawyer specializing in shariah cases] wanted to bring a case of apostasy against a guy – "bring me an Islamic state and then we could do it", I said.' Such a crime has no place in the Lebanese personal status arbitration system. Similarly, *zinā* (adultery, fornication, incest) and its punishment, crucial armatures around which much else concerning personal status turns in Islamic law, fall outside the religious courts' competence, being viewed as a criminal matter as 'adultery' more narrowly conceived, as in the French precedents on which the civil code is based. Conversely, foreigners can be surprised by those portions of 'shariah law' that can be argued for: an American or European woman married to a Lebanese Muslim could, in the event of a marital dispute, find herself deprived of custody of her children, for instance, following Islamic precepts giving fathers precedence in this respect at a relatively early stage in the children's lives.[10]

While the nature and function of the religious authorities of the various communities are formally very different – a Catholic patriarch is not a Mufti of the Republic nor an imitator of the supreme ayatollah – there has been a tendency for them to become more like each other, as Greek Orthodox Archbishop George Khudr, a noted political thinker and writer on the Lebanese scene, describes in an article published in the Lebanese newspaper *Al-Nahar* (28 March 1998) in response to the civil marriage debate (reproduced in Traboulsi 2000). He begins with an allusion to Ayatollah Khomeini's famous interpretation of the Shiite principle of 'the sovereignty/guardianship of the jurisprudent' (*wilāyat al-faqīh*), whereby political rule is to be exercised by those qualified in God's law:

> Every historical community has a *walī faqīh* [sovereign jurisprudent] managing it, bearer of the hidden truth and explainer of it in its particulars to the people of the earth. *Wilāyat al-faqīh* in our country is not a monopoly of he who follows the ideology prevailing in Iran. No man of religious learning has remained pure in Lebanese Islam. The scholar has become a 'man of religion', which Islam rejects. I think that the importance of the French Mandate in its Catholic culture is that it made the clergy master over every sect, and set up in

return muftis in Christianity ... From this perspective, political Islam has been Lebanised so far as to lose its 'rebellious' individuality
in accordance with traditional Lebaneseness, and political Ma-
ronitism has been destroyed in a new conservative combination:
'Christlamism'.[11] (Cited in Traboulsi 2000: 307–8)

Religious thinkers form a community in themselves, frequently
meeting for 'religious dialogue' and often referring to their 'friends'
among the other faiths. My meeting such people and asking them
their opinion about assisted reproduction was not an outlandish thing
to do: such matters as medical ethics are an arena where they can debate, as representatives of their faiths and communities. Round table
discussions, often televised, are an opportunity for them to come together, albeit on a somewhat competitive footing. I was given, for
example, a book published by the society for Islamo-Christian dialogue (Markaz al-Dirasat wa-l-Abhath al-Islamiyah-al-Masihiyah
1999) devoted to discussions of cloning, with articles by all the big
names. Indeed, I rarely emerged from a meeting without one of the
man's published volumes – 'Have you read my book?' – or even
piles of them, resulting in an onerous mound of reading. Such people write, and in great quantity. But they also have a personal relationship with their communities, whose members visit and telephone
with enthusiasm. I endeavoured to make contact with religious authorities from all the major communities, and gratefully received assistance from all. Having said that, however, my requests for
legalistic responses to ethical questions were much more compre-
hensible to Sunni and Shiite authorities than to Christian, or even
Druze, ones. This was due, no doubt, to the widely recognized role
within Sunni and Shiite Islam of the mufti, a religious specialist who
issues fatwas (religious opinions), on which more shall be said
shortly. Although the Maronite Church, for example, as part of the
Catholic Church, certainly has a position on such matters – the position of the Vatican – it seemed to make less sense that I, as a foreign
researcher, should wish to consult a local priest about it.

As was mentioned above, there is an element of competition here.
Different authorities have greater or lesser influence; their political
roles and actions are subject to scrutiny; their public and professional reputations may vary. Further, theology and personal status
law may be taken up as tropes to express rivalry within and between
the various communities. As a nominal Christian, I was often asked
by Muslims how I could possibly intellectually uphold the doctrine
of the Trinity. Personal status laws, matters of 'morality', were a

common focus: Christians might take Muslims to task for the admissibility of polygamy; Muslims might note the problematic nature of divorce for Christians. Sunnis pick on the possibility of temporary marriage for Shiites; Shiites might point to Sunnis not requiring that witnesses be present for a divorce to be binding. Many Shiites pride themselves on their religion being the most progressive of all, the most in touch with the modern world, which they ascribe to their authorities' freedom in their use of 'independent reasoning' (*ijtihād*) in interpreting the fundamental texts, a topic examined below (Deeb 2006: 14ff., 70ff.). It was commonly put to me by people of all religious affiliations, incorrectly in formal terms in fact, that Shiism 'has' *ijtihād*, while other creeds do not.[12]

To get ahead of myself somewhat, one can see this perception of the different communities in the attitudes of doctors, who are constantly faced with 'moral' issues. Christian doctors often commented that Islam was 'liberal' in comparison with churches that forbid even contraception, for example:

> There are two religions here. Islam allows everything – whatever medicine can do to help, you can do it. Christianity – they don't allow IVF, so how can they allow egg donation?!|[13]

> The difference in religion is between Christianity and Islam. The Pope is against these techniques, but Christians, even if they're religious – I mean if they go to church, call themselves religious – they won't inquire much into whether or not ... Islam is different, but the good thing is that Islam approves these procedures. They might ask about donor procedures, because these aren't acceptable. But now there's a new fatwa for Shiites allowing them to have donor egg procedures.

And a pious female Shiite doctor, 'in Hezbollah' as her colleagues described her, remarked that she had seen that 'in the debates, the round tables, the Christians are behind here'. Religion, it seems, can be seen to impede 'progress' to a greater or lesser extent; and it is Islam, and especially Shiite Islam, that is often seen as the more progressive.[14]

Islamic legal authority

We need to focus a little more tightly on the Islamic religious specialists who are our special concern. According to Muslims, God has not left us without guidance as to the shariah (*sharī'ah*), the 'right path' through life, a '"total" discourse', misleadingly, if conventionally termed 'Islamic law', a gloss that diminishes its 'flexibility and interpretability' Messick (1993: 3), albeit one I myself stick to throughout. This is not, then, akin to the statutory law of the nation-state, although the emergent states of the modern Middle East often attempted to present their new European-style law codes in Islamic dress (Anderson 1976), nor can it be reduced to the limited portions applied in religious courts in Lebanon. It should in principle be possible to ascertain God's will as to the right or wrong action in any situation, the object of the Islamic science of *fiqh* ('jurisprudence', as it is conventionally translated). Where a Muslim needs guidance when faced with a problematic issue, such as is posed by medical innovation for instance, she or he can seek the opinion (fatwa) of someone recognized as competent in the religious law, a mufti ('jurisconsult').[15]

While in many historical settings the role has been relatively uninstitutionalized, informal even, many states have, from early times, instituted official positions of mufti, and Lebanon, as we have already noted, has a (Sunni) Mufti of the Republic, as of 1955. For a Muslim who lives within such a state, these official authorities may have their uses, but they are in no way considered superior to such a figure not associated with the state; in fact, more often the reverse is true. As a follower of Lebanon's own Ayatollah Fadlallah put it: 'Even if they offered Fadlallah the position of head of all the religions in Lebanon he wouldn't take it: because then he would just be a *muwazzaf* [employee, civil servant], paid by the state.' Lebanese Sunnis may turn for guidance to any of the internationally known religious authorities, such as Shaykh Yusuf al-Qaradawi,[16] but equally to their own local and trusted shaykhs. Modern times have seen the emergence of specialized and authoritative fatwa-producing committees within Sunnism, the global majority school, such as those of al-Azhar University in Cairo, the Muslim World League in Mecca and the Organisation of the Islamic Conference in Jeddah, as well as the European Council for Fatwa and Research in Dublin, founded in 1997. There are innumerable local and international fatwa shows on television and radio, where people can phone in with their queries, as well as fatwa-giving Internet sites. 'Islamic law' is, then, to stress the point, both a realm of discourse infinitely larger than the rulings of Hanafi law dispensed by state-employed shaykhs in Lebanon's Sunni personal status courts, and a site for debate between the various currents of contemporary Sunnism: the more 'progressive' Islamism of the Muslim Brotherhood (in Lebanon, the Jama'ah Islamiyah), as against the more 'conservative' Salafism of Saudi Arabian inspiration, for instance.[17]

Shiite jurisprudence is different again; here a more formal and hierarchical structure has evolved. For a scholar to be of real consequence, he must have been recognized as being capable of exercising 'independent reasoning' (*ijtihād*) in matters of *fiqh*. The opinion that counts here is that of his teachers and peers at one of the great centres of Shiite learning such as Qom, in Iran, or Najaf, in Iraq. From among these *mujtahids* (those capable of *ijtihād*) will emerge a 'model', a 'source of imitation' (*marja' al-taqlīd*), whose fatwas can be followed by 'lay' Shiites with confidence (Walbridge 2001a). His standing will then depend on how many followers he (and he should, in most opinions, be a man) attracts. He will usually write a comprehensive guide to the shariah for Muslims, his 'epistle' or 'treatise' (*risālah*); nowadays he will most often have his own website. At times in the Shiite world there has been one supreme such figure, although at present there are tens. Shiites, formally speaking, in the majority view, should follow the fatwas of one such authority in all matters, and should follow one living rather than deceased, although people may in practice pick and choose between the opinions of different authorities.[18]

An individual *marja'*'s following and influence varies geographically, and in Lebanon I was commonly told that three are important: Grand Ayatollah Sayyid[19] 'Ali al-Khamene'i, Supreme Leader of the Islamic Republic of Iran (since 1989) and thus widely followed by Lebanese Shiites under the umbrella of Hezbollah, the Lebanese Shiite military, social and political organization supported by Iran; Grand Ayatollah Sayyid Muhammad Husayn Fadlallah, the only *marja'* based in Lebanon, who enjoys high local standing and affection due to the munificence of his local charitable organizations and his outspoken comments on and interventions in national and international politics, underpinned by the freedom of speech and action his independence from the state provides (see e.g. Sankari 2005);[20] and Grand Ayatollah Sayyid 'Ali al-Sistani, based in Najaf, Iraq, who rose to global prominence during the American invasion and subsequent occupation of Iraq, is widely regarded as the most learned of current *marāji'* and is commonly said to have 'succeeded Khu'i', i.e. the late, great Ayatollah Abu-l-Qasim al-Khu'i, to become the most widely followed *marja'* in the Shiite world, including Lebanon (see e.g. Khalaji 2006). While Sistani is perceived as a more 'traditional' figure, both Khamene'i and Fadlallah espouse a politically and socially engaged form of Islam. All of them have offices in Beirut, where they are, with the exception of Fadlallah who is himself present, represented by a number of shaykhs, their *wakīls* ('authorized representatives'), who give 'the same opinion', or 'the opinion of the sayyid'. And their books are widely available, their websites well known.

This is a fiercely competitive arena. While Khamene'i's position as Supreme Leader of the Islamic Revolution gives him great popular standing among Shiites in Lebanon, his standing in jurisprudential circles is not so lofty, and his elevation to the status of *marja'* at the prompting of the Iranian government in 1994 was controversial (Clarke 2007a; Walbridge 2001b). As one Shiite (a follower of Fadlallah) put it to me: 'Khamene'i is officially a *marja'*, but not really. Look, a doctor gets his certificate, then specializes, gets a doctorate, becomes a professor etc. Khamene'i never did his doctorate. There's politics here too – Hezbollah follow Khamene'i, they don't follow Sayyid Fadlallah.' Khamene'i's position regarding the use of donor sperm (he allows it) in particular raised more than a few eyebrows when I discussed it with other sources.

Again, while Fadlallah is widely respected and regarded with much affection in Lebanon, even among non-Shiites (Deeb 2006: 92–93), he is a controversial figure in juridical circles for a number of reasons (Aziz 2001). Where his supporters laud his ability to 'keep up with times', his critics perceive a certain hastiness: notoriously, as soon as human cloning became a hot topic in the global media he came out in favour of it.[21] A top Sunni jurist told me that 'the press were ringing up wanting to know my position – "Sayyid Fadlallah says this is a great thing, what do you think?" At least give me some time to read about it, understand and think!' I was thus recommended by many within Shiite jurisprudential circles to check the opinion of other jurists, especially Ayatollah Sistani, as well as Ayatollah Muhammad Sa'id al-Hakim, also based in Najaf.[22] I did so, but was not wholly convinced that juridical standing necessarily translated into direct relevance to the Lebanese fertility scene. During our discussions of religious opinions of assisted reproduction, one doctor, probably the leading Shiite practitioner of such techniques in Lebanon, told me: 'You should check out Sistani – he doesn't agree with any of this maybe. He's the ultimate.' But he could not tell me Sistani's opinion, while that of Ayatollah Khamene'i is notorious and that of Fadlallah, who has delivered celebrated and well-received lectures to Lebanese medical audiences (Fadlallah 1995, 2002b), readily available.[23]

Fatwas

Classically, the relationship between mufti and petitioner is a relatively direct and formalized one: one approaches the mufti and presents a question, orally or in writing, and will then receive a reply, orally or in writing (in print, most often, nowadays[24]). Such was often my own method. But contemporary religious opinion appertaining to our present interests is disseminated in many ways. Personally, it is delivered either through conversation in the flesh, or in modern times remotely by telephone, fax or email, even through the medium of the television or radio phone-in (Messick 1996). Equally, this opinion is available impersonally, whether it is to the audience of those phone-ins, or to readers of books, magazines or websites. Newspapers and magazines carry fatwa columns. Collections of fatwas are published, although one sometimes wonders if the questions they reply to are authentic or purely conventional (Skovgaard-Petersen 1997: 20). The ulama publish liberally, including monographs on subjects such as assisted reproduction.

We are presented with a problem of register. The level of discourse employed by the shaykhs by necessity varies according to their audience: Arab or British, non-learned Muslims, fellow jurists or non-Muslim foreign researchers. An email question, a telephone call, an interview and a book all have different dynamics. Vardit Rispler-Chaim (1993: 2), who writes on Islamic medical ethics in the wider Muslim world using published fatwas, argues that '[f]or the study of twentieth century Islam [the published fatwa] is almost the only channel through which Muslim scholars' attitudes and legal opinions can be learned'. But in the case of contemporary jurists, one can also ring them up, send them an email or go and talk to them, and ask whatever one wants to know: one would be obtaining a fatwa, but a tailor-made one, as it were. She continues: 'One of the greatest advantages of the fatwa literature … is that it assumes a dialogue between lay people and scholars' (1993: 4).

But when trying to understand fundamental, underlying notions, it might be somewhat misleading to work solely with material produced for lay people. In the case of assisted reproduction, there is a world of difference between Ayatollah Sistani answering in the affirmative a petitioner's question as to whether or not he is allowed to undertake IVF treatment with his wife, and his son Sayyid Muhammad Rida al-Sistani's[25] (2004) magnum opus on the issues raised by assisted reproduction, which is a nearly 700-page work of *fiqh is-tidlālī,* that is to say a work of jurisprudence where all the evidence and reasoning is presented. Further, crucially, one talks of 'X's fatwa on Y subject' in the sense of X's public opinion on Y that X has disseminated through one medium or another. But X may, in the case of an individual petition, within the context of particular circumstances, give an opinion as to Y in Z circumstance that might seem at odds with his public pronouncement as to Y in general terms. I present an example below; but we should stress here an important point: that 'the Islamic position on such-and-such' is not only diverse and a matter of opinion, but may vary according to circumstance. Clearly this has ramifications for any anthropological theories deduced from 'the position of Islamic law'. Also, there is a great deal of material produced regarding 'Islamic law' which may or may not be written by widely recognized authorities and may not constitute a fatwa in the strict sense, yet may be of interest to the anthropologist.

Sitting in the office of Shaykh Amin al-Kurdi, head of the fatwa department of Dar al-Fatwa ('the fatwa centre' or 'the seat of the mufti', i.e. the [Sunni] Mufti of the Republic)[26] in Beirut, I saw all manner of requests: a shaykh's work is manifold. This includes general advice and assistance. One man came to ask about his son, who had mental problems: he heard voices and when he went walking in the street he thought that people were staring at him. The shaykh directed him to a nearby doctor, who, he assured him, was not only a qualified medical practitioner but also a shaykh, and had a Masters degree in Islamic Studies from Britain. A lady came in with her teenage daughter to ask about registering her in the shariah college, which is linked to Dar al-Fatwa and of which Shaykh Amin is dean. 'No problem,' Shaykh Amin promised. *'Yā shaykh-nā* ['our shaykh', as people commonly say], she is an orphan [*yatīmah*][27] – we don't have the money.' 'No problem, we can help.' (He told me afterwards that strictly speaking they should not, as formally one stops being an orphan when one reaches the age of majority.) 'We live opposite a different college. Do you have connections there?' the lady wondered. But other requests are for fatwas proper. So, for example, during Ramadan he was visited by an old lady who had a problem with her eyes. 'Does putting eye drops into my eyes mean I have broken my fast?' she asked. 'No', replied Shaykh Amin, whereupon she pressed further: 'Can I get a written fatwa to that effect?' Why, one wonders, did she need to have the written (printed) fatwa? Presumably not to help her remember, or to keep for God's benefit. Shaykh Amin declined to speculate, although I hazarded that it must be for the benefit of wider society, proof that she is not breaking her fast, proof of her piety.

Shaykh Amin told me that most such requests come by telephone, especially concerning these matters of religious duties, but the majority of requests in person for formal, written fatwas concern matters of personal status, subject to religious courts in Lebanon: property, family matters, inheritance and custody. These are questions of a conflict over rights (*huqūq*), Shaykh Amin explained. We should note, however, that a fatwa is not binding in a legal sense; clearly it has moral authority, or people would not use it for purposes of arbitration, but it has no coercive power. The ruling of a judge (*qādī*), on the other hand, apportions blame and redress sanctioned by the state's coercive apparatus: the man who does not pay his wife maintenance in defiance of a judge's ruling can be sent to prison; if it is feared a spouse will violate a custody ruling by leaving the country with the children, they can be placed under a travel ban and will not be able to pass the borders.

A fatwa can be a way of resolving family differences without pursuing the costly and painful path of the courts; equally, phrased as a general statement of principle rather than referring to individuals, it does not apportion blame. And people frequently have recourse to the shaykhs regarding such problems in less formal manner. During a court session, someone might come and sit in a chair beside the judge for a discreet word: '*Yā shaykh-nā*, my daughter married a man and there were problems from the start. Yesterday he divorced her out of the blue. What can we do?' The shaykh will dispense some words of wisdom, usually in favour of reconciliation, drawing more often on his knowledge of the local community and common sense social observation than religious texts and principles: 'Look, you don't want there to be a scandal. You don't want to bring a case to the courts: your differences will just become more bitter and you will end up spending a lot of money,' he might advise. Such meetings are not confined to the office or the court: often people will come to a scholar's home. 'Until eleven at night', one distinguished but very elderly shaykh complained to me. To concentrate overly on the formal, written fatwa as a distinct phenomenon, then, is perhaps unwise, for opinion is dispensed by the shaykhs on all manner of matters, and in all manner of ways. As Islam is notionally formally implicated in all aspects of life, so the shaykh can be consulted on any matter. One can receive that advice in any number of ways, and do with it as one wishes.

Furthermore, as we have already noted, it is clear that rulings as to the shariah can vary according to circumstance. A Lebanese friend, a young Christian man, was most insistent that I brought out this aspect of the mufti-ship: 'This is very important, that people realize this about Islam, that people are going to the mufti and asking if they and their girlfriend can have an abortion, and they are saying "yes". Islam is flexible.' Abortion is only possible under certain circumstances in Islamic law, one of the most important of which is where there is danger to the woman's life: it may be argued that such a danger could arise for an unmarried, pregnant woman in communities where the honour ethic takes its most violent forms.[28]

Regarding another medical ethical issue, I was sitting in once with a Sunni *qāḍī:* the court sessions had finished, but a small group of people came in to seek the judge's advice, an old lady, a middle-aged man – her son – and a young man. They sat a little awkwardly, and then the judge asked what they wanted. The young man explained: he worked for the family, and had done for a long time, as a gardener, and general handyman. But now the old lady was ill and needed a kidney transplant. 'I want to give her one of my kidneys', he said. 'God bless you' said the judge. 'The thing is,' he continued, 'I don't have very much money, and she would like to give me a present for my help. Is this acceptable?' 'Well…' the judge began; here the old lady and her son interjected as to how well they knew the young fellow, and he too insisted on how well he knew them and what great bonds of compassion and long acquaintance bound them. 'Yes, well it seems that you are a very good young man, and want to do something very good. God bless you.' The question of money had been raised, and although not explicitly condoned by the shaykh, he seemed satisfied that the circumstances were not those of exploitation and commercial gain, but rather of acceptable recompense for a praiseworthy deed. This was notable, for according to the majority of opinion, both Islamic (Rispler-Chaim 1993: 38–39) and Christian, money should not be involved in such matters for fear of encouraging trade in organs. A Christian Lebanese doctor specializing in organ transplants told me of the difficulties in such cases of an 'unrelated donor':

> This is against Lebanese law. You can't say, 'I bought a kidney.'
> When I started doing this kind of thing, my father's cousin, who is
> very high up in the Church, said: 'As long as he's not forced, okay.

It's his own decision. Even if there's some amount of money, as long as it's like a gift.' But that's personal, not official. Religious laws are personal for us. Islam is similar. It is unsaid. No one dares say that he is doing it for the money. They always pretend it's free of money. I ask for a paper from the shaykh – it will say: 'I don't oppose this procedure.' They never mention the money. You'll never hear a religious man say, 'even if there's money, no problem'.

Here again, actors find 'flexibility', both through attention to the individual circumstances of a particular situation, and through allowing some things to go unsaid.

As a further, telling example of the circumstantial particularity of religious opinion, take this testimony from a gynaecologist working in a predominantly Shiite town in the south of Lebanon:

I had two patients, both twelve weeks pregnant, both foetuses had a severe malformation, anencephaly – they were non-viable, would die two hours after delivery. I told them they have to have an abortion. Both were very attached to religion, Hezbollah especially. 'Can we refer to the shaykh?' they asked. Exactly similar cases – one patient gets the permission, one not. It was the same shaykh, at Khamene'i's office. Six months apart, in the same year. I was very puzzled – I asked someone, and they said that the way of telling the story is the important thing. Maybe the shaykh felt that one didn't really want to have an abortion. Same village, same *marja'*, both my patients. The other woman delivered the baby; it died during the delivery. I have had so many similar examples.

We should be careful then not to take the 'official' statements of such opinions as overly concrete. Indeed, it is not always easy to tie down exactly what a given authority thinks, as we will see when we examine their opinions in detail: they change their mind, an answer given in one context may not exactly match that given in another, intermediaries may relay a somewhat different version, and of course much depends on the rigour of the question. In the course of my interview with Ayatollah Fadlallah, I put one of my own pet theories to him: should a gestational surrogate, given the nourishment and nurture she provides the foetus, not be regarded as at least equivalent to a 'milk mother', whose breastfeeding of a nursling earns her, in Islamic law, some of the rights of a mother (see Chapter 1)? The sayyid answered immediately in the affirmative. But in an interview with a member of the sayyid's fatwa-giving department directly afterwards, the shaykh was rather taken aback, and rang the sayyid to check: 'Yes, he has a new opinion.'

I was at the time concerned that perhaps I had myself influenced the course of Islamic law – this was not, I thought, quite the participant observation of the classical anthropology of my training. In retrospect, this was a foolish and arrogant assumption: the question has been debated in Shiite jurisprudential circles, as we will see, and the sayyid keeps his own counsel. But the directness of engagement and spontaneity of opinion were striking, and far removed from the steady textual studies of scholars such as Rispler-Chaim that I had taken as my model. Islamic jurisprudence is a living, ever-changing tradition, immediate even if its object is eternal. As we noted above, Sayyid Fadlallah is sometimes criticized for a certain hastiness, but, in this regard, it is interesting to note Messick's (1993: 138) portrait of a mufti: 'When a question is posed, the mufti's response is always immediate. Far from pausing to refer to a legal manual or, seemingly, even to reflect, he answers all questions without hesitation. This is remarkable in view of the range and complexity of the questions he receives.' Messick's account is of a mufti in the highland Yemen of the 1970s. Sayyid Fadlallah's concerns are rather wider.

Adoption, fostering and foundlings

To round off this attempt to set religious law in its Lebanese context, I now turn to adoption, as an example directly concerning kinship, our especial focus, and one implicating religious precepts and institutions as well as their relation to the state. In Islamic law, as we noted in Chapter 1, *nasab* (filiation) is nominally only acquired procreatively: 'adoption' (*tabannī*), in the fullest sense of taking in an unrelated child and considering him or her to be one's own in every way, is prohibited. 'He who knowingly calls himself of other than his father, paradise is to him forbidden', as the Prophet said (Zuhayli 2002: 7248). One's name and inheritance rights cannot be bestowed on anyone other than one's 'real' child. Leading Syrian Islamic scholar Shaykh Wahbah al-Zuhayli (2002: 7248), in a discussion of the topic in the course of his comprehensive legal handbook, emphasizes that 'Islam is the religion of truth and justice' that 'obliges the relation of the child to its true [*haqīqī*] father, not to his counterfeit father' and warns of the dangers of the 'foreign element [*al-'unsur al-gharīb*]' within the family. Sexual relations would not be religiously prohibited with an adopted family member, resulting in a situation potentially corrosive to the family's sexual morals. As a Sunni

Muslim doctor said to me: 'Suppose you adopt a girl and she becomes very beautiful. Say you're forty-three and she's eighteen – could you marry her?' Under Islamic law you could, raising not just the worry of moral corruption, but also the problem of veiling and seclusion (Inhorn 1996: 192; 2006b: 108). Relations between men and women who can marry have to be regulated, and cannot partake of the intimacy of normal domestic life.

Prohibited in Islamic law, adoption is thus legally impossible for Lebanese Muslims under Lebanon's personal status regime. In Christian thinking, on the other hand, adoption is allowed. Both Maronite and Greek Orthodox Christians in Lebanon, for instance, can adopt children, giving them their name and inheritance rights, subject to certain conditions: that an adoptive parent is of a suitable age and capable of providing them with an adequate upbringing (see Traboulsi 2000 for a full account). Just as in Britain, for example, proving this capability can be an onerous task. Unlike in Britain, however, under Lebanon's personal status regime matters of adoption for Christians are handled by their religious courts. Many of the fertility specialists I spoke with told me that they recommended adoption as a possibility to their patients, Muslim and Christian, but were pessimistic as to their chances, were they to go by the book. Rather, there was a general expectation that people might have more success if they circumvented the toils of bureaucracy altogether. As one doctor had it: 'The Church accepts adoption, but legally it's very complicated – the paperwork is difficult. It will say "adopted" on the birth certificate. But that's 1 per cent of adoptions. 99 per cent make an illegal birth certificate.' This assumption that people liberally the bend the rules to further their personal projects, that they subvert a state 'system' that is widely perceived as barely functional, is an important one for us to bear in mind.

To return to formal Islamic precepts, while adoption is forbidden this is not to say, however, that fostering (*takafful*)[29] is prohibited: on the contrary, such a worthy deed is explicitly commended by Islam and legally permitted for Lebanese Muslims. The Quran is frequently concerned with the lot of orphans – Muhammad was one himself – and aiding them is especially laudable. However, a distinction is drawn between full adoption, where one takes a child as one's own, and fostering, where one does not and the child's unrelated status is remembered and the appropriate Islamic rulings followed.[30] Confusingly, the two categories are often subsumed under the heading 'adoption' (*tabannī*), both in everyday Lebanese discourse and even occasionally in the writings of Islamic authorities,[31] and people commonly move freely between the terms *tabannī* and *takafful*. A whole realm of practice thus lies beyond the doctrinaire statement that 'adoption [*tabannī*, always] is forbidden in Islam', although that is 'the position of Islam' and must be honoured in official, public discourse. Again, one must be wary of seeing overmuch rigidity and sharpness in the boundaries of that official discourse. One doctor was most direct: 'I advise adoption for many patients, and I have letters [which I was not permitted access to] I have sent to religious authorities explaining the patient's situation and asking about adoption. In many instances they say okay – the Muslims, that is.' I sought to pin down exactly what was being approved. '*Tabannī* not just *takafful*', he insisted, although one cannot but suspect some blurring of the lines here.

'Adoption' in a loose sense is thus in reality more common among the Lebanese Muslim communities than the formal Islamic prohibition of adoption would suggest, due to tolerant interpretations of fostering (*takafful*) 'the exchange form [*shakl badīl*] that Muslims rely on', as it was put in a newspaper article ('Laws concerning children' 1983) written in the midst of the disruption of Lebanon's 1975–90 civil war and Israel's 1982 invasion and subsequent occupation. Those were times of particular worry over the number of children being lost and orphaned,[32] but these practices undoubtedly continue, although one would no doubt not wish to exaggerate their frequency (Chahine 2004a; Inhorn 2006b).[33] Fostering is itself not monolithic. Paradigmatically, such arrangements, which often seem to shade into adoption proper, take place within families.[34] As one lawyer put it, 'In Lebanon, if my brother has six children and I have none, he will give me one.' A friend's brother's wife suddenly died, leaving my friend's brother with two young children that he was ill qualified to care for. The children were sent to live with my friend's sisters, their aunts. My friend (Syrian), who was investigating the possibility of adopting a child in Lebanon on the insistence of his (European) wife, joked that he had already adopted two, since it was he who financed his sisters' household. We should note, however, that within the family, nephews and nieces – prohibited in marriage – fall within the boundaries of intimacy. Such 'adoption' is then relatively unproblematic, religiously and socially.

To read it another way, there is a family responsibility – religious, legal and social – to look after needy relatives; to pass them on to other, unrelated persons would be a moral failure. As Rugh (1995:

121) remarks, 'Institutionalized orphans are a category of people that, strictly speaking, should not exist in Arab society if the popular notion is correct that Arab family responsibility is all pervasive.' However, that ideal does not always translate into reality, and in Lebanon, as elsewhere in the Middle East, modern times have seen the advent of orphanages for the supervision and care of such children, and indeed the advent also of bureaucratic obstacles to those individuals who might wish to take them in themselves. Sonbol (1995: 59), in her regional survey, remarks that '[o]rphanages were and continue to be one of the most effective showpieces of the modern state'. In Lebanon, though, orphanages are religious or communitarian institutions par excellence: although the state supports them, they are much more a 'showpiece' for religion than the state; in fact their potency is a reminder of the ineffectiveness of the state for many. Such 'charitable institutions' (*jam'īyāt / mu'assasāt khayrīyah*), usually religious foundations, Christian and Islamic, hold great power within Lebanon's sectarian system, controlling very considerable sums of money.[35]

Orphans are an emotive issue and a focus for fund-raising in a country scarred by civil war and occupation (Deeb 2006: 197–98).[36] They were also the subjects of intense international charitable interest during the 1975–90 war itself. That interest diminished with peace, although the infrastructure it created remains: it is said that Lebanon has the most orphanages per capita in the world, and the state, weak as it is, clearly relies on their assistance in coping with Lebanon's social problems.[37] A manager at Dar al-Aytam al-Islamiyah ('the Islamic home for orphans'), the largest orphanage-cum-charitable institution in Lebanon[38] and part of the Sunni community, told me that the government is pressing them to provide services covering the full panoply of social problems, except addiction and prostitution, which Dar al-Aytam is not prepared to deal with 'for religious reasons'. This extends even to education. Many less well-off families place their children in orphanages to benefit from the superior education on offer, so much so that apparently 'well under half the children in so-called orphanages have lost one parent, and only a very small percentage have lost both' (Hunter 2003). Several of the managers of orphanages that I spoke to were proud to tell me that there is no longer any stigma attached to children who have been educated in such establishments. 'Quite the opposite given the standard offered by Sayyid Fadlallah's schools', said a shaykh working for the sayyid's charitable organization.

When 'fostering' of and by Muslims takes place beyond the con-
fines of the family, then, it most often has to be mediated through
such institutions. The usually recognized method is to give a gift to
the orphanage, or perhaps sponsor a specific child resident there:[39]
the child will live in the orphanage and not with the sponsor, although a manager at Dar al-Aytam al-Islamiyah did tell me of some
extra-orphanage fostering arrangements. Obtaining children from
Christian institutions is not necessarily any easier. The situation
seems highly unsatisfactory to some, too weighted towards (religious) institutional interests, rather than those of their wards, or even
the state. One doctor complained to me that '[t]hey put orphans in an
institution where people keep the children and get paid. With adoption, those people would lose out. Ask yourself this, why is it so difficult to adopt in Lebanon?' If what is wanted is something beyond
fostering, closer to adoption proper – a child to take away and perhaps even register as one's own – rules may have to be bent, even
broken. This is an area where, despite good faith, bureaucratic constraints enjoin official deniability, and the consequent lack of trans-
parency leads to rumours of commercial motives.[40] The 'baby trade',
including unwanted babies delivered by doctors and immediately
transferred for adoption by Western couples, was a source of great
concern during the upheaval of the 1975–90 civil war, and that concern persists.[41] This is a sensitive subject: 'I don't want to say too
much', a Christian doctor told me, regretting his previous frankness,
'I'll get into trouble.'

Foundlings

Not all 'orphans' are equal. In particular, we should note a distinction between the 'orphan' (*yatīm*), who has lost their father, and
maybe mother as well, and the 'foundling' (*laqīt*), who has no
known parentage. Lebanese society is deeply suspicious of children
of unknown origin. They are assumed to be illegitimate (*ghayr
shar'ī*), and probably to have resulted from sexual misdemeanour.[42]
Fostering-cum-adoption of such children, who would seem ideal
candidates in many respects, is thus complicated by their stigmatized
status. An article in a Lebanese daily, for instance, tells the story of
Nadia, who with her husband adopted a child during a visit to
Lebanon in the war: 'One thing that really bothered me while I was
in Lebanon was people's initial reaction when we decided to adopt
Nabil ... They kept asking us how we could even think of adopting
a child, when we didn't even know if he was Christian or Muslim'

(Chahine 2004a). And, as my friend who had 'adopted' his brother's children told me: 'The point is they would want to know where the child came from – if it was my brother's child then that's no problem, they accept that. But if it's a stranger [*gharīb*], then they'll say, "oh maybe it's a bastard" [*ibn harām,* lit. 'forbidden child', 'child of a prohibited act']. They'll want to know if it's legitimate [*ibn halāl*] or a bastard [*ibn harām*].'

Like Europe (Boswell 1988), the Islamic Middle East has long been concerned with the issue of children 'picked up' (the root meaning of *laqīt*) after having been abandoned, parents unknown. Handbooks of Islamic law include sections on the *laqīt* and his or her rights. In religio-legal terms, then, the *laqīt* is blameless, even if he or she is considered by society at large as identical to the despised bastard (*walad zinā* / *ibn harām* etc.), who in fact has a very different and particular status in Islamic law. As we noted in the previous chapter, the bastard cannot claim kinship to its father (nor mother, under classical Shiite precepts), and, most importantly, has no rights of inheritance over his estate. As the issue of a heinous act, one not 'pure [*tāhir*] of *nasab'*, the bastard is barred from certain religious functions: among Shiites, they cannot become a *marja'*, for example, and they cannot lead the Friday prayers. The bastard is reviled by wider society;[43] to call someone 'bastard', and thus accuse their mother of sexual misdemeanour, is the most terrible insult. Such ignoble provenance cannot be known in the case of the *laqīt,* and thus these legal rulings should not apply. Nevertheless, even knowledgeable religious authorities sometimes slip into equating the two.[44] It is generally assumed that foundlings, or 'street children' in another, deeply pejorative, expression, have come to be such through some parental failing: 'the *laqīt* is the result of an error, a mistake [*ghalat, khat'*]', as one shaykh put it to me. Without 'relatedness', such a person has an anomalous and difficult position within society – indeed, no position at all, according to an Islamic vision of society as being built upon the fundamental relations of *nasab* (filiation) that tallies with a broader concern for 'family values'.[45]

That anomalous position and prejudicial attitude is also reflected in state bureaucracy, which equally has a vision of the individual's relationship to society as mediated through their parentage. Lebanese identity papers, which have to be carried with one at all times and produced at every bureaucratic hurdle, state the name of an individual's mother and father. A foundling or bastard's failings in this regard are thus readily discernible. In an interview with a

Lebanese daily newspaper (Abou Nasr 2004), Dr Sa'id Mekkawi,
president of the Muslim orphanage of Sidon, explains that the
biggest problems come when the child must start school, as it is not
easy to obtain an identity card for them, 'a seemingly minor point
that can create bureaucratic and emotional hassles'. Even though
their orphanage does usually manage to obtain the relevant materials, children still face the problem that the expression 'mothers and
fathers unknown' is written on their identification papers. As Dr
Mekkawi comments, 'This expression has a very bad impact on a
child's morale ... society has no mercy on them, and does not respect them.' There may be further bureaucratic complications: a
journalist quotes elsewhere from an interview with a bank manager:
'A single mother is not allowed to open a bank account for her child,
for instance ... Usually when a bank account has to be opened for a
child, it's the child's father who has to sign the papers' (Chahine
2004b). A law was passed in 1996 forbidding the use of the expression 'illegitimate [*ghayr shar'ī*] child' or suchlike on the identity
card, including any reference to their father or mother being unknown, and I have seen records of cases brought since by orphanages to change children's identity papers to state, for public
consumption, imaginary names for their parents, in order to 'safeguard their dignity and feelings from the psychological and social
problems their lack of known parentage causes'.[46] One doctor I
spoke with compared the position in the modern West, through a
striking (if neither wholly apposite nor accurate) account of the
parentage of some prominent Americans: 'Clinton was raised by a
woman not related to him, and then became President. Senator
Mitchell, the head of NATO, was raised by a Lebanese woman, but
isn't related to the Lebanese community at all. Here in Lebanon a
laqīt can't exist, let alone be President!'

An unwanted child – either of sex outside marriage, or of parents
who feel unable to support the child – will be left abandoned, perhaps on the steps of the appropriate institution, or at the door of a
church or mosque, or perhaps even, most symbolically, on a rubbish
tip, as in this newspaper report from the civil war era:

> In the middle of last April, a car stopped in front of a rubbish heap.
> A man and a woman got out, both carrying a rubbish bag tied with
> string, and threw them on the heap. Then they quietly returned to the
> car and took off for who knows where. The couple's movements
> aroused the curiosity of the local residents. Some of them rushed to
> investigate the bags fearing that they might find explosives inside.

They undid the first bag and were astonished to find a child inside. They hurried to the second bag and there was a second child ... twins, a boy and a girl, not more than 48 hours old. (al-Hosri 1987)

This was a persistent theme of reporting at the time, when the large numbers of such abandoned children were seen as symptomatic of the deep malaise, moral and economic, of Lebanese society. Newspaper reports reflect an atmosphere of moral panic at 'this level of moral decay' ('... and a foundling in Sidon' 1987) and 'deterioration of values' ('The Islamic orphanage' 1987).[47] Orphanages make strenuous appeals to the parents of such children to make their identity known, in order to rescue the children from the terrible fate of being of unknown parentage. During the civil war Dar al-Aytam al-Islamiyah made the following announcement:

> Last Wednesday, 22 July 1987, there appeared a newly born foundling girl, left inside an open Mercedes in Ain-al-Mreise ... We ask the mother and family of this sweet innocent child that they think about this child, who will suffer from being of unknown parentage and a foundling [*majhūlat al-abawayn wa-laqītah*], that they might recognise her as theirs. If the abandonment is due to a matter of [sexual] morality [*sabab akhlāqī*], always know that God is forgiving and compassionate ... If the reason were poverty and need, then Dar al-Aytam is prepared to undertake the care and maintenance of the child; what is important is that she be of known parentage [*ma'rūfat al-abawayn*] and belong to a family ... Just the sight of this beautiful girl engenders feelings of her innocence and calls upon every person of character from her family to accept her belonging to them, and that is her right [*haqq*] given by the shariah and justice. ('Appeal from Dar al-Aytam' 1987)

Sometimes the efforts succeed. In another case, 'two of the mothers came forward and identified their children and confessed that the births were illegal [*ghayr qānūnīyah*], and asked the workers at the orphanage to keep them as they could not look after them'. The orphanage had tried to find out who the men were whom they had had relations with, in order to remove the stigmatizing label of *laqīt* from the children. 'We tracked one down and convinced him to marry the mother, and then separate from her afterwards if he wished, in order to get an identity for the child that carries the name of his mother and father' (al-Hosri 1987), something of a legal fudge as the children had already been born and, formally speaking, *nasab* is established by conception within a marriage contract.

While the two Sunni orphanages I visited, in Beirut and Sidon, have *laqīt*s among their inmates, one of the shaykhs responsible for managing Sayyid Fadlallah's orphanages told me they had none, although he was at pains to point out that this was a mere accident and not policy. When I discussed this with Shiite friends, however, some could not resist drawing the implication that this is because one does not encounter such depravity amongst the Shiite community.[48] One joked that all such children end up in Christian institutions. As we had long been engaged in friendly banter, I replied that that just goes to show the superiority of Christianity. 'What, to take in all the bastards?' he rejoined.[49] While this was a joke, it does illustrate the dilemmas posed by the plight of such children, at once pitiable and contemptible, when sexual propriety is a key stake in social identity and rivalry, and a core theme of the rhetoric of contemporary moral degradation. At the Druze orphanage at Abey I was told they had had no *laqīt*s to date, 'but the way society is going, who knows?'

Fooling bureaucracy.

Not all 'adoptions' within Lebanon take place as 'fostering' arrangements. A number of people obtain an unwanted child by one means or another, maybe from a helpful soul at an orphanage, or through a doctor delivering the baby of an unmarried woman. This child is then registered as theirs, perhaps – or so I was told – after simulating a pregnancy, or returning from a trip away.[50] Shaykh Muhammad Kana'an, then head of the Sunni courts of Lebanon, told me:

> Adoption is possible – it happens, that is, not that it's allowed – but secretly. If a man and wife don't conceive, then they go to institutions for street children, or even see a child on the street and take it. Then they go to the *mukhtār* [sheriff] and say 'Oh, we've got a child.' 'Congratulations!' He registers it and so on. They don't go to the court and say we want to adopt this child, that's against Lebanese law. Sometimes we get inheritance cases in court where there's a secret adopted child taking the main part of the inheritance – the real children complain.[51]

Shaykh Kana'an describes a straight fiction here, but there are other ways of effecting such adoptions by bending, rather than breaking, the law, as a lawyer described: 'There is no adoption in Islam – so what does the Muslim do? He uses a *hīlah shar'īyah* [legal ruse]. He comes to court and says, "I was previously married to a woman, she bore a child and I didn't register it. If it is acceptable, I would like to register it in my name." He gets a ruling in his name, and then it goes into the documents, records, etc.' Another such legal device is that of the 'claim' (*iqrār*) that a child of unknown provenance is in fact your own legitimate child, providing that no evidence exists to the contrary.[52] As a newspaper account, again from the civil war era, notes: 'This method superficially resembles adoption in introducing a child as a son into a family not his original family, but differs in its results, as the claimed child is a son to the claimer and the rights of parent and child are established between them. And as the majority of cases of accepting children into families for fostering take place because these are foundlings of unknown parentage, so the great majority of Muslim families adopting make claim of their relation' ('Laws concerning families'1983).

Kinship has an important bureaucratic dimension, and the state has much at stake. These matters are intensely political: not only because the Lebanese state is, like others, jealous of its membership, but also because of its communitarian organization. One lawyer outlined a scenario: 'Say for example a man and woman are married nine years, with six kids, without registering any of it: it's all undeclared. One day the school demands an I.D. They go to register the kids. The Officer of Civil Status asks, "Are you married?" According to the 1951 Inscription of Marriage Act, any amendment of your family booklet [*daftār al-'ā'ilah*] more than one year after the event needs a court decision. A judgement from the Christian or Muslim court is not binding; you need a civil court decision.' As for the reason for this particular legal interest: 'It's because of the Palestinians: they're afraid you're adopting or inserting such people.'

Within any nation-state, nationality is a key issue and focus of control. Within Lebanon it takes on an extra dimension. As we have seen, demography is a sensitive issue and there are, for example, some 400,000 Sunni Muslim Palestine refugees registered in Lebanon: were they to become Lebanese citizens it would have a profound effect on the demographic communitarian balance and thus challenge the conventional distribution of political power (Norton 2007: 82–83; Rougier 2007: 1ff.). The legal status of these refugees is wretched; they are deprived of rights to own property or work. There are thus instances where bureaucracy is fooled in order to give a child an otherwise ignominious status, as illegitimate but Lebanese rather than legitimate and Palestinian: one lawyer told me about 'a ruse used by [Lebanese] mothers married to Palestinians, to pretend they were single because otherwise their kids wouldn't have Lebanese citizenship.' Another possible trick is to exploit the status of the foundling: if you are born in Lebanon of unknown parents then you should be able to take Lebanese nationality. So another lawyer told me that Palestinian refugees 'put the kids at three or four years old by the door of the orphanage and run away – the Mufti has been raising the question of why they're not being given Lebanese nationality, not being given their rights as a *laqīt'*, although this suggestion was dismissed by the official I spoke with at Dar al-Aytam al-Islamiyah.

In sum, while we will find it hard to avoid considering the sectarian identities and institutions whose origins Makdisi (2000) helpfully locates within a genealogy incorporating nineteenth-century European Orientalism and Ottoman modernization rather than atavistic rivalries, most significant for our own purposes in investigating the relations between religious precepts and kinship thinking and practice is the communitarian bureaucratic and legal organization bequeathed by the French Mandate. In matters of personal status, which covers much of what anthropologists call 'kinship', Lebanese citizens are subject to religious courts and precepts, whether they count themselves as religious or not. Even if religiously committed, in the case of Muslims, for instance, 'Islamic law' in any case cannot be reduced to a set of codified rulings: its explicit content is a matter of opinion and circumstance, and while religiously committed Lebanese Muslims are no doubt very much concerned to 'do the right thing', that is neither necessarily given nor necessarily congruent with the workings of the courts, religious or otherwise. An authority such as Sayyid Fadlallah, for instance, may have progressive opinions in many such areas, but they are not necessarily applied in the Shiite courts, which in fact broadly accept the authority of Sayyid Sistani. The travails of Lebanon's recent history have left many with little faith in or even respect for the state, handicapped as it has been by the relative independence of the religious communities, constitutionally essentialized under the auspices of French colonialism. In order to obtain rights citizens of other countries take for granted, Lebanese citizens may have to resort to 'legal ruses', or out and out fictions. Conversely, those with a commitment to certain avowedly Islamist projects may see little harm in ignoring the state altogether. We are presented, then, with a complex picture, where diverse intellectual interests – 'Islamic law', for instance – and personal projects interact within the constraints of a particular legal system with a particular political history. That complexity need hardly discourage us, but we should keep it in mind when we turn to the more abstract realm of Islamic legal debate.

Notes

1. Among the many excellent accounts of Lebanon's modern history available, I have found Picard's (2002) a particularly useful resource for my purposes here. On constitutional and legal matters, Rabbath (1986) is essential. I have drawn on both throughout this section.

2. Norton (2007: 122–23) argues that the influence of religious institutions and leaders has increased in recent years.

3. The Christian communities: Maronite, Greek Orthodox, Catholic Melchite, Armenian Gregorian (Orthodox), Armenian Catholic, Syrian Orthodox, Syrian Catholic, Assyro-Chaldean (Nestorian), Chaldean, the Latin Church, Protestant, and, later, Coptic Orthodox. The Muslim communities: Sunni, Shiite, Druze, Ismaili, Alawi.

4. Four are generally recognized: Hanafi (now prevalent in the Middle East, India and Pakistan), Hanbali (Saudi Arabia), Shafi'i (East Africa and Southeast Asia) and Maliki (North, Central and West Africa). The substantive differences between them are generally not large, and their role in the everyday experience of Muslims nowadays is perhaps limited; the existence of separate, and thus divisive, schools of law came under attack from modernist reformers. But the ulama have cause to cite the different opinions when writing carefully for a knowledgeable audience. It is thus important to note, against some contemporary stereotypes, that Sunni Islamic law is not monolithic: diversity of opinion is recognized and has been historically institutionalized.

5. After their sixth Imam, Ja'far al-Sadiq (d. AD 765). In 1959, the then Shaykh al-Azhar, Mahmud Shaltut, issued a fatwa recognising (Twelver) Shiite law as a fifth school alongside the four Sunni schools (Bearman, Peters and Vogel 2005: xii). The differences between Shiite and Sunni law are again not large: the basic rights and duties are almost identical. There are, however, some (in specific cases notorious) differences that we will have occasion to mention again, regarding, for instance, the inheritance of daughters and the possibility of 'temporary marriage'.

6. This has proved a key site of contest: the recent ascendancy of Islamist politics throughout the region has led to attempts at more 'Islamic' reformulations in many countries (see Chapter 6).

7. See e.g. Traboulsi (2000: 273ff.). On the most recent civil marriage proposal, see Traboulsi (2000) and El-Cheikh (2000).

8. For a more considered account of Islamic courts elsewhere, see, for instance, Rosen (1989) or Mir-Hosseini (1993).

9. Lawyers commonly observe that such 'mixed' marriages pose the most complex and trying issues under the Lebanese legal system; but it might

be refreshing, given the emphasis on communitarianism here, to note that such intercommunity and anti-sectarian marriages are common.

10. According to the most commonly applied standards, at seven years for a boy and nine for a girl in the Sunni courts, and at two and seven years respectively in the Shiite courts.

11. My translation of *naslāmīyah,* his neologism, a compound of *nas-rānīyah,* 'Christianity', and *islāmīyah,* 'Islamism'.

12. Notoriously, an influential position developed among some Sunni jurisprudents in about the twelfth century AD that the fundamental principles of religious law had been evolved to perfection, and thus that the 'gate of independent reasoning' (*bāb al-ijtihād*) should be closed: with respect to the fundamentals, successors should imitate and not innovate (Hallaq 1997: 143ff.). To what extent this held in reality is controversial (Hallaq 1984), and limited forms of *ijtihād* are in any case indispensable for the Sunni mufti's work (Hallaq 1996). The possibility of, indeed need for, renewed *ijtihād* of a more extensive kind has in the modern era become a point of focus for reformist and traditionalist debate (Hallaq 1997: 207ff.). Among the Shiites, a struggle in the eighteenth century between partisans of a close adherence to the traditions of the Prophet and the Imams ('Akhbaris') and those of an approach that privileged human reason ('Usulis') was won by the latter (see e.g. Cole 1983). Whatever the scholarly debate, it is this contemporary Shiite pride in the relative freedom of their religious authorities to exercise *ijtihād* that is important for our purposes here.

13. While both Sunni and Shiite Islam allow medical intervention in reproduction – Sunnis with the proviso that no third parties are involved (as in the use of donor gametes, for example) – the Maronite Church, as part of the Catholic Church, forbids all such intervention (al-Maktabah al-Buliyah 2006: 93ff.). The other main church in Lebanon, the Greek Orthodox Church, similarly forbade such intervention, although it has recently relaxed its position. As we saw in the previous chapter, Islam has long allowed contraception, in contrast with its prohibition by the Vatican.

14. Contrast, on the one hand, the defensive tone of Father Maron al-Lahham in the introduction to a collection devoted to Christian medical ethics (al-Maktabah al-Buliyah 2006: 5–6), who notes that some are surprised by the strictness (*tashaddud*) of the Church and accuse it of not keeping up with daily life, with, on the other, the unbridled optimism of Shiite thinker Sayyid 'Abd al-Karim Fadlallah (2007: 8–9) in his book on IVF and cloning, issues the Muslim can face with 'a complete legislation: whence the importance of *ijtihād,* source of the vitality of religion and its utility through the passing of the ages'.

15. I have drawn freely here and below on Masud, Messick and Powers (1996).

16. Based in Qatar, Shaykh Qaradawi is perhaps the world's best-known Islamic scholar, largely through his appearances on al-Jazeera's weekly programme *Al-sharī'ah wa-l-hayāt* (*The shariah and life*). He is also head of the European Council for Fatwa and Research mentioned below. His jurisprudence is of a relatively progressive cast, by some lights.

17. This dichotomy is barely adequate, and the 'conservatism' of many Salafi groups needs heavy qualification: their fundamentalist approach to jurisprudence, centring on close adherence to the textual traditions regarding the Prophet, may lead to 'conservative' opinions on many social issues, but is in itself particular and an attack on the historical mainstream, as are the interpretations of some politically radical groups of the concept of *jihād* and their propensity to accuse others of apostasy (*takfīr*). Rougier (2007) provides an admirable account of these currents among Lebanon's Sunnis.

18. Something permitted, exceptionally, and under certain conditions, by Ayatollah Fadlallah.

19. Ayatollah, 'miraculous sign of God', is the highest of a hierarchy of religious titles that have relatively recently emerged in Shiite Islam (Mottahedeh 1987: 232–33). 'Sayyid' is another honorific, frequently employed among the Lebanese Shiite community, used to refer to descendants of the Prophet Muhammad. All the ayatollahs we will encounter here (Sistani, Khamene'i, Fadlallah and Hakim) are sayyids, and I use both titles.

20. Ayatollah Khamene'i, in contrast, is also head of state of a major power, which has its constraints, and Ayatollah Sistani long had to be careful of his public pronouncements, living as he did in Saddam Hussein's Iraq.

21. See e.g. Ghusn (2001), Fadlallah (2002a: 20ff). That is, he sees it as holding great potential, a potential that should be explored (see also Fadlallah 1999 and his interview with Kuwaiti daily *al-Ra'y al-'Amm* cited on his website at http://english.bayynat.org.lb/Issues/cloning02012003.htm); one doctor told me that Fadlallah had in fact blocked proposed legislation banning such research in Lebanon. Sayyid Fadlallah is particularly insistent on paying heed to scientific advance: he alone of the *marāji'* determines the beginning and end of the lunar months of the Islamic calendar by use of astronomy rather than the naked eye (the debate hinges on the interpretation of a key text containing the word *ru'yah,* 'seeing') (Aziz 2001: 211; Deeb 2006: 93).

22. Ayatollah Hakim has comparatively few followers in Lebanon, but does have an office in Beirut where he is represented by his son, with whom I spoke on a number of occasions.

23. One would like to be able to give a clearer idea of each figure's relative popularity, but statistics would be hard to produce, and scholarly impressions vary widely: Deeb (2006: 71), who carried out extended fieldwork in Beirut's Shiite suburbs, reports that most of her pious Shiite acquaintances followed either Fadlallah or Khamene'i, with a few choosing Sistani and some continuing to follow Khomeini or Khu'i after their deaths; Norton (2007: 151), one of the leading Western scholars of the Lebanese Shiite community, notes the difficulties but finds Sistani as the most widely followed, by at least 60 per cent, with Fadlallah next and only a very few following Khamene'i.

24. Messick (1993), whose work I have found most useful here and below, makes much of the transition from the previous, 'calligraphic' mode. I also draw on Masud et al. (1996).

25. Throughout, to avoid confusion, I refer to Muhammad Rida Sistani by his full name, and to his father as simply 'Ayatollah Sistani' or 'Sayyid Sistani'.

26. And also the administrative centre of the Lebanese Sunni community.

27. It is sufficient to have lost one's father to be considered an orphan.

28. I.e. so-called 'honour crimes'. Although more associated with other parts of the region, such killings do occasionally take place in Lebanon: there were 22 cases between 1995 and 1997 according to the Lebanese authorities; other sources have 36 such crimes reported between 1996 and 1998, mainly in small towns and villages (Chahine 2004c). Sayyid Fadlallah, for instance, who condemns 'honour crimes' unreservedly (2002b: 16), explicitly allows abortion in such circumstances (1995: 12–14).

29. The synonymous *kafālah* is commonly encountered in the secondary literature, as in 'the *kafālah* system'.

30. Compare Howell's (2006: 173–74) description of legal distinctions between 'simple adoption' (or the *adoption simple* of the Code Napoléon), where a complete break with the child's former parents is not effected, and 'strong adoption', where it is. Islamic resistance to 'strong adoption' led to most Muslim countries refusing to sign the 1993 Hague Convention on Protection of Children and Co-operation in Respect of Intercountry Adoption.

31. Former Shaykh al-Azhar Mahmud Shaltut (1965: 321–22), for instance, writes of 'two forms' of 'adoption' (*tabannī – takafful,* 'fostering', is not mentioned), one where one takes in another's child and treats them well, and the other, the 'general understanding of the word', giving the adopted child full *nasab,* the vital relation of filiation that gives them their place in wider Islamic society. Inhorn (1996: 191) notes for Egypt that many of the urban, illiterate poor are in fact unaware that adoption is

religiously prohibited.

32. A Lebanese doctor specializing in genetic testing gave me a fascinating and moving account of women who had lost their children during the upheaval of the civil war, became convinced they had found them and came to him seeking proof. I quote at length: 'About three years ago I had a call from a magazine journalist, from *Shabakah* [a woman's magazine], saying there was a case they would like me to help with. There was a man in prison, who claimed he was the son of a certain woman. She came to the prison to visit him: that went on for six months; she was poor but brought him gifts. It started to affect her marriage, and a court order was issued for me to settle the matter. Before the test, she came to me, and told me that she had lost her son in the war, in 1976: he was five or six years old. He went to buy bread, and disappeared. There was a story in the magazine, which this man read: he told the guard, "I'm the son." She went with her sister to visit him: "The minute I saw him I knew it was him," she said. So they brought him to me in manacles – he fainted when we took the blood! The mother came for the results. I asked her, "What made you so sure? Because he's not your son." Then she flipped 180 degrees: "I knew he wasn't my son! My son had a mole, and this guy didn't. My sister said maybe it disappeared with age. I'm glad because I couldn't afford it anymore." I had another case: a woman was getting on the bus, and saw a kid, and thought "That's my son." She'd lost her son in the war, and the boy was about the right age, seventeen. She followed him home, and then told her sister. She agreed: "Yes that's your son." The kid had parents, a mother and father – he has like seven or eight children. It's ridiculous. They did the test – it wasn't hers of course.'

33. While the influence of Christian precepts and the terrible travails of the war may make Lebanon a particular case, reports from across the region suggest similar patterns: see Sonbol's (1995) historical survey, Rugh (1995) and Inhorn (1996: 189ff.) on Egypt and Bargach (2002) on Morocco.

34. In a collection of 'contemporary fatwas', Zuhayli (2003: 285–86) comments on two queries that reveal potential conflicts over property in such arrangements, one as to whether the guardian can use the orphan's property to pay for communal food and drink (yes) and another as to whether an orphan working for the family business must be paid for the work (yes).

35. Sayyid Fadlallah's organization, for instance, the Mabarrat Association (Deeb 2006: 88ff., 177), runs six orphanages, fifteen high schools and three technical and academic training facilities, serving 17,500 students, as well as two hospitals, other medical facilities and a chain of not-for-profit petrol stations and restaurants. In 2003 the association spent some $7 million (U.S.) on its 3,500 orphans and 350 handicapped

dependents (El-Ghoul 2004; www.mabarrat.org.lb). This charitable network was damaged in the 2006 war with Israel.

36. According to Norton (2007: 109), commenting on fund-raising amongst the Shiite community in particular, as much as $2 million (U.S.) may be collected in one night during Ramadan.

37. A recent article in a Lebanese daily provides some useful statistics: 'Back in 1946, only 14 orphanages and two residences for handicapped children existed in Lebanon. The number expanded by 40 percent during the 1975–1990 civil war, and there are now over 200 such institutions, housing 40,000 children. Save the Children UK reports that in 2000, "of just over 875,000 children aged under 14, between 3 and 4 percent find themselves in residential care." Well over half of the Social Affairs Ministry's yearly budget of roughly LL100 billion is spent subsidizing the care of children in institutions' (Hunter 2003).

38. Running 39 institutions in 22 locations (Hatoum 2004), and also known officially as the 'Social Welfare Institutions'.

39. This is *kafālat al-yatīm* ('sponsoring an orphan'): this would commonly entail a gift of $500 to $1000 per orphan per year in the case of the Mabarrat Association, for instance (El-Ghoul 2004).

40. Such adoption is said to be expensive: I was given estimates by doctors for adoption costs ranging from $5000 to $60,000, although, as one doctor said, 'it could be a few hundred dollars through some good sister who might help them', that is, a nun working at a Christian orphanage. According to a manager in one Muslim orphanage, Christians came to them seeking to adopt in the hope that it might be cheaper.

41. Years later, many such children are returning to Lebanon to discover their 'roots'. These stories have not gone away since the end of the war: witness a newspaper report ('Baby trading' 2004) from the period of my fieldwork, concerning trading in newborn babies. Three people were arrested, among them two women, as part of an investigation into the selling of a newborn child for $5000; the investigation included the mother of the child. 'Three pregnancies from fornication are ascribed to her, indicating that she was pregnant with the aim of selling the child,' the article reports, continuing, 'Among those arrested was a former nun.' The moral concern, especially with the role of religious figures, thus persists.

42. See Inhorn on Egypt (1996: 191; 2003: 272) and Lebanon (2006b), Bargach (2002) on Morocco.

43. See Sonbol (1995: 60), Bargach (2002 passim). Notable Syrian Islamic authority Shaykh Muhammad Sa'id Ramadan al-Buti is asked in his fatwa column in Syrian medical magazine *Tabibak* (no. 476, Dec. 1997) by one misguided petitioner whether it is obligatory to kill such a child;

he is, one should note, at pains to point out that such an act would be abominable.

44. As does Shaykh al-Azhar Jad al-Haqq (1997: 3216) in his discussion of artificial insemination and IVF (see the following chapter).

45. However, to set alongside that, a manager at Dar al-Aytam al-Islamiyah told me that people come seeking to marry *laqītah*s, foundling girls, precisely because of their lack of relatedness: 'it is easier because of the *mahr* [bride-price] and there's no family to deal with.' Such girls can be got on the cheap.

46. I quote from one such case copied for me by a generous lawyer. In Morocco, a 1993 law also banned the use of the term *ibn zinā* on a child's identity papers and allowed the use of a fictive surname, but fictive fathers' names are still legally contested (Bargach 2002: 110ff.).

47. Although the numbers may have declined, the phenomenon persists even now, as does the moralizing discourse. During fieldwork I collected a considerable number of newspaper reports of babies found abandoned (Clarke 2005: 139 n. 178).

48. As Shiites consider themselves the best of God's followers, a Shiite bastard is tantamount to a 'logical absurdity', according to Kohlberg's (1985: 237) survey of classical Shiite literature.

49. Others suggested that if one wanted to wash one's hands of such a child then, as a Muslim, one would leave it in a Christian area, and vice versa.

50. Compare Rugh's (1995: 131) account of concealed adoption in Egypt: 'prospective foster mothers affected a false pregnancy with the aid of gradually increasing thicknesses of sponge rubber until such time as the baby was "delivered" by ministry officials'. Exactly the same ruses and bureaucratic falsifications are reported in cases involving the new fertility treatments.

51. For such a case, and others illustrating the further points made below, see Homsi (2003: 109ff.).

52. The man should be married; no other man should be making the same claim; it should not be known that the child is in fact illegitimate; the difference in age between child and claimant should be plausible; and the child should themselves accept the claim.

Part II

CONVERSATIONS

When we talk about medicine and religion, it may seem at first sight as though we are talking about things unrelated to each other. But this confusion ceases once we understand that religion came to serve humanity, and that medicine is the science that works for humanity. And things also become clear if we understand that religion is not just a spiritual state opening onto the transcendental … Religion does not deny the body, because the body is a truth.

Ayatollah Muhammad Husayn Fadlallah (1995: 1)

Chapter 3

TEST-TUBE *FIQH:* ISLAMIC LEGAL REACTIONS TO THE NEW REPRODUCTIVE TECHNOLOGIES

Islamic medical ethics

Medically assisted conception has become a prominent theme of Islamic legal literature as part of a wider blossoming of global Islamic legal scholarship on medical ethical issues (Rispler-Chaim 1993). To restrict ourselves to the literature in Arabic, the terms employed include: *al-talqīh al-sinā'ī / istinā'ī,* 'artificial fecundation' or 'artificial conception', most usually but not exclusively applied to artificial insemination;[1] *atfāl al-anābīb,* a straight calque of 'test-tube babies', and, by extension, 'in vitro fertilization'; and *wasā'il al-injāb al-musā'idah,* 'techniques of assisted reproduction'. Shaykh Yusuf al-Qaradawi, one of the world's most famous Sunni jurists, now based in Qatar, entitles a fatwa on the topic 'Transplantation of the embryo' [*shatl al-janīn*], commenting: 'I have chosen this name to distinguish this from what has been reported in the press for years concerning "test-tube babies" [*janīn unbūb al-ikhtibār*] and all the bugbears that accompany that' (Qaradawi 1990: 562). These thinkers are, for the most part, careful and discriminating in the categories and vocabulary they use, even if their audience, ordinary people making use of their opinions, are no doubt not always, just as the ethnographies of assisted reproduction in the West often reveal ordinary people obliterating the fine distinctions anthropologists would like to draw, preferring to see themselves as just 'giving nature a helping hand'.

This interest in medical ethics is linked to a wider portrayal by Muslim writers of Islam as harmonious with modern science, not opposed to it in the way that they consider Christianity to have been, with what are thought to be disastrous consequences for the place of religion in Western life. Islam is, rather, the religion of knowledge and science: the Arabic for 'science', *'ilm*, equally refers to religious knowledge; the derived agent noun, *'ālim / 'ulamā'*, could refer to religious scholars or to scientists; the glories of medieval Islamic science, which were indeed remarkable, are a source of contemporary pride. Much effort is expended by Islamic thinkers to show how the findings of modern science were prefigured in the Quran and other Islamic texts, in order to 'prove that Islam is true' (Hoodbhoy 1991; Stenberg 1996). A favourite, and pertinent, example is the Quranic account of embryogenesis, which is seen to concur exactly with the modern scientific explanation.[2] However, almost invariably the titles of popular religious books capture the idea of IVF or cloning, say, as standing 'between' two monoliths, usually 'religion and science', or 'science and the shariah' or 'science and *fiqh*', indicating, despite the fervent protestations to the contrary, an ambivalent relation between the two.[3]

'Islamic society'

We will need to bear in mind the context of the ideas with which these scholars are working, in particular that of the fundamental bond of relatedness, *nasab*. Islamic legal thinkers, broadly speaking, share a vision of an Islamic society as a system of rights and obligations where the primordial set of relations comprises, as we have noted, those of *qarābah,* meaning 'closeness' or 'kinship and alliance', of which the most important, because non-contingent, element is *nasab,* variously translated as 'consanguinity', 'kinship relations' or 'relations of filiation'. While the most commonly understood meaning of *nasab* is 'membership in an agnatically defined group', in jurisprudence it encompasses other types of kin relation, with the mother and her relatives. That is, Islamic notions of kinship are cognatic, although agnatic ties are emphasized and given hierarchical superiority (Conte 1991, 1994b).

Here let me present the account given to me by Shaykh Muhammad Kana'an, then head of the Sunni higher appeals court and manager in chief of the Sunni religious courts in Lebanon, an account with which he began his explanation of the Islamic position on assisted reproduction and which was clearly intended as a simple introduction to the issues involved:

> Humanity is distinguished by *nasab,* and the nobility [*karāmah,* perhaps 'self-respect', or 'dignity'] of a person issues from the nobility of his *nasab;* thus the person without *nasab* has no nobility, the bastard [*walad al-zinā*] or foundling [*laqīt*] for example. Thus nobility of *nasab* is a human right [*karāmat al-nasab min huqūq al-insān*] in the shariah. So this is the aim of marriage in Islam, making *nasab* between kin.[4]

As opposed to animals, humans are aware of their filiation from their parents and use this relation as the key means of structuring society, a distinctively human phenomenon. It is this distinction which Shaykh al-Azhar[5] Mahmud Shaltut (born 1893, Shaykh al-Azhar 1958–63) sees modern 'material philosophy' as confounding:

> It would be fitting for [such thinkers] to remember that humanity – and they themselves – has societies, peoples and tribes,[6] made up of individuals organised by one tie, by which people are recognized and related; and they are, in their humanity, not like the individuals of animals and plants which remain separate in life, not gathered together by bonds, and do not feel the need for bonds in their lives. The one is peculiar to animals and plants, and the other is peculiar to people. (1965: 327)

Possession of a proper such relation is vital to human dignity, and is thus considered in Islam a 'human right': the bastard and the foundling of unknown parentage are cheated of this vital aspect of humanity. Marriage is the institution by means of which proper filiation is established. Shaykh Kana'an continued:

> Ties are first to the family then to society and then to humanity [*al-rābitah li-l-'ā'ilah thumma li-l-mujtama' thumma li-l-insānīyah*]: as the Prophet said, 'You are all from Adam'. This is the genealogy of humanity [*al-nasab al-insānī*]. This is the link from man to man, not the link of money, work and so on but the tie of kinship [*rābitat al-nasab*]. It makes a network [*shabakah*]. So for the person who does not have *nasab,* it is as though he is on his own.

Again, society is fundamentally constituted from relations of filiation: deprived of such relations, one is cut off from the network of society.

Nasab comes from the father. As for the mother, she shares in it. But the party to whom the *nasab* belongs, its primary owner, is the father. One says, 'I am the son of so-and-so' [*anā ibn fulān*]. In animals, it goes back to the mother.[7] Just as in Britain, you do not register the son to the family of the mother. A person is first an individual, then part of a family, then a 'tribe' [*qabīlah*], then a people [*sha'b*]. So the Ottomans came from 'Uthman, the Ayyubids from Ayyub, and they gave rise to the Ottoman and Ayyubid states.

Shaykh Kana'an presents the typically agnatic rhetoric that colours the cognatic basis of 'Islamic kinship', and that will be useful to remember when we come to see how sperm and eggs are treated in the debates over assisted reproduction: unlike in Western biomedical and anthropological discourse, where the two are often subsumed under the heading 'gametes', the use of donor sperm is a much more sensitive matter than that of donor eggs in Islamic debates, and the distinction between the two is generally preserved, linguistically as well as analytically.

To reiterate: *nasab* accrues to those conceived within a union of marriage. As *nasab* is what gives one full membership in society, it is a right: this is a common theme in discussions of illegitimate sex and so forth – a child has a right to legitimacy. Without it, he or she will be severely disadvantaged, deprived of the support, financial and otherwise, that a father and his relatives owe to a child, and also of the inheritance from him and his relatives,[8] as this is apportioned in fixed measure, according to a divinely appointed system that looms large in the Islamic imagination.

As *nasab* is the principle on which this whole system is founded, and is acquired through sex within marriage, illicit sex (*zinā*) threatens the whole framework of Islamic society. *Zinā* includes all sex between people between whom there is no marriage contract (or right of ownership in the case of slaves, now redundant), and is one of the very few crimes against God for which He demands a set punishment (*hadd*): death by stoning for the married and lashes for those not. According to Coulson (1979: 68),

> Sexual relations outside marriage, therefore, in the contemplation of Muslim jurisprudence can lead to only one result. They will create outlaws, or at least distort and confuse the lines of *nasab*. Hence they pose the greatest threat to the family law because they undermine its very foundation. From this broad, and I believe correct, perspective, *zinā* properly appears as the gravest of offences which merits the gravest of punishment. The laws governing sexual behaviour are the

protective wall which buttresses and safeguards the whole fabric of shariah matrimonial and family law.[9]

The legitimate child, on the other hand, is a 'blessing' (*ni'mah*) for its parents, as the Syrian Shaykh 'Abd al-Hamid Tuhmaz (1987: 35) says, quoting the Quran (16:72): 'God has given you spouses from among yourselves and, through your spouses, sons and grandchildren. He has provided you with wholesome things: will they then believe in falsehood and deny God's favours?' And children are an 'ornament', as in this Quranic verse (18:46), which I heard many times in the course of my research: 'Wealth and children are the ornament of this life [*al-māl wa-l-banūn zīnat al-hayāt al-dunyā*].'[10] Qaradawi has a rousing description:

> The child is an extension [*sirr*: the translation here is a little removed from the basic meaning of 'heart', 'inmost part'] of his father and the bearer of his characteristics. During his lifetime he is the joy of his father's eyes, while after his death he represents a continuation of his existence and an embodiment of immortality. He inherits his features and stature as well as his mental qualities and traits, both the good and the bad, the beautiful as well as the ugly, from his father. The child is a part of his father's heart and a piece of his body [*kabd*: 'liver', 'heart', 'centre']. (Qaradawi 1994: 221, for the Arabic see 1993: 431)

And so the plight of infertile couples seeking fertility treatment is viewed with great sympathy: they are deprived of a key element of human social flourishing. Without children, the entire social vision of Islam breaks down: their place within society will be incomplete. Thus while the Western discourse surrounding assisted reproduction has leaned heavily on ideas of individual rights, Islamic discourse takes a social vision as its starting point.

Sunni opinion

Sunni Muslims are, in terms of world Islam, the majority, and in the matter of assisted reproduction are broadly in agreement. I thus take their position first, and then, in the following chapter, consider the Shiite positions, some of which are importantly different. Amid the profusion of material, some sources are considerably more authoritative than others: the Islamic Fiqh Academy (Majma' al-Fiqh al-Islami) of the Organisation of the Islamic Conference (OIC), based in

Jeddah, Saudi Arabia, is perhaps currently preeminent; al-Azhar University in Cairo, which now has its own research council (Majma' al-Buhuth al-Islamiyah), has long been regarded as definitive; the Muslim World League also has a jurisprudential body (al-Majma' al-Fiqhi al-Islami), based in Mecca. *Al-fiqh al-islāmī wa-adillat-hu,* the comprehensive treatise of Shaykh Dr Wahbah al-Zuhayli (2002), head of the department of *fiqh* at the University of Damascus, is consulted as an authoritative source by Dar al-Fatwa, the administrative body that regulates the affairs of the Sunni community in Lebanon and issues 'official' fatwas (as described above, Chapter 2). I have taken the opinion of these as the foundation of the presentation here; for additional material, the monograph on the topic by Ziyad Salamah (1998), a teacher at the Schools of the Islamic Scientific College in Amman, Jordan, has often proved invaluable.

In any case, regarding assisted reproduction, there is more or less a consensus within Sunni Islam across a very wide range of material. I describe that consensus here, while including some dissenting voices. Much of the material I refer to dates back to the 1980s, when these questions were most thoroughly debated within Sunni Islam, as a reaction no doubt to the international interest in the advent of IVF.[11] The consensual position that was reached has weathered the subsequent years well, and most Sunni thinkers I talked to about these matters considered them settled.[12] When I asked for material on IVF in Islamic bookshops, the proprietors would dismiss the topic as old hat and direct me to the mass of new books on cloning.

For our purposes, an attempt to deduce kinship assumptions from reactions to new reproductive technologies, the following procedures are immediately relevant: artificial insemination by husband (AIH) or by donor (AID, or DI – 'donor insemination'), in vitro fertilization using the gametes of the couple or those of donors, gestational surrogacy arrangements and the postmortem use of gametes. These are the techniques that present the possibility of unfamiliar modes of reproduction and patterns of relatedness, and that have excited debate in the West and in the Islamic world, particularly those techniques that involve fertilization outside the body: sperm and eggs from any individual, even after their death if the gametes have been kept in suitably refrigerated conditions, can be combined and transferred to a woman's body. Reactions to the possibilities of human cloning are also interesting, although of purely theoretical concern as yet.[13] A new reproductive technology that has great practical relevance in the Middle East, although not immediately useful for

our present purposes, is sex selection.[14] There are other ethical issues
that have excited much debate in the West, such as the destruction of
frozen embryos and the use of embryos for experimentation, that are
not perhaps immediately relevant to kinship; these have been discussed in the Islamic literature but have aroused relatively less excited debate (Inhorn 2003: 112). I do not consider those here.

So, with regard to the issues of immediate interest, in broad
strokes, the salient points of this Sunni consensus are as follows (cf.
Inhorn 2003: 97–98):

1. Islam is pro-medicine and pro-science, and favours any advance that
   does not contradict fundamental religious principles.
2. Fertility treatment can be resorted to in case of necessity, but should be
   confined to married couples.
3. Procedures involving the couple's sperm and eggs are not prohibited in
   themselves, in so far as they do not contravene other Islamic regulations:
   due caution must be observed regarding the sight and touch of the private parts of others, for example.[15] Children of such procedures are considered legitimate.
4. No techniques that involve a third party are permissible: that is, paradigmatically, artificial insemination by donor, and also IVF using donor
   sperm, egg donation and surrogacy arrangements, i.e. the use of gestational carriers.
5. With regard to the latter two proscriptions, the possibility of polygyny
   in Islam raises the question whether they might be permissible where
   both women are married to the same man: although initially allowed by
   some, this ruling was subsequently altered to prohibition.
6. Such arrangements involving third parties are analogous to, if not identical with, illegal sex, *zinā;* children born of them are illegitimate, hence
   have no paternal relation: the maternal relation is ascribed to the birth
   mother by most, but not all, Sunni authorities.
7. Such arrangements, like *zinā* in general, are pernicious because they up-
   set and confuse the clear genealogical relations that God has laid down
   as the basis for the organization of human society, underpinning such
   important institutions as, for example, Islamic inheritance law.

Thus such new possibilities are far from being rejected out of
hand (as they have been by the Catholic Church, for example):
rather, these new techniques are welcomed and accommodated,
within certain limits. For a minority of Islamic thinkers, especially
in earlier years, they remain beyond the pale: Tuhmaz (1987: 57) de-
plores what he sees as a wave of Muslims taking their wives to clinics 'where the doctor turns the woman around just as he likes, and

inserts medical inspection devices into her privates and stares at her and touches her all over ... and some do not content themselves with doctors from Islamic countries, but take [their wives] to the countries of unbelief and debauchery'. For him, the leading causes of infertility are sexual diseases, a delayed age of marriage, abortion, sex during menstruation, and women working outside the house and taking part in energetic sports and dances – it is not fertility treatment that will help here but adherence to Islam, which prohibits such activities (1987: 70). 'Abd al-Halim Mahmud (1981–82), Shaykh al-Azhar in 1973–78, takes it that 'growing babies in test-tubes' will leave them devoid of humanity, love and compassion:[16] what need is there for such abhorrent practices, given the present problems of global overpopulation, Mahmud asks? However, such opinion is a small minority outside the broad consensus outlined above.[17]

IVF and artificial insemination

Zuhayli cites the rulings of Majma' al-Fiqh al-Islami (see above) concerning assisted reproduction, noting the importance of and wide interest in the rulings of the council, the fruit of long research and discussion in which he was himself involved (Zuhayli 2002: 5076). In the council's first ruling concerning 'test-tube babies' (*atfāl al-anābīb*), arising in their conference of 22–28 December 1985 in Jeddah, the matter was discussed from medical and jurisprudential perspectives and it became clear that further study would be required. They therefore resolved to postpone a decision until their next sitting (Zuhayli 2002: 5084). That duly appeared as a result of the conference of 11–16 October 1986 in Amman in Resolution no. 4, again entitled 'Test-tube babies' (Zuhayli 2002: 5099–100). Therein, they specify seven known means of 'artificial conception' (*al-talqīh al-sinā'ī*):[18]

1. Fertilization takes place between sperm taken from the husband and an egg taken from a woman who is not his wife, and then the embryo is placed in his wife's womb.
2. Fertilization takes place between the sperm of a man other than the husband, and an egg taken from the wife, then the embryo is placed in the womb of the wife.
3. Fertilization takes place externally [i.e. by IVF] between the gametes [*bidhratay*] of the spouses, and then the embryo is placed in the womb of a woman volunteering to carry it.
4. Fertilization takes place externally between the sperm of a man who is not the husband [lit. 'a stranger', *rajul ajnabī*][19] and the egg of a woman

who is not the wife [*ajnabīyah*], then the embryo is placed in the womb of the wife.

5. Fertilization takes place externally between the gametes of the spouses, and then the embryo is placed in the womb of another wife [i.e. of the husband, see below].

6. Sperm is taken from the husband and an egg from his wife, and fertilization is effected externally, then the embryo is planted in the womb of the wife.

7. The husband's sperm is taken and injected into a suitable place in the cervix or womb of the wife for internal fertilization.

They judge that the first five are forbidden, either in themselves or for their consequences, namely the mixing up or confusion of lines of filiation (*ikhtilāt al-ansāb*), the loss or destruction of motherhood (*dayā' al-umūmah*) or other matters that the shariah objects to. That is, IVF using donor sperm and eggs, and surrogacy arrangements, are forbidden. The sixth and seventh scenarios, that is, IVF using the husband's sperm and his wife's egg and womb and artificial insemination using the husband's sperm (AIH), can be resorted to in case of need if the necessary precautions are taken. These are not explicitly stated here, but all sources are agreed that one must be mindful of precepts forbidding the uncovering of the private parts before anyone other than one's spouse, except where necessary – and fertility treatment may indeed be of an example of such a necessity. According to a ruling from the Muslim World League's organ al-Majma' al-Fiqhi al-Islami (2007a [1985]: 166), such treatment should be undertaken with a female Muslim doctor if possible, or else a non-Muslim female doctor, trustworthy male Muslim doctor, or, as a last resort, non-Muslim male doctor; a chaperone should be present. Great care should be taken that the spouses' gametes are not confused with those of other patients in the course of the laboratory procedures.

We should note that the council's ruling here is very bare. No evidence is cited, and very little explanation is given. However, it is clear elsewhere that children of permitted procedures are legitimate. There is indeed a possible precedent for AIH in the medieval legal handbooks: were a husband to ejaculate, and his wife, or indeed his female slave, to insert the sperm into her vagina and conceive, the child would gain *nasab* to the husband or slave-owner (Jad al-Haqq 1997 [1980]: 3218–19).[20] There is no indication in the council's ruling, however, as to whether or not the forbidden procedures are analogous to adultery, or rather, in Islamic terms, the broader category of *zinā*, an important theme as we shall see. Zuhayli himself does not comment, although he includes in his handbook a section of his own on *al-talqīh al-sinā'ī*, here clearly referring to artificial insemination specifically: between husband and wife this is permissible, but with the sperm of a 'stranger', i.e. between an unmarried man and woman, it is forbidden because it is 'with the meaning of *zinā*', which is the delivery of a man's sperm into the womb of a woman with whom he has no marriage relation. In addition, this is contrary to the level of behaviour expected of humanity, akin rather to reproduction in plants and animals (Zuhayli 2002: 2649). We might note generally that while these Sunni thinkers forbid the use of donor sperm in both insemination and in IVF, the two practices are distinguished from one another.

To turn to the opinions of the Shaykhs al-Azhar, Mahmud Shaltut, in what is an early (1959) fatwa on *al-talqīh al-sinā'ī*, here, prior to the advent of IVF, clearly referring only to artificial insemination, is equally stern in his verdict on the use of donor sperm in such procedures:

> Without doubt it casts man into the realm of animals and plants, and removes him from the human plane, that of noble societies which weave together their lives with publicly proclaimed marriage contracts ... In the eyes of the Islamic shariah, which possesses the noble means of regulating humanity, it is an abominable sin, and a mighty one. It meets with *zinā* in one frame: their essence is one. And their result is one, and that is the placing of foreign male fluid intentionally in a tilth between which and that man there is no legally binding marriage contract, which natural law[21] and the divine shariah preserve. (Shaltut 1965: 328)

With 'tilth' (*harth*), Shaltut is referring to the Quranic verse (2:223) 'Women are your fields: go then, into your fields whence you please', that is, consider your wives fertile ground in which to sow your seed.[22] Many of these writers slip easily into such monogenetic metaphors for procreation, but most are well apprised of the modern scientific account and its duogenetic consequences.[23]

Former Shaykh al-Azhar and Mufti of Egypt 'Ali Jad al-Haqq Jad al-Haqq, in his fatwa of 23 March 1980, '*Al-talqīh al-sinā'ī fī-l-islām* [artificial reproduction in Islam]', agrees that 'impregnation of the wife with the husband's sperm, without doubt of its being exchanged or mixed with the sperm of another, be they human or any animal,'[24] is allowed in the law, and will establish *nasab* relations. Meanwhile, the use of the sperm of a man other than the husband is forbidden and is 'within the meaning and consequences of *zinā'*, and likewise, with regard to IVF procedures, those involving the husband and wife alone are permissible (1997 [1980]: 3213–14). Jad al-Haqq elaborates on the consequences of the use of sperm from a third party:

> As for the husband who adopts any unrelated child born of one of these forbidden techniques, the child is not his child in law, and the husband who accepts that his wife carries the seed of another man, whether by actual *zinā* or what is within its meaning, is what Islam has called a *dayyūth* ['cuckold/pimp'].[25]

> Any child resulting from the methods of artificial reproduction decisively forbidden is perforce not filiated [*lā yunsab*] to a father, and is filiated to she who bore him and delivered him due to his being considered in the condition of a normal birth as an actual bastard [*walad zinā*] exactly. (1997: 3214)

Jad al-Haqq goes on to expand on these principles at some length, the fatwa being some sixteen pages, rather than the two of Majma' al-Fiqh al-Islami for example, and styled as the responses to questions from a doctor; he adduces textual evidence from the Quran, Sunnah and noted jurisprudents for his positions. As in the ruling of Majma' al-Fiqh al-Islami, he notes that techniques that involve a third party other than the husband and wife are pernicious because they entail mixture or confusion of ancestry (*ikhtilāt al-ansāb*); Islam rather is solicitous of the purity or healthiness (*salāmah*) of ancestry (1997: 3217–18).[26]

So, just as husband/wife IVF is like normal sexual reproduction between them, so the use of donor sperm and eggs and surrogacy arrangements are, for many authorities, like adultery, *zinā* in Islamic terms, 'with its meaning' (*bi-ma'nā-hu*, i.e. 'subsumed under it', 'considered as such'). The involvement of a third party, or the use of such techniques by unmarried persons, is thus forbidden because it is akin to *zinā*, covering all sexual relations outside a marriage contract, and a heinous crime.[27] Its consequences are like those of *zinā*: the bringing into the world of people who are children of unmarried parents, without a properly defined place in society, and thus destructive of it. Thus the legal consequences for relatedness share in those of *zinā*: the child is akin to a 'bastard', a child of *zinā* (*ibn / walad zinā*), which carries a strong stigma and certain legal consequences – in Sunni law, no relation (*nasab*) is constituted between such a child and the 'father', although it is with the mother.[28] Such a child is also often likened to the 'foundling' (*laqīt*), who has no known ancestry, and is thus similarly socially impoverished (as we saw in the previous chapter), although, again, most scholars do attribute *nasab* to the mother. Who is to be considered the mother, in cases of donor eggs and surrogacy arrangements, is a separate issue, considered below.

As something of a qualifier here, we should note that while Zuhayli and Shaltut liken donor insemination to *zinā,* and Jad al-Haqq extends that analogy to IVF involving donor sperm – and 'folk' notions are in accord – the ruling from Majma' al-Fiqh al-Islami does not, although it does cite 'lineage confusion' as a reason for prohibiting both. Not all scholars are convinced that the analogy between these medical procedures and *zinā,* illicit sex, holds, especially in the case of IVF: distinguished Syrian Shaykh Muhammad Sa'id Ramadan al-Buti (2002: 77) finds this without basis, 'a fantastic notion far from the rulings of the shariah'. And it is nowhere suggested that carrying out such procedures *is* an instance of *zinā:* that would, it should be noted, entail a possible ruling of execution for the wife and the donor.[29] But all scholars seem agreed that the use of donor sperm, through insemination or IVF, is prohibited on similar grounds: the introduction of a third party between husband and wife, and the confusion of kinship relations (see Salamah 1998: 87 for a full list of references).[30] The rulings of Majma' al-Fiqh al-Islami and Jad al-Haqq further agree that this prohibition is extended to the use of donor eggs in IVF procedures, and that is the consensus position. But, as we will see shortly, these are not identical cases: the use of donor sperm and donor eggs are distinct issues, as are, again, donor insemination and the use of donor sperm in IVF procedures. Finally, surrogacy arrangements are forbidden on the majority of opinion on similar grounds (on all of the above, see Salamah 1998 for copious additional references).[31]

What of the saying of the Prophet that we encountered in Chapter 1, 'the child to the [marriage] bed, and to the adulterer the stone' (*al-walad li-l-firāsh wa-li-l-'āhir al-hajar*): could this not provide a precedent for arguing that a child of donor sperm could be legitimately related to the 'social father', the husband? Jad al-Haqq indeed mentions the principle early in his fatwa, as part of a general exposition of how solicitous Islam is of the preservation of the family and kin relations. There are ways of interpreting the saying that might obviate such a suggestion, but he is quite explicit: 'when a woman who has a husband is pregnant by *zinā* with another man or through rape, her pregnancy is related [*yunsab*] to her husband, not to he who committed *zinā* with her or raped her' (Jad al-Haqq 1997: 3217). That is the last we hear of the matter from Jad al-Haqq, but Salamah's (1998: 146) useful survey is more explicit: 'this child will be related to the husband, because the marriage bed is his, although it is a mighty sin that the husband accept this situation, and he can dissolve his relation to this child through repudiation [*li'ān*] of his wife, who delivered it by means of *zinā*, "for one should not relate a child to oneself that is not one's own"', here citing classical jurist Ibn Taymiyah (d. AD 1328). Certainly, one should stress, none of the Sunni thinkers referred to here use the Prophetic saying to argue a case for donor insemination: the use of donor sperm is beyond the pale.

Donor eggs, surrogacy and the maternal relation

While the focus of the debate above over 'donor gametes', as much Western discourse would have it, was on the use of donor sperm, the prohibition on its use was extended to the use of donor eggs and surrogacy arrangements on similar grounds: that it confuses lines of filiation. The child of donor sperm is equated with the bastard, who has no father, but is related to his mother. The question of maternal relation in the unwelcome event of a procedure using a third, female party – an egg donor or gestational carrier – remains problematic: should the mother be the genetic mother, the source of the egg, or the gestational carrier?[32] This has proved a thorny question in the West as well: witness the custody battles ensuing in the US after gestational surrogates refuse to hand over the children they have carried to term for other women (Ragoné 1994; Dolgin 1997).[33]

Qaradawi (1990: 563) poses the problem in his own terms, bringing in the distinctively Islamic institution of 'milk kinship' (see Chapter 1), which gives an extra dimension to these Islamic debates:

> We are familiar with the milk mother and the rulings concerning milk siblingship. Now we have realised that people have two ties to their mother, a tie of creation and inheritance [*silat takwīn wa-wirāthah*] whose origin is the ovary [*asl-hā al-mabīd*], and a tie of pregnancy and nurture [*silat haml wa-hadānah*] whose origin is the womb [*asl-hā al-rahim*]. Until now, the tie of the womb was applied to both by extension. But what if now the two relations [*nisbatān*] branch out, the creation from one woman and the nurture from another? Where does the tie of the womb stand vis-à-vis ovary filiation [*bunūwat al-mabīd*]?[34] What are the rights of the nurturer and what are the legal consequences?[35]

Qaradawi leaves the question unanswered here, although elsewhere he plumps for the gestational carrier (Shah 1995: 114). Indeed
most, although not all, Sunni authorities have been reluctant to ascribe any relation to the genetic mother in these cases, and have preferred to ascribe full maternity to the woman who bears and delivers
the child.[36] So Shaykh Muhammad Kana'an in my interview with
him cited the Quranic verse, 'Their mothers are those only who gave
birth to them [*waladna-hum*]' (58:2), telling me that this shows that
wilādah, parturition, is the operative principle, and another verse,
'With much pain his mother bears him, and with much pain she
brings him into the world' (46:15). 'So the mother is she who carries
the child, and tires herself', Shaykh Kana'an concluded.[37]

Tuhmaz (1987: 27) – not an enthusiast of assisted reproduction in
general, as we have seen – argues likewise, but admits the difficulties in the case of a surrogate mother, who carries a child for a
woman who cannot do so herself, in Arabic a 'hired mother',[38] a further example of the 'social and moral chaos' that NRT have brought
to the 'enervated societies of the West' (1987: 71). What if the surrogate refused to hand over the baby?

> What then is the extent of the relation of the provider of the seed
> [*nutfah*] with the child?[39] Is there not some type of relation of part
> and whole [*juz'īyah*] between her and the child?[40] If the swallowing
> of a little milk taken by a nursling from the breast of any woman cre-
> ates a relation of legal motherhood [milk kinship, again] ... then still
> more appropriate is it in this case that there be instituted a relation
> of motherhood and part and whole between the seed-sowing woman
> [i.e. the genetic mother] and the child.[41] Thus in the modern age the
> child could have three mothers: the deliverer, the seed-sower and the
> breastfeeder. But how can this child be related to the husband when
> there is no link of marriage between him and the hired surrogate?
> (1987: 72)[42]

A minority of Sunni thinkers do indeed ascribe motherhood to the
genetic mother, the egg provider, in such hypothetical scenarios.[43]
But, again, these novel possibilities of relatedness are not pursued:
rather, such procedures are disallowed. The 'logic of substance' is
not followed through. It is rather the issue of the presence and absence of socially legitimated relations between the parties involved
that is emphasized: in particular, reproductive relations have to be
sanctioned by marriage.

Here a further issue arises due to the permissibility of polygamy
in Islam. This raises the possibility of procedures involving more

than two people, where ties of marriage exist between those individuals: a husband's sperm can be used to fertilize the egg of one wife and the embryo implanted in the uterus of a second wife.[44] If the problem lies in procedures involving persons not linked in marriage, why should this not be allowed? Indeed, many minor, less well-informed shaykhs whom I questioned on this matter could see nothing wrong with it: the social logic seems satisfied. A 1984 fatwa from al-Majma' al-Fiqhi al-Islami, the organ of the Muslim World League, based in Mecca, allowed such a 'two wives' procedure (my term, not theirs) in the course of its seventh session.[45] However, this was then rescinded in the eighth session in 1985, when it was prohibited to implant an embryo in a second wife.[46] The stated reasons for the change were that the gestational carrier, the co-wife, might have had sex with the shared husband around the same time that the embryo formed of the other wife's egg and the husband's sperm was transferred; one would have no way of knowing if a resulting pregnancy was the issue of the transferred embryo or of the egg of the gestational carrier herself, thus entailing the problematic 'confounding of the lineages' (al-Majma' al-Fiqhi al-Islami 2007a: 161–62). As Salamah (1998: 102 n. 1, 103) points out, this would only be a problem if motherhood was to be attributed along genetic lines, a position clearly implied by the council's initial ruling. He is clear that he finds this mistaken, preferring rather the majority opinion that it is gestation and delivery that constitute maternity; he is equally clear that such arrangements should nevertheless be prohibited, the current consensus position, as we have seen. When we go beyond these Sunni opinions to those of some Shiite authorities, however, we will find the latter more willing to take up these possibilities.[47]

To finish with some still more abstruse issues, the concern regarding the confusing intrusion of third parties extends to the possibility of sex organ transplants that might transfer the genetic characteristics of their previous owner to a resulting child (such transplants are medically feasible, if practically unattested, as far as I am aware). Thus Majma' al-Fiqh al-Islami resolved to prohibit such operations (Resolution 59/8/6, 'In the matter of transplanting reproductive organs', from the sixth session in Jeddah 14–20 March 1990, cited in Zuhayli 2002: 5183), citing the findings of a medical organization in Kuwait (probably the Islamic Organisation for Medical Sciences mentioned above) and noting that 'the testicle and the ovary continue to bear and secrete the inherited characteristics', even after transplantation, which is therefore forbidden.[48] Here, then, 'genetics' are paramount. Those reproductive organs that do not carry inherited characteristics could, however, be transplanted, and this then includes the uterus, as the doctors who carried out the world's first uterus transplant in Saudi Arabia noted: 'The Islamic religious position on uterine transplantation was clarified in March 1990, before initiation of this project, when the Islamic Jurisprudence Council [i.e. Majma' al-Fiqh al-Islami] approved the transplantation of reproductive organs that do not transfer genetic coding' (Fageeh et al. 2002: 246).[49]

To sum up so far, while we have here a rich and varied set of debates, there is a broad consensus among Sunni writers regarding artificial insemination and IVF treatments: they find medical intervention to help resolve problems of fertility admirable, so long as it follows the paradigm of reproduction within a marriage contract. Procedures involving a party other than the husband and wife are, roughly speaking, assimilated to sexual relations outside the bounds of a marriage contract (*zinā*), strongly prohibited. The use of donor sperm is thus paradigmatically unacceptable, and by extension so is the use of donor eggs and gestational surrogates, despite the possibilities opened up by the permissibility of polygamy in Islam. In the case of the latter procedures, maternity would, in the majority view, be awarded to the gestational carrier and not the genetic mother, although the Sunni thinkers see difficulties here, as have legislators elsewhere.

Notes

1. There is a tendency in the Islamic literature for artificial insemination and IVF to be run together under this heading.

2. A very distinguished fertility specialist working in London told me that when contributing to a BBC documentary on these issues he had noted that, in Britain, research on embryos is not allowed after fourteen days, when the embryo is considered a living being. A Sunni cleric who was there to contribute leapt from his chair, crying '*al-hamdu lillah*', 'Praise be to God! In Islam it is said that the soul [*rūh*] comes on the fourteenth day!' The issue is controversial, and important for discussions of the permissibility of abortion: classically, the soul entered the foetus after 120 days, but this is increasingly contested.

3. Witness: *Atfāl al-anābīb: bayna-l-'ilm wa-l-sharī'ah* ('Test-tube babies: Between science and the shariah') (Salamah 1998); *Al-istinsākh: bayna-l-'ilm wa-l-dīn* ('Cloning: Between science and religion') (Mis-

bah 1997); the almost identical *Al-istinsākh: bayna-l-dīn wa-l-'ilm* ('Cloning: Between religion and science') (Yasin 2000); the very, very similar *Al-istinsākh al-jīnī: bayna-l-'ilm wa-l-dīn* ('Genetic cloning: Between science and religion') (Taha 2000); and *Al-istinsākh: bayna-l-'ilm wa-l-fiqh* ('Cloning: Between science and *fiqh*') (Sa'di 2002). As variants, we have *Al-istinsākh al-basharī: bayna-l-tahlīl wa-l-tahrīm* ('Human cloning: Between permission and prohibition') (Hamid 1999), and the edited collection *Al-istinsākh: jadal al-'ilm wa-l-dīn wa-l-akhlāq* ('Cloning: The debate between science, religion and ethics') ('Ulwani 1997). Cloning also provides the opportunity for 'interfaith' dialogue, as in *Al-istinsākh: bayna-l-islām wa-l-masīhīyah* ('Cloning: Between Islam and Christianity') (Markaz al-Dirasat wa-l-Abhath al-Islamiyah-al-Masihiyah 1999).

4. Rather reminiscent of Fortes's (e.g. 1953) notion of 'complementary filiation', one cannot help but observe.

5. I.e. the shaykh in chief at the distinguished al-Azhar University in Cairo.

6. *Mujtama'āt, shu'ūb wa-qabā'il:* Shaltut is alluding to the famous Quranic verse (49:13): 'We made you into nations and tribes, that you might get to know one another.'

7. As another shaykh remarked to me, 'in the human the orphan [*yatīm*] is who has lost his father, in the animal it is who has lost its mother'. And compare Jad al-Haqq (1997: 3228): 'The orphan from a son of Adam is from the death of his father and from the animal from the death of its mother.'

8. Maintenance and inheritance may also be due from the maternal side; here circumstance and legal variation play a part.

9. Anees (1984: 112) quotes this same passage in his own Islamic analysis of donor insemination.

10. Of course, this could also imply that they are not a necessary part of the life of the individual, although they are necessary for the continuation of the human species. Tuhmaz (1987: 37) discusses this, and notes that children may also be an affliction and source of discord (*fitnah*).

11. 'It was among the most prominent issues of the hour in the world' (al-Majma' al-Fiqhi al-Islami 2007a [1985]: 162).

12. Although a fatwa, issued in 2001 by the al-Azhar committee headed by current Shaykh al-Azhar Tantawi and prohibiting surrogacy arrangements and the use of sperm postmortem, reached the global media (Hawley 2001). Some issues are clearly still alive (see Hamiyah 2004: 95 n. 2). I have heard persistent accounts of more recent debates still within al-

Azhar concerning surrogacy arrangements and the basis for the ascription of maternity (see below), but I have yet to track down published materials.

13. As distinguished Syrian Shaykh Muhammad Sa'id Ramadan al-Buti (2001: 193) remarks in response to a question on the topic: 'When this theoretical possibility becomes applicable and a practical reality, then is the time for questions about the notion which is running around your imagination ... As for now, seek delivery from much of your ignorance regarding your present concerns.'

14. The following is a representative opinion: 'There was an agreement that the Islamic legal viewpoint is that fetal sex selection is unlawful when it is practiced at a national level, while on an individual basis, some of the scholars participating in the seminar believe there is nothing legally wrong with the attempt to fulfil the wish of a married couple to have a boy or a girl through available medical means, while other scholars believe it is unlawful for fear that one sex might outnumber the other' (from the Islamic Organisation of Medical Sciences, 'First seminar: Reproduction under the light of Islam', websource available at www.islamset.com). Clearly this is something of a fudge, although one backed by some practitioners (e.g. Kilani and Haj Hassan 2001), who would like to be free to assist in 'family balancing'.

15. The genitals and anus should not be revealed to anyone but one's spouse. Another problematic issue is that of masturbation in order to produce sperm for analysis and use in treatment: self-masturbation is considered by the majority of scholars to be prohibited, as a form of sexuality beyond that between a married couple (as Musallam [1983: 34] notes, masturbation by the wife's hand is licit). However, it is worth noting that generally allowances are made in Islam in case of necessity (*darūrah*), and also, in the Shiite texts I work with here, severe difficulty (*haraj*), under both of which headings infertility may fall.

16. Mahmud's vision being rather a literal one of what this might entail. Clearly this was in the very early stages of awareness as to what these procedures involved (cf. Inhorn's [1994: 337–40] reports of such early fears amongst lay people in Egypt; similar misapprehensions are apparent in the early reactions in Britain [Pfeffer 1987]). Compare Qaradawi's subsequent, more discriminating use of terminology and comment on 'test-tube babies', cited above.

17. Some further examples would include that of Shaykh Buti of Syria, who is reluctant to allow any form of IVF on the grounds that it opens the door to all manner of unwholesome prospects, notably the 'confounding of genealogy' we will encounter below (Buti 1998: 240, 242; 2002: 77, 88; but Salamah 1998: 90 seems to suggest otherwise). See Salamah

(1998: 89ff.) for some other contrarians.

18. Note again that the published ruling of the council conflates IVF and artificial insemination under the one heading of 'artificial conception'.

19. This, besides such periphrases as 'a man other than the husband', is the characteristic way of referring to what are in English termed sperm (or egg) 'donors' (although *mutabarri'*, a straight translation of the latter, is sometimes used), or 'third parties': this use of the 'stranger' (*ajnabī* or *gharīb,* also 'foreigner') is part of the broader rhetoric that opposes the 'near' (*qarīb*) and intimate to the 'distant', with whom relations are problematic. One might note how the English 'donor' implies a discourse of alienable property, while the Islamic 'stranger' invokes rather a vision of the disruption of social relations. I have explored these issues more fully elsewhere (Clarke 2007b).

20. Tuhmaz (1987: 67) is most critical of the use of this precedent in discussions of contemporary artificial insemination and IVF treatment: he points out that the argument occurred in a very different context, and argues that it cannot be used to imply that such a procedure is lawful.

21. *Al-qānūn al-tabī'ī.* 'Nature' has been a key theme in anthropological debates over medically assisted reproduction in Euro-America (Strathern 1992a). Islamic thinkers make frequent use of *tabī'ī,* 'natural', 'normal', which alludes to God's 'stamping' of each part of His creation according to His model. Human nature is to do good, people being tempted into sin, illicit sex for example, only by Satan. So although 'nature' is a feature of this Islamic discourse, it is not in the sense of a fundamental animal component of human behaviour over which is laid 'culture'. A bastard would not then be a 'natural' child: such behaviour is decidedly unnatural from an Islamic perspective.

22. This 'monogenetic' image of procreation, which has resonances in 'folk' ideas, has been extensively discussed by Delaney (1991: chap. 1). Jad al-Haqq gets into difficulties, as it seems to me, by extending the 'tilth' to refer to a donated egg: if the egg of another woman were used then 'the wife would not be a tilth in this condition for her husband'; conception would result from 'the husband and a woman forbidden to him and not really a tilth' (1997: 3221). The fatwa bears witness to some distinctly unscientific thinking, as in this discussion of the hypothetical gestation of a human embryo in an animal womb: 'This creation will acquire the characteristics of this female ... Have you not seen when the donkey mounts the horse and it conceives, is their fruit that of just one of them!!? It is another creation in form and nature ... if [the embryo] were removed after its creation and animation, and were returned to the womb of the wife, there is no doubt that it may have acquired many of the characteristics of the female animal whose womb contained it ... this

creation would issue other than human in its nature, indeed like that whose womb nurtured it, because of the inheritance of its characteristics and nature' (1997: 3222–23). One should equally avoid marrying a beautiful woman of dubious morals, for virtue and vice may likewise be inherited.

23. Tuhmaz, who in these matters is the most consistently rebellious of the published shaykhs I have read, is reluctant to cede ground to modern scientific notions so easily: 'some of [the early Arabs] thought that the foetus grows with the sperm of [the man who has sex with a pregnant woman], and increases its hearing and sight, and the foetus is like the son of the first man who had sex, by whom the woman was pregnant, and of the second. But doctors today deny that, and do not think that the sperm of a man having sex with a pregnant women has any effect on her foetus during its time inside her womb, as the foetus is inside the protective covering which surrounds it completely and separates it from the outside environment, and the foetus obtains its nourishment during the period of pregnancy from the mother's blood circulation through the placenta ... But the noble sayings of the Prophet ... are right ... How often it is that the facts which scientists refused and denied in the past are subsequently established by science' (1987: 23).

24. The concern that animals might become involved in these processes is a persistent theme throughout the fatwa (cf. Salamah 1998: 114ff., 147f.). I could not say what has inspired it.

25. Jad al-Haqq explains the term in a footnote (1997: 3214 n. 1): 'he is the man who has no sense of *ghayrah* [honour/self-respect/jealousy] over his family' (compare his subsequent [1997: 3224] comment that donor insemination destroys the *karāmah* [nobility/self-respect] of men). Cf. the *hadīth:* 'Three persons shall not enter the Garden: the one who is disobedient to his parents, the pimp [*dayyūth*], and the woman who imitates men' (cited Qaradawi 1994: 233). It would seem that these are the worst disturbers of the social order.

26. 'Mixing' (*ikhtilāt*) is a problematic issue more generally, preeminently in the case of the mixing of men and women, which is carefully regulated, by use of separation and veiling, in order to avoid the occurrence of illegal sex.

27. Such sentiments are not just 'Islamic'. It may be worth bringing in a Maronite Christian perspective (al-Maktabah al-Buliyah 2006: 99ff.): while all medically assisted conception is prohibited under Catholic precepts, recourse to a third party is a clear violation of the union between the couple. As a matter of manners (*adabīyan*), it is forbidden; indeed it is a type of *zinā* and leads to the corruption of family relations. Artificial insemination by husband, on the hand, while forbidden by the Church

(*kanīsīyan*), is morally (*akhlāqīyan*) permissible.

28. Cf. the discussion by Ibrahim (1990: 155), who cites Shaykh 'Abd al-Latif Hamzah as a lone exception arguing that the child does not inherit from the mother either, incorrectly, in Ibrahim's considered opinion, and against the consensus. Contrast this comment from a (Shiite) doctor: 'It's not *ibn zinā* if everyone knows about it'. That is, such procedures could become socially sanctioned, although he is perhaps unduly optimistic: as we will see, patients undergoing donor treatments in Lebanon are, according to the doctors I spoke with, generally extremely concerned about confidentiality in such matters precisely because they fear the opinion of wider society.

29. Both Dr Abu Sari' 'Abd al-Hadi (1994: 72ff., 99), professor of *fiqh* in the Women's College of Riyadh, and Tunisian author Muhammad Bin Ibrahim (1990: 155), for instance, explicitly note that the use of sperm is 'like adultery' (*ka-l-zinā*), but not an instance of it that necessitates the *hadd* punishment. *Zinā* requires actual sexual relations.

30. So in technical terms, Buti (1998: 240, 242; 2002: 77, 84) relies on the principle of *sadd al-dharā'i'* ('the blocking of means' [to evil]).

31. Hamiyah (2004: 95 n. 2) cites a Dr 'Abd al-Mu'ti Bayumi of al-Azhar as allowing (in 2001) surrogacy as akin to a contract hiring a wet-nurse (see next chapter for comparable Shiite arguments). His opinion was rejected by his colleagues.

32. Or neither or both, of course, as some Shiite commentators note (Ridawi 2002: 87; M. R. Sistani 2004: 424; 'A. al-K. Fadlallah 2007: 59).

33. This question has also provoked rabbinical debate, complicated by the matrilineal transmission of Jewish identity (Kahn 2000).

34. Qaradawi's choice of terms here is interesting as he seems to privilege the ovary by using *bunūwah,* 'filiation', in connection with it rather than the vaguer *silah,* 'tie' or 'relationship', which he uses of the womb.

35. It is worth noting that Qaradawi situates the origin of the relation in either the womb or the ovary, in the organs themselves, rather than in the egg or the gestational carrier's blood for example: we will find no easy explanations of the 'substance' type here.

36. As is the case in British law. A Shiite doctor specializing in the use of donor eggs (as we will see below, some Shiite authorities allow this) commented: 'The Sunni position on maternity – it's not logical, to say that the mother is the woman who carries the child and then not allow egg donation.'

37. This is a common argument; so too e.g. Shaykh 'Ali Tantawi among many others (Shah 1995: 114; Salamah 1998: 137).

38. *Umm musta'jarah;* or 'hired womb' (*rahim musta'jarah*). This leads Sayyid Muhammad Rida Sistani (2004: 314ff.) to devote a learned section to whether or not such an arrangement might legitimately be the subject of an Islamic contract of hiring (cf. Salamah 1998: 127ff.). The womb is also sometimes said to be 'borrowed' (*musta'ārah*); the occasional *umm badīlah* (lit. 'exchange mother') looks like a straight calque of 'surrogate'. Compare the rabbinical 'innkeeper' (Kahn 2000: 154), and the French *porteuse*.

39. Elsewhere also the ovum (*buwaydah*). Note that *nutfah* can refer to both the male and the female reproductive contribution, although it is most readily associated with the male.

40. This idea is often used where English might talk of consubstantiality: it alludes to the saying that the child is a 'part from the whole' (*juz' min al-kull*), or a 'portion' (*bid'ah*) of the parent (cf. Benkheira 2001a: 9 n. 15).

41. Ibrahim (1990: 156–57) cites one Shaykh 'Abd al-Basit writing in *al-Wa'i al-Islami* as suggesting, rather counterintuitively one cannot help feeling, that while full motherhood should be awarded to the gestational carrier, the provider of the egg should be considered as a milk mother.

42. I have examined the parallels between surrogacy and milk kinship in more detail elsewhere (Clarke 2007d).

43. See Salamah (1998: 135ff.). Zuhayli (2003: 223), for instance, awards motherhood on genetic lines in the case of surrogacy arrangements specifically, which he prohibits, as does sometime professor of *fiqh* at Amman University Shaykh Mustafa al-Zarqa', in his own earlier discussion of surrogacy arrangements; he further awards milk motherhood to the gestational carrier (cited in Ibrahim 1990: 156). Buti (2002: 78, 85) holds that motherhood must be both genetic and nurturant and therefore a child of donor eggs or a surrogacy arrangement should be considered a foundling (*laqīt*) with respect to its mother. Shaykh 'Abd al-Khaliq Nasir of al-Azhar finds both women to be mothers of the child (cited Hamiyah 2004: 96, note).

44. Although, as one doctor noted, such a procedure is 'not practical. Why do it when you can just get the other wife pregnant anyway?' The possibility within Shiite Islam of temporary marriages to egg donors gives this debate added impetus, as we will see.

45. The council's resolution was avowedly based on the presentation of Shaykh Mustafa al-Zarqa' (al-Majma' al-Fiqhi al-Islami 2007a: 162; Salamah 1998: 101), who is thus presumably the authority Tuhmaz (1987: 72–73) refers to as 'one of the great modern Islamic thinkers', who proposed the two wives solution; Tuhmaz confesses that he is 'as-

tonished how such a suggestion could come from such a man' and how the Fiqh Council could have adopted such a suggestion, even though it later revoked it. Ibrahim (1990: 158) cites, with approval, Shaykh 'Abd al-Basit (see note above) as permitting such a scenario.

46. Yacoub (2001: 244) cites Egyptian medical sources as implying that the verdict was changed to agree with Jad al-Haqq's 1980 fatwa, although Yacoub finds that Jad al-Haqq's discussion here centred on animals, not humans (cf. Omran 1992: 299, n. 1031). Yacoub also cites Qaradawi as suggesting womb transplants (see below) as an alternative to surrogacy arrangements.

47. To pre-empt that, Salamah (1998: 103–4) cites a Shiite Shaykh Muhammad 'Ali al-Taskhiri as suggesting that the co-wife gestational carrier's sexual relations with the shared husband could be regulated so that no such possibility might arise (and see Hamiyah [2004: 95 n. 2] for a similar argument by a shaykh at al-Azhar); Salamah dismisses the possibility as contravening the principle that law is not founded on reason alone and the well-attested precept that a man may have sex with his wife when he wishes.

48. See also Hathout (1991: 116). I have also found two fatwas concurring with this from Shaykh Salih al-Ghanim al-Sadlan, a professor at the Imam Muhammad bin Saud Islamic University in Saudi Arabia, in the Arabic women's magazine *Sayyidati* (vol. 22, no. 1106, 18–24 May 2002), so the topic holds some popular fascination. Yacoub (2001: 267), a commentator rather than a religious specialist, agrees with regard to testicle transplants, but toys with the idea that ovary transplants between women married to the same man might be less problematic.

49. But against this, Dr Ahmed al-Tayyib, president of al-Azhar University, writes in women's magazine *Sayyidati* (vol. 23, no. 1185, 22–28 Nov. 2003) that womb transplants are impermissible as, among other reasons, they entail 'confounding of relations' (*ikhtilāt al-ansāb*).

Chapter 4

MORE TEST-TUBE *FIQH*

S hiite religious authorities share the Sunnis' commitment to science and medical progress; indeed, the Lebanese Hezbollah, like
their Iranian models, have made such a commitment a core part of
their revolutionary platform (Abisaab 2006: 233). Shiite authorities
likewise for the most part find assisted reproductive procedures involving a husband and (one) wife unproblematic as long as care is
taken regarding the uncovering and manipulation of the private parts
by those normally forbidden to do so.[1] However, we find a diversity
of opinion regarding the use of third parties in assisted reproduction,
and the consequent relations. Some of these opinions are strikingly
less restrictive than the Sunni consensus. Where unsure of the correct ruling, Shiite scholars sometimes have recourse to enjoining
caution upon their followers rather than making a definitive pronouncement. As previously discussed, the structure of religious authority is rather different in Shiite Islam: we are primarily interested
in the opinion of their 'sources of imitation', the *marāji'*. The structure of the chapter reflects this: rather than deal with the issues topic
by topic, I take the opinion of each *marja'* in turn. In Lebanon, as I
was told, the most important sources to be considered are Ayatollahs
Khamene'i of Iran (and Supreme Leader of the Islamic Republic),
Fadlallah of Lebanon and Sistani of Iraq, although I was also advised by some in jurisprudential circles to consider the opinion of
Ayatollah Muhammad Sa'id al-Hakim, also based in Najaf, Iraq, as
a reliable control, as it were. In terms of Shiite scholarship more
widely, this is a small and rather idiosyncratic selection, but it is rea-
sonably representative of the spectrum of opinion and should serve
to make the important points. I draw on published and unpublished
writings, Internet sites and email correspondence, and interviews,
the latter with Ayatollah Fadlallah himself and with those shaykhs

who represent the other *marāji'*. I concentrate on the positions of these figures, although I also draw on a wide range of other sources and conversations.

My Shiite sources are more recent than the Sunni ones, and many of the fatwas seem more immediately reflective of the real-life problems of these authorities' followers than do the pronouncements of the Sunni muftis and councils we encountered in the last chapter. This may be coincidental, but perhaps reflects the more personalized relation of *marja'* to follower compared with the general pronouncements of organizations like Majma' al-Fiqh al-Islami and state muftis like Shaykh Jad al-Haqq: these Shiite opinions are not attempts at regulation, while much of the 'Sunni consensus' described in the previous chapter would seem to be just that. We are dealing with rather different genres, then, but the plurality of competing authorities, as opposed to the ostensible consensus reached (and valued, formally speaking) by Sunni jurisprudents, also perhaps lends, for the outside observer, a seemingly greater diversity and dynamism to these debates. As Lebanese Shiite Shaykh Muhammad 'Ali al-Hajj (2006: 6) has it, in a useful booklet devoted to legal opinions concerning the freezing of gametes that I draw on frequently here, 'There is great wealth in the differences of interpretation of our scholars in this matter.'

Khamene'i

If we turn first to the opinion of Ayatollah Khamene'i, we find a radical departure from the Sunni consensus regarding assisted reproduction.[2] Here I have two key sources, first and foremost his book *Ajwibat al-istiftā'āt* ('Responses to fatwa requests' [Khamene'i 2003]). This is widely available in Lebanon and commonly cited: one Christian doctor pulled it from his bookcase in the course of my interview with him, saying that it allows him to reassure Shiite patients who are worried about the religious ramifications of the procedures he offers. Unlike the legal handbooks of the other key *marāji'*, this does not constitute a *risālah 'amalīyah*, a many-volume, comprehensive compendium of Islamic rulings (Clarke 2007a: 291–92). Khamene'i's book is rather a collection of fatwas that take the form of replies to questions from petitioners. However, on inspection of two editions, 2002 and 2003, his answers (and the questions) vary slightly; there is, then, a certain artificiality to the format.

I note the important differences and take the more recent as definitive. Secondly, I consulted the ayatollah's general juridical representative (*al-wakīl al-shar'ī al-'āmm*) in Lebanon, Shaykh Muhammad
Tawfiq al-Muqdad, whom I interviewed in 2003.[3] The shaykh's
statements are, formally speaking, to be regarded as representative
of the ayatollah's: in Shiite jurisprudence, only the most highly qualified of scholars, a *marja'* or *mujtahid*, can give an authoritative
opinion as to the religious law in their own right (see Chapter 2).
However, as discussion deepens, so the lines between the published
position of a *marja'* and his representative's own reading of it may
perhaps become blurred.

In the collection of fatwas, in a section headed 'artificial conception' (*al-talqīh al-sinā'ī*), Ayatollah Khamene'i is first asked (2003,
part 2: 69) if IVF is religiously permissible for a married couple, using, that is, the husband's sperm and the wife's egg. He replies that
it is, although enjoining the avoidance of associated actions forbidden in (religious) law such as the sight and touch of the patients' private parts by those not so permitted – that is, by anyone except one's
spouse. Again, this condition, very restrictive for those wishing to
have fertility treatment, could be lifted where such procedures were
considered as a matter of necessity for the patient, although
Khamene'i does not remark upon that possibility here.[4] We might
note that in the 2002 edition his answer is more expansive, stating
that it is not permitted for a 'stranger' (*rajul ajnabī*, i.e. a man other
than the husband) to carry out the procedure if it were to involve
such looking and touching. Although the import is the same, the later
edition seems perhaps to strike a tone more accommodating of patients' needs by diminishing the emphasis on this point. He then
notes that 'the child is related [*yulhaq*, here and subsequently] to the
spouses, *the producers of the sperm and the egg* [*sāhibay al-nutfah
wa-l-buwaydah*, my emphasis]'. This is the characteristic way, in
both Sunni and Shiite texts, of referring to the 'genetic' or 'biological' parents, as they are usually now termed in the West.[5]

He is then asked whether, given that a wife's inability to reproduce due to a lack of ova can lead to the breakdown of her marriage,
it is permissible in this case to use donated eggs, fertilized with her
husband's sperm by IVF and then transferred to her womb. He re-
sponds: 'There is no problem in the shariah in itself, except that the
child born in this way is related to the sperm and egg producers, and
its relation to the owner of the womb is problematic, and they [dual
form: the husband and wife presumably] must take care to exercise

caution [*ihtiyāt*] regarding the particular legal rulings of *nasab*.' In a subsequent question (2003, part 2: 70), Khamene'i is asked about such procedures involving two women married, permanently *or temporarily*, to one man: Shiite Islam, unlike Sunni Islam, allows temporary marriages for a defined time period in addition to permanent unions; such marriages involve lesser rights and duties than marriage proper (Haeri 1989). As a man, one could marry the egg donor for a day, say, or even an hour, for the duration of the procedure. Is this scenario permitted, and who would then be considered the mother of the child? Also, would one wife's fear of having a child with disabilities transmitted by her own genes allow her to use the egg of the other, if this were not allowed in itself? This has all by implication already been allowed, given that no condition of marriage was made above, and Ayatollah Khamene'i confirms that and the kinship relations that would result. We might note here that such a marriage with the egg donor does serve to remove the suspicion that such procedures are prohibited for many authorities (see below), not least of whom was Khamene'i's predecessor and mentor, Ayatollah Khomeini (Salamah 1998: 102),[6] and that temporary marriages in cases of egg donation are indeed common practice in Iran, according to Soraya Tremayne (2006, n.d.). The 'two wives' scenario is thus widely accepted, as it was not by the Sunnis, and indeed the device of temporary marriage with an egg donor is a neat legal ruse (*hīlah shar'īyah*) to avoid concerns as to impropriety. Removing the condition of marriage, on the other hand, as Khamene'i has done, clears the way for a sister to donate eggs, a common scenario. This would otherwise have been impossible as Islam prohibits marriage with two sisters simultaneously.

This is a radical change: on this position, the potentially troubling use of donor gametes, in this case eggs, is allowed; the problematic confusion of lines of filiation seems to be obviated by making it clear that relation follows genetic relation, although the stated principle involved is the vague one of being the 'originator' of the sperm or egg. It is the relation with the gestational carrier – in this case the married woman seeking to remedy her infertility – that Khamene'i sees as problematic: clearly he does not find the textual arguments relied on by those Sunnis, the majority, who award her maternity wholly convincing, although, one might note, many other Shiite authorities in earlier years did so (see below). While this would seem to raise problems for a woman wishing to profit from the possibility of using donor eggs, the way would seem to be cleared for surrogacy arrangements, although that is not explicitly stated.[7] From the same starting point as the Sunni authorities, Ayatollah Khamene'i has drawn a very different conclusion: one should be wary, then, of attempting to isolate an underlying, unitary 'Islamic kinship system'. Were a married couple to take advantage of this opportunity to use donor eggs, Khamene'i's position has important consequences. Associated with *nasab* relations are concomitant rulings that entail rights of maintenance and inheritance, and are also key to matters of domestic privacy and veiling. If it is to be the egg donor that a resulting child is to be related to, then a very complex set of relations will ensue.

Khamene'i is then asked: 'Is it allowed to fertilise the wife of an infertile man with the sperm of a stranger [*rajul ajnabī*, i.e. a man other than her husband], by placing the sperm in her womb?' He replies:

> There is no legal obstacle [*lā māni' shar'an*] to the fertilisation of the woman with the sperm of a stranger in itself, but forbidden preliminary actions such as prohibited looking and touching and so on must be avoided. And in any case if a child is born in this way, it is not related to the husband, but to the producer of the sperm and to the woman, who is [here] the owner of the egg and the womb.[8]

This is really astonishing when compared with the Sunni positions we examined above, where the insemination of a married woman with the sperm of a man other than her husband was deemed clearly unacceptable, tantamount to 'adultery' (*zinā*). Shaykh Muqdad, as the Ayatollah's representative, explained: 'The key principle to understand here concerns the nature of *zinā*. The fundamental principle is that it concerns the physical act of sexual intercourse. So artificial insemination with the sperm of a man other than one's husband, and similar procedures, are not instances of *zinā*. Although it is important to bear in mind that the husband's permission must be obtained.' While Khamene'i is almost unique in allowing donor insemination,[9] it is not of course that other authorities necessarily equate these medical procedures with *zinā*: they have other reasons for prohibiting them (see below and previous chapter). For Khamene'i, and, incidentally, for most other Shiite authorities, whether or not they allow the procedure (Hajj 2006: 34), the child is legitimate (*shar'ī*). This then raises the problem of whom the child is related to. Certainly what a couple resorting to treatment with donor sperm or donor eggs would be hoping for is that the child be related to them both; but no, the child is related to the genetic parents, to the 'owners/producers' of the sperm and egg, and not to the social parents, not even, it would seem, a wife carrying a child conceived of a donor egg, although Khamene'i recommends caution here.

Again, this stipulation that *nasab* will follow genetic lines has complicating consequences for family life, as, in Islamic law, kinship and its absence entail distinct rights and duties: the child and his or her genetic parents will have mutual inheritance rights; conduct between the child and the couple who have sought treatment will have to be carefully regulated, as relatedness engenders marriage prohibitions, which further determine rules of seclusion, bodily concealment and comportment. Thus if one is forbidden to marry a woman – one's sister for example – one can be in a closed room with her unaccompanied, see more of her body – her hair for example – than unrelated men, and generally deal with her in more familiar fashion. Where such a relation is lacking, as it would be for one or both spouses for couples using donor gametes on Khamene'i's position, the expected intimacy of domestic life would be severely disturbed. It is hard to imagine people following these stipulations to the letter, and I challenged a Shiite doctor, a follower of Khamene'i who provided donor gamete procedures for his Shiite patients, on this point. Clearly keen to demonstrate that these complexities are not a practical barrier to undertaking such procedures, he pointed out that there are other legal rulings that will serve to alleviate such problems: 'If the child were male, then there's no problem because the mother suckles.' A boy raises potential problems for the wife: she would have to veil in front of him when he reached puberty. But if she had become pregnant by use of a donor egg and, having given birth, breastfed the child, then a milk kinship relation would be established removing the problems of intimacy, a legal device we saw employed in some cases of 'fostering' (see Prologue).[10]

I then challenged him as to the situation if the child were female. He thought for a moment: 'There's a way... Yes, you can't marry your wife's daughter.' If the child is female then there is potentially a problem between her and the husband: in the case of the use of donor sperm where he is not considered the father, we understand. But here the girl will be in the position of a *rabība*, 'stepdaughter' or 'ward', that is, one's wife's daughter by another man: the *rabība* is forbidden to the husband so long as he has had sex with her mother[11] (on both counts, see Chapter 1). The doctor continued: 'Anyway, the real problem is inheritance – but you can give

them the money beforehand, make a will and so on. This can be done
in normal circumstances, if you favour one son over the others, or
don't like one and wish to exclude them. This is perfectly normal, it
even holds up in government courts. If you die before doing that
then, okay, yes there is a problem. But people *are* religious; they follow all the rules.' It is not, then, that people simply ignore the consequences of these legal opinions – they do not, but there are ways
and means of circumventing their potential problems.[12]

Shaykh Muqdad explained the Ayatollah's position regarding the
use of donor gametes as 'a good way of *tabannī* [adoption]', indeed
'the best type' [*ahsan naw' min anwā' al-tabannī*]. I queried this,
given my understanding that adoption is formally forbidden in Islam, whereupon we entered the realm of ambiguous distinctions between full adoption and fostering that we encountered in Chapter 2.
Shaykh Muqdad had been using the term *tabannī* loosely. 'Yes, yes,
but in Islam we mean something different – *tabannī* is rather *tar-
biyah*, bringing a child up, but not giving it your name, pretending
it's yours like in the West. So, in the case of donor sperm, you must
not say that this is my son, rather it is not, but it is that of a known
father. If the father is known, then this is better for psychological, religious, moral and other reasons. If he grows up not knowing his father, this could be upsetting. If he's related to an unknown father,
then that's another matter.'[13] 'So is that a problem?' I asked. Shaykh
Muqdad elaborated: 'No, not a problem, but known [*ma'rūf*] is definitely better. It could even be unknown [*majhūl*], but it is much better if it is known. The sperm could be obtained from someone *qarīb*
['close', a relative] or *ba'īd* ['distant', not a relative], *min al-arhām*
or *ghayr al-arhām* [from the inner circle of relatives or otherwise].
Artificial insemination by husband has been around for ages, but by
donor [*rajul ajnabī*] it's new.' So long as the social relationships are
clear, then, all is well. Given the issues of inheritance and intimacy
raised, one might well surmise that the ideal donor would be a near
relative: Shaykh Muqdad raises the possibility without giving it special prominence, but doctors do indeed report instances of close relatives donating sperm, as we will see.

Shaykh Muqdad also had some further comments regarding
the maternal relation, for I was keen to clarify Sayyid Khamene'i's
position regarding a gestational carrier of the egg of another woman.
If maternity is to follow genetic lines, this leaves the question of the
'nurturing' role of the gestational carrier, which could perhaps parallel that of the 'milk mother', with whom a kinship-type relation is es-

tablished through her nourishing a child with her breast milk; as we saw in the last chapter, such a possibility was raised in Sunni discussions, but passed over. Shaykh Muqdad was clear that such a comparison was invalid: 'The producer of the egg is the mother. The second woman is just a place [for the foetus] to grow: she needn't even be a wife. Maybe my wife is sick and cannot carry a child, for example. I've seen American films about such procedures. The relation with the womb mother is not even like milk kinship.'

Ayatollah Khamene'i also allows the use of sperm after death, in which he is, again, unusual.[14] He is asked (2003, part 2: 70): 'If sperm were taken from the husband and after his death an egg from his wife were fertilised with it and then placed in her womb, then, firstly, is that deed legally permitted? And secondly, is the resulting child the child of the husband and legally related to him? And thirdly, does the child inherit from him?' Khamene'i replies that '[t]here is no problem [*lā ba's*] with the stated procedure in itself', and finds the relationship to the mother clearly established, although he is less clear on the child's relationship to the dead husband, finding it merely 'not unlikely' that filiation is also established here, but without rights of inheritance. And he is later (2003, part 2: 71) asked, in still more detail: 'Is it possible to fertilise the wife with the sperm of her dead husband in the following circumstances? A: after his death but before the end of the *'iddah* [the 'waiting period' before remarrying enjoined on a widow or divorcee]. B: after his death and after the end of the *'iddah*. C: if she were to marry another husband after the death of her first husband, then would it be possible for her to conceive using the sperm of her first husband? And is it possible for her to conceive using the sperm of her first husband after the death of the second husband?' Again Khamene'i readily grants permission, finding that '[t]here is no obstacle to that in itself, with no difference between what is before the end of the *'iddah* and what is after it, nor between if she were married or not.' It also makes no difference whether the fertilization with the first husband's sperm is after the death of the second husband or during his life; if the second husband is alive, however, then he has to give his consent.

To reiterate, these positions are, in the context of global reactions to these procedures, and especially in the context of the Sunni positions we have just seen, surprising. Ayatollah Khamene'i has, in the matter of assisted reproduction, seemingly decided on some fundamental principles – namely, that these procedures do not constitute *zinā* and that *nasab* relatedness is congruent with genetic relatedness

– and has followed them through, regardless of the novelty of some of the ensuing relations. Of course, the arguments are more complex than this. The brevity of the fatwa format renders the ayatollah's reasoning rather opaque, and Shaykh Muqdad's explanation was clearly pitched at a relatively low level for my benefit. However, in his own survey of Shiite opinion, Shaykh al-Hajj (2006: 21–22) gives a slightly more expansive account, noting that, as a general principle of Islamic jurisprudence, everything that is not explicitly prohibited is permitted (see also 'A. al-K. Fadlallah 2007: 14), and that Khamene'i finds that those evidences used by others to prohibit the use of donor sperm, for example, are in fact themselves only applicable to instances of *zinā*; that is, it is not just a question of whether or not assisted conception involving donor gametes can be assimilated to 'adultery', but also a question of the exact meaning and reference of the pertinent religious texts.

While the terms of the debate more generally can hardly be gleaned from the yes/no format of the fatwa literature, I do have two very full accounts: the large and, for me, rather difficult volume by Sayyid Muhammad Rida al-Sistani (see below), and a much briefer and easier work by Sayyid 'Abd al-Karim Fadlallah, supplemented by my own conversations with the latter, who is, I should stress, not part of Ayatollah Fadlallah's school even if he is a member of the same extended family,[15] and a scholar of note and director of higher studies at one of Beirut's Shiite seminaries (the Hawzah 'Ilmiyah). While a lengthy exposition would perhaps prove tedious, it is clear from these discussions that the issues are far from cut and dried. A key Quranic reference, for instance, is the verse beginning 'And tell women believers to cast down their eyes and guard their private parts [*yahfazna furūjahunna*]' (24:31) – but guard them from what? While some scholars argue that this can be extended to include donor sperm, for example, others argue that the context would imply that this is restricted to fornication and lustful looks; after all, a woman is allowed to insert water or medicines into her vagina ('A. al-K. Fadlallah 2007: 16).

Another key text is the saying of the Prophet Muhammad: 'He who will receive the worst tortures on the day of judgement is the man who placed his seed in a womb forbidden to him.' Again, its application is debatable; it is far from clear, for instance, that the embryo transferred to a woman's womb after IVF is the same as a man's 'seed', and some authorities in fact use this point to legitimize embryo donation ('A. al-K. Fadlallah 2007: 18–21; and see below).[16]

Sayyid 'Abd al-Karim Fadlallah himself feels that by far the most powerful argument for prohibiting any of these procedures is the well-established principle of 'obligatory caution in genital matters' (*wujūb al-ihtiyāt fī-l-furūj*; see 'A. al-K. Fadlallah 2007: 22ff.). While the general principle is to permit all that is not explicitly prohibited, in certain restricted fields – such as the taking of human life, for example – the gravity of the matter is such as to enjoin avoidance as a matter of course. Sexual issues are one such area, as they are bound up with the reproduction of society, where one must err on the side of caution.[17]

Clearly Khamene'i finds none of these arguments wholly convincing.[18] His position regarding donor sperm in particular is notorious, and by all accounts created quite a stir when it was first issued; it was cited by many I talked to in jurisprudential circles in knowing fashion, with the suggestion, I thought, of his supposed relative lack of legal scholarship and acumen (see Chapter 2). I cannot comment on this, save reemphasizing the political dimension to such suggestions, but it hardly seems credible that the ayatollah, with the very considerable clerical apparatus behind him, would simply blunder. One can ultimately only speculate as to the reasons for his notable lack of restriction here,[19] but it has had a considerable impact on the practice of assisted reproduction in Lebanon, as has no doubt the position of Lebanon's own Ayatollah Fadlallah, whom we consider next.

Fadlallah

Ayatollah Muhammad Husayn Fadlallah, as the only Lebanese *marja'*, is very influential within Lebanon. I had the privilege of interviewing him at his Beirut offices in 2004, consulted published and unpublished writings and his website, and enjoyed many conversations with Shaykh Muhsin 'Atwi, the head of his fatwa-issuing department. Shaykh 'Atwi, although a very considerable scholar himself, was always careful to present the sayyid's opinion rather than his own: again, under Shiite precepts, only the most senior of clerics, an acknowledged *marja'* or *mujtahid*, is qualified to make a definitive statement as to the religious law. In our earliest meetings Shaykh 'Atwi would frequently ring the sayyid on the internal telephone to make sure of his position. When, for example, I asked about the ascription of maternity in the case of the use of a donor egg, he replied: 'In Sayyid Fadlallah's opinion it is the egg donor who is the mother.' 'And in your opinion?' I asked. 'I don't have one,' he responded. No doubt he has his own perspective on the debate, but in the context of our discussions it would not have been appropriate for him to mention it.

I started my interview with Ayatollah Fadlallah himself by asking him about assisted reproduction in general. He began by saying that it can be seen as a way of solving problems with reproduction in the natural (*tabī'ī*) fashion, by using IVF for example. This is permitted in Islam as long as the sperm is from the husband[20] and not from a stranger,[21] in which case the procedure is not allowed, whether the woman is married or not. Immediately it is clear that his position is opposite to that of Ayatollah Khamene'i in this respect. It is not that 'Shiites allow donor sperm': there is a diversity of opinion, even on what would seem to be clear-cut issues such as this. 'People might say, "A blood transfusion for my wife – no problem. But sperm – no way!"' Shaykh 'Atwi joked one time when we were sitting in his office, along with another man who had come to ask the shaykh's advice on a different matter. 'Still, legally speaking, a woman could divorce her husband, then marry another man temporarily, for an hour or so, get pregnant and then return to her husband', he mused. 'But there could be a problem with the *'iddah* [waiting period before remarriage]', ventured the bystander. 'Yes, true. It could be his brother, not a stranger [*gharīb*], someone inside the family, so as to avoid gossip. There could be money involved.'

I was subsequently given a comprehensive compilation of Sayyid Fadlallah's responses to individual petitions regarding assisted reproduction sent via email to his website:[22] the staff of his offices, including Shaykh 'Atwi, then answer the queries in accordance with the sayyid's teachings and the sayyid himself checks them all before they are sent in return. Exactly such scenarios arise. One woman asks (in Arabic):

> I live in the U.S. and have been married for five years, but without having had any children. I underwent IVF five times, without success. My husband's sperm count is low, and our chances of having a child slim. We are thinking of divorcing, and then I will make a marriage contract with my husband's brother and do assisted conception with him. And then if, God willing, I get pregnant, his brother will divorce me after the nine months of the pregnancy and I will remarry my husband and register my child in his name. Is that religiously permitted? (Fatwa no. 39,336)

The reply from the sayyid's offices reads that, so long as the marriage to the brother is sound, this course is allowed, except that registering the child in the name of the woman's first husband would be impermissible: it should rather be registered in the name of the brother, the child's father as the provider of the sperm. In other fatwas where people have written asking if they can use donor sperm tout court, the sayyid's staff have made it clear that they may not, but have again mentioned this solution, that it would be possible for the husband to divorce his wife, she wait the obligatory waiting period of three months or so and then marry the sperm donor temporarily; then, if she falls pregnant through AI or IVF using the donor's sperm, she must wait the necessary waiting period [*'iddah* again] for a pregnant woman, which is until delivery of the child, and then she can remarry her original husband; the child will, however, be that of the sperm donor.

While this may sound almost unfeasibly complicated, and I was, I should say, told of no such cases in Lebanon by my medical informants, anthropologist Soraya Tremayne (2006, n.d.) does report exactly this solution being used by infertile couples in Iran.[23] One cannot help but think that straight donor insemination would be easier. 'Do people do such things [i.e. use donor sperm]?' I wondered to Shaykh 'Atwi. 'Those who do would have to ask Sayyid Khamene'i's office. We don't know what people actually do with our advice, but they would ask here and there'. The experts themselves assume, then, that people test the limits of the shariah and seek out the legal possibilities that best suit them, in fear of the judgement of wider society ('gossip') as well as that of God.[24]

Sayyid Fadlallah continued our interview by explaining the background to his position. In his view, *zinā* has two aspects: that of the act of sex, and that of reproduction (*injāb*), which must take place within the marriage relation. He would seem, then, to be working with a somewhat different notion of *zinā* from Khamene'i, although again, his exposition here was pitched at a relative layman's level. Nevertheless, Fadlallah, like others, does not regard donor insemination or IVF using donor sperm as *zinā* per se, and a resulting child is related to the sperm donor, but is not deemed a bastard.[25] As he said to me, 'From a legal point of view he is his son, but the deed is wrong.' To turn to his published work, in his treatise[26] *Fiqh al-sharī'ah* (2003, vol. 3: 521), he states: 'The child is legitimate in every case in which the entry of the man's sperm into the woman's womb is effected by other than sexual intercourse, or they are fertilised together outside the womb, whether the sperm was the husband's or that of another man, and whether this insertion or fertilisation was permitted or forbidden.'

And again, were one to use another man's sperm or commit some other forbidden action in the course of the procedure, 'it would be sinful [*āthiman*], and the child is not a bastard [*ibn zinā*], and *nasab* with him is realised as well' (2003, vol. 3: 524). Such a child is analogous to a child born of other, forbidden sexual acts: intercourse during the menstrual period, the Ramadan fast or the Hajj pilgrimage to Mecca, for instance. Such children are also legitimate: bastardy is a status realized only under certain conditions, the result of *zinā* proper (M. R. Sistani 2004: 9–15). As regards 'the entry of the man's sperm into the woman's womb ... by other than sexual intercourse', we might note here that the Shiites have their own premodern artificial insemination tradition, a report of a ruling by the Prophet Muhammad's grandson, Imam Hasan, interestingly different from the Sunni equivalent cited in the previous chapter: it concerns the child of 'lesbianism' (*musāhaqah*), where a woman, after intercourse with her husband, engages in lesbian activity with a virgin, transferring his sperm to her in the process and making her pregnant – no doubt more an example of scholastic debate than a frequent occurrence in reality. The child is considered that of the husband.[27]

Besides finding artificially conceived children to be legitimate, Fadlallah further agrees with Khamene'i that relatedness is congruent with genetic relation, as regards the maternal as well as the paternal relation. So he writes:

> The origin [*asl*] of the relation [*nisbah*] of the child to its father is its being from his sperm [*nutfah*], just as for us [i.e. Fadlallah, thus indicating that this point is controversial], the origin of the relation of the child to its mother is its being from her egg, without there being a role for her nurture of it in her womb and its being delivered of her. So if an infertile couple, seeking a child, were to resort to the procedure known as 'the hired womb' [*al-rahim al-musta'ārah*, i.e. surrogacy], that is, that a sperm is taken from the man and an egg from the woman, who is suffering from problems in her womb which prevent her from bearing a child, and the two gametes [*al-nutfatān*] are placed in the womb of a second woman and she delivers a child, then the child born of this second woman is definitely the son of the sperm producer, and as for its mother it is clear that she is the egg pro-

> ducer, not the woman who has nurtured the child in her
> womb and delivered it. (2003, vol. 3: 523)

Fadlallah has none of the reservations on this point that Khamene'i noted then. And in our interview, we considered the use of donor eggs: 'In the matter of the egg, if we postulate taking the egg of one woman, fertilising it with the sperm of a married man and placing the fertilised egg in the womb of that man's wife, there is an opinion that says that there is no problem with that [see below]. But there is a legal debate as to who the mother is. Sayyid Abu-l-Qasim al-Khu'i, for example, held that the mother is the woman who bears the pregnancy [*al-hāmil*]. Our opinion is that the mother is the egg producer. In any case, the child is legitimate.'

Ayatollah Khu'i was generally considered to be the most widely followed *marja'* in the world until his death in Najaf in 1992, and was teacher and mentor to many of the contemporary leading figures, including both Ayatollahs Fadlallah and Sistani.[28] He based his opinion here, as the Sunni authorities cited in the previous chapter, on the Quranic verse (58:2), 'Their mothers are those only who gave birth to them [*waladna-hum*]' ('A. al-K. Fadlallah 2007: 60).[29] Fadlallah (M. H. Fadlallah 1995: 10), on the other hand, argues that the egg is 'the foundation in the creation of the child, and the sperm and the egg both have an integral role here'; the gestational carrier is 'merely a vessel'. In my compilation of fatwas from the sayyid's website, this is always made clear to those asking about the use of donor eggs: in Sayyid Fadlallah's opinion a resulting child will be the child of the egg donor. So, for example, a woman writes: 'I have been married for more than ten years, but we have not been blessed up to now with children. So I have agreed with my husband that he will marry another woman, and she will give me one of her eggs so that it can be transplanted inside me and fertilised by my husband. Is there any shariah problem from this angle?' (fatwa no. 75,082). The reply comes that there is no problem with this scenario, but she should be aware that the true mother is the provider of the egg. But the reply goes on to note that '[this is] according to our opinion, but our teacher Sayyid Khu'i (God rest his soul) thought that it is the woman who bears the pregnancy that is the mother', and by mentioning this the door is perhaps opened to those who might wish to adopt that reading, if it were more convenient for them and they were not strictly bound to the opinion of another *marja'* (see Chapter 2). Sayyid Fadlallah, we should note, unusually, allows his own followers a certain latitude with regard to their 'imitation' (*taqlīd*) of his rulings.

This genetic position, shared by Khamene'i, Fadlallah and Hakim (see below),[30] struck me as the majority view, although in conversation, Sayyid 'Abd al-Karim Fadlallah (introduced above and, again, not part of Ayatollah Fadlallah's school), who had investigated the matter in depth, felt that this was something new. Previously, most authorities had sided with Khu'i ('A. al-K. Fadlallah 2007: 59):[31] the genetic position was the coming thing, and would, in his considered opinion, fairly shortly – 'after two or three years' – become the new consensus. In his own book on IVF, Sayyid 'Abd al-Karim Fadlallah, who shares this view, cites some of the sayings of Imam 'Ali, cousin and son-in-law of the Prophet and a figure of great importance to Shiite jurisprudence, which anticipate, in the sayyid's opinion, many of the findings of modern science in this field. For instance, 'The two seeds struggle in the womb and whichever is the greater, its likeness issues: if the seed of the woman were greater then he will resemble his maternal uncles, and if the seed of the man were greater then he will resemble his paternal uncles' (2007: 73). How amazing it is, Sayyid 'Abd al-Karim Fadlallah comments, to think that Imam 'Ali not only knew of the existence of the ovum, but also of the workings of dominant and recessive genes, centuries before these were established scientifically (2007: 75–76).[32]

To return to my interview with Ayatollah (Muhammad Husayn) Fadlallah, I asked the ayatollah, as I had asked Shaykh Muqdad, if, were one to suppose the genetic mother the legal mother, one could not draw a parallel between the gestational carrier and the 'milk mother', who breastfeeds the child (see Chapters 1 and 2). In an unpublished but celebrated lecture at the Middle East Hospital, Beirut in 1995, Fadlallah was cautious, noting that this was an issue still under debate at the time and not giving his own opinion (Fadlallah 1995: 11). But in our interview in 2004, Sayyid Fadlallah promptly agreed with my suggestion, noting that he has discussed in his legal treatises how it is that breastfeeding institutes a relation that entails marriage prohibition. The basis of that relation is the constitution (*takwīn*) of the child, its flesh and bone being generated from the nourishment provided by the breast milk. This is also present in pregnancy, and so there is a school of thought, which the Sayyid holds to be correct, that a relation of prohibition is instituted in this case also.[33] Others, however, he noted, differ in this matter. After the interview, I sought to confirm the point with Shaykh 'Atwi, who checked with the sayyid: 'Yes, he has a new opinion. The mother is the egg producer, but the gestational carrier resembles women prohibited in marriage through breastfeeding. Her legal ruling becomes that of the milk mother; through the nurture in the womb she becomes the nurture mother [*umm al-hadānah*]. A new ruling.'[34] This ruling also appears in my compilation of website fatwas, where the sayyid's offices note in reply to a question from 2007 (no. 71,509) that the woman bearing the child is 'ruled as the milk mother'. But in the most recent reply of all, from 2008, fatwa number 101,180 since the beginning of the database, they write that 'she has no relation at all unless she suckles the child after it is delivered, whereupon it becomes her milk child'. Again we see the dynamism of these debates: such opinions are continuously evolving.

Ensuing relations aside, the question still remains as to whether these procedures are permissible. In his 2003 discussion of surrogacy arrangements cited above, Fadlallah goes on to remark that these would be permitted if both women were married to the man (see also Fadlallah 2001, vol. 1: 273), and if there was no requirement of prohibited masturbation (i.e. by other than the wife's hand)[35] on the part of the man or uncovering of the woman's private parts (*'awrah*) before a male doctor, although one assumes that medical necessity would be considered sufficient justification for these latter as elsewhere. Were the procedure carried out otherwise, that would constitute committing a forbidden act (carrying the seed of a man other than one's husband), but the child would not be considered a bastard and would acquire *nasab*. Here, then, a marriage contract is required – the 'two wives' procedure is allowed – without it, a surrogacy arrangement is forbidden.[36] So a petitioner wrote to the sayyid's website asking:

> I have a friend who cannot have children due to a problem in her womb, and the doctors advised her to 'rent' the womb of another woman. She has been able to find a surrogate in whom will be transplanted her – i.e. the woman with the sick womb's – egg, fertilised with the sperm of her husband. Is it obligatory for the surrogate to get divorced from her own husband and marry the sick woman's husband, even knowing that the egg will have been fertilised in the laboratory by the husband of the sick woman, the source of the egg? (Fatwa no. 64,460)

The sayyid's staff confirm that the marriage would indeed be necessary, but go on to note that 'the couple may find other scholars who allow it [without such a marriage], and with an eye to the necessity of the procedure, it is possible for the couple to follow [*taqlīd*] their opinion in this matter'. Again, we should remember that this latitude in the sayyid's understanding of *taqlīd* is relatively unusual.[37]

But what of the use of a donor egg, fertilized with the husband's sperm and transferred to his wife's womb: if the husband married the egg donor, that would be permitted, under the ruling above, but what about without such a marriage? After all, this is not a case where the sperm of a 'stranger' is being introduced into a woman's womb. There is some evidence to suggest that the sayyid finds this procedure permissible without such a marriage:[38] in the 1995 lecture he was quite clear that 'this deed is not prohibited [*hādhā al-'aml laysa muharraman*]' (Fadlallah 1995: 10; also cited by Hamiyah 2004: 94–95); Shaykh al-Hajj (2006: 32), who seems to have worked quite closely with Sayyid Fadlallah in the writing of his own survey, also reports that he allows it. In our interview (in 2004), quoted above, the sayyid merely noted that 'there is an opinion that says that there is no problem with that', although to my subsequent chagrin I neglected to clarify with him whether this was an opinion he shared: nevertheless, I sought to do so with the sayyid's offices immediately afterwards and understood that 'the Sayyid has a new opinion, regarding the donor egg there is now no need for marriage'. But the balance of evidence I have at my disposal suggests that the settled, official view is otherwise, that marriage, even if temporary, between the egg donor and the husband of the recipient is required. That is the position declared on the sayyid's website, and that given to me by Shaykh 'Atwi on a later visit (in 2007), and that made clear time after time in the fatwas in my unpublished collection, where such a marriage is enjoined, or at least made the subject of 'obligatory caution' (*al-ahwat wujūban*).[39] The latter advice requires the sayyid's followers to take the most cautious path here rather than run the risk of sinning, effectively preventing them from undertaking the procedure without such a marriage, but also serving as a tacit admission that the jurist is not wholly convinced of the requisite ruling: if they were, a more definitive statement would be made. Donation between close, non-marriageable relatives is thus ruled out, as it was not by Ayatollah Khamene'i.[40]

We have, then, a complex and nuanced picture as to the legality of this procedure. For one thing, the distinctions to be made here are fine and exact: where Western academic discourse is interested in 'donor gametes', these Islamic debates distinguish between egg and sperm, and single and married. And it seems the sayyid may have changed his thinking on this matter; certainly he finds the right ruling far from obvious. In any case, complete consistency across the whole of his organisation in harmony with his developing thinking, while clearly desirable, is no doubt not easily achieved. There may too be a difference between relatively conservative public pronouncements, mediated through an array of public outlets, and private suspicion and comment that more relaxed positions may be nearer the truth. Whatever the case, establishing the exact ruling at a given time is perhaps less important for our purposes here than observing the complexity, contingency and dynamism of what is, one should again stress, more a realm of opinion than 'law'.

Finally, Sayyid Fadlallah has also considered the issue of the post-mortem use of sperm and finds that a resulting child would be related to the genetic parents, although it would not inherit from the father.[41] However, 'the permissibility of the wife undertaking this deed is not unproblematic, and it is more fitting that she exercises obligatory caution [as above] by not placing the sperm in her womb after her husband's death' (2003, vol. 3: 524; see also Hajj 2006: 54–58).[42] In our interview, he noted that there has been debate over this matter in Shiite circles, and told me that he is one of those of the opinion that 'this is not allowed, because the wife has been separated from her husband by his death, and so the sperm is not actually from her husband, just as she could not use his sperm after being divorced from him'. And Shaykh 'Atwi confirmed this for me, ringing up the sayyid: 'Have you changed your opinion? No, we remain there.'[43]

Sistani

That the opinions of Khamene'i and Fadlallah had the highest profile during my field researches was due no doubt to the prominence of these two figures in the Lebanese Shiite imaginary – the one the official *marja'* of Hezbollah, the other Lebanon's most substantial religious authority – although also due, perhaps, to the fact that they allow certain controversial procedures, or at least may be thought the most likely to, as relatively 'progressive' figures. However, as I have noted, I was advised to cast my net a little wider, and in particular to consider the opinions of Ayatollahs 'Ali al-Sistani and Muhammad Sa'id al-Hakim, both based in Najaf, Iraq, and both generally considered of a more 'traditional' cast than their explicitly Islamist counterparts Khamene'i and Fadlallah. As we will see, however, that 'traditionalism' does not make them any less alive to these new scientific and medical issues, or indeed necessarily more restrictive in their rulings on them.

Sistani's opinion was, at the time of my fieldwork at least, not common knowledge. I have already quoted (in Chapter 2) the otherwise well-informed Shiite doctor who called Sistani 'the ultimate' but was not sure of his opinion regarding IVF and the use of donor gametes. The doctor's suspicion was that his position is more restrictive than those of Khamene'i and Fadlallah, which perhaps explains his own relative lack of interest. I speculate; but I in fact found it more difficult to establish Sistani's opinion in detail here, and only obtained direct statements of it some time after my initial researches, through email correspondence with his branch offices in Qom (Iran) and London. This may of course be due to the vagaries of fieldwork; Sistani's institutional machinery in Lebanon was, in 2003–04 at least, more limited than that of Khamene'i or Fadlallah. I did speak to one of Sistani's representatives in Lebanon, who was reluctant to commit himself on what he saw as very complex issues and preferred to present me with a copy of the recent work devoted to the topic by Sistani's son Sayyid Muhammad Rida Sistani, a renowned jurist in his own right but also a spokesman for the Sistani school in particular.

The book, *Artificial reproductive techniques* (*Wasā'il al-injāb al-sinā'īyah*), presents some 700 pages of dense jurisprudential analysis that took me months to work through. Sayyid Muhammad Rida Sistani offers what must be a fairly comprehensive survey and critique of the possible arguments and evidence, but time and again, he finds the textual proofs that are commonly advanced inadequate for a definitive answer: this is clearly to be seen as a difficult and obscure area where caution – again, a recognized and respectable position for the Shiite jurist to adopt – is advisable. However, such reticence also reflects both the genre in which he is writing, where one looks at the arguments from all sides, and the difference in status between himself, most distinguished scholar though he may be, and a *marja'* such as his father, who has taken on the burden of giving definitive and authoritative responses to the questions of the masses. Despite Ayatollah Sistani's prominence, then, as perhaps the most widely followed Shiite authority of all, my account of his position here is, unfortunately, less full than that of those above.

From Arabic works I obtained during my fieldwork it was clear that Sistani does allow assisted reproduction using the spouses' sperm and eggs (AI and IVF), but he prohibits donor insemination, although were it carried out inadvertently (if different men's sperm became confused in a clinic, perhaps) a resulting child would be the legitimate child of the sperm donor and inherit from him. If the procedure were carried out deliberately, then 'it is not unlikely' that the child will also be legitimate and enjoy inheritance rights over the estate of the donor: it is only the child of *zinā* proper that is denied inheritance (Sistani 2000: 256; 2002, vol.1: 459–60; Hajj and Jawad 2007: 501).[44] In my initial researches, I did find mention of procedures where the egg of one woman is fertilized with a man's sperm and then transferred to the womb of another woman, as in the use of donor eggs and surrogacy arrangements, but in the context of the question as to who is to be considered the mother.[45] In his *risālah*, Sistani (2002, vol. 1: 460) notes that there are two possible answers to this question: he finds it debatable that motherhood could be attributed to the provider of the egg, even if caution would advise not abandoning this possibility. In a fatwa quoted elsewhere (Hajj and Jawad 2007: 501–2), Sistani again finds the issue problematic and advises care, this time finding it not unlikely that a relation of marriage prohibition is established between the gestational carrier and the child, even if it were not ruled that a full kinship relation applies.[46] This latter point was confirmed in more positive form in subsequent (2007) email correspondence between myself and Sistani's official website, based in Qom, which stated that 'the child born to the woman who gave birth is *mahram* (*mahram* means the woman is not required to wear hijab ['the veil'] in front of him when he grows up – if he is a boy that is)'; but 'in respect of all other rulings precaution must be exercised towards both parties'.

So, if I may extrapolate, Ayatollah Sistani is (understandably) perhaps not absolutely certain as to whether or not, in God's law, maternity is attributable to the egg donor, and thus advises acting as though it is, just in case: as her relative, for instance, one should avoid marrying a child conceived of her egg, for fear that this may indeed be a prohibited act. Sistani is more explicitly decisive with regard to the (hypothetical) question of 'artificial wombs': were an embryo grown in and delivered of such a device, then it is 'clear' (*zāhir*) that the child is related to the providers of the sperm and egg (Sistani 2002, vol. 1: 460; Hajj and Jawad 2007: 501). Here, then, a 'genetic' principle seems to be favoured. This may seem a rather recondite issue: perusal of Hajj and Jawad's (2007: 461) comparative presentation of the fatwas of Sistani and Khu'i reveals that this is a commentary on the position of Sistani's mentor, who held that in such cases (which he deemed permissible) the child, while related to the sperm provider, is regarded as having no mother.[47] One has the impression here of learned, measured debates in the scholastic centres of Najaf and Qom.

These texts are, however, silent on the more practical issue as to whether infertile women can benefit from egg donation, on the one hand, and surrogacy arrangements on the other. In my email correspondence, I asked about the permissibility of a series of scenarios, including egg donation with and without marriage to the egg donor, and 'hiring the womb' of a woman other than the wife – a surrogacy arrangement, that is – and the brief reply to these stated that 'The matters mentioned are all allowed'. Given my previous impression of a relatively circumspect approach on the part of the Sistani school, this was surprising and did not reflect the vaguely felt expectations of Lebanese fertility circles, as mentioned above.[48] Appended were some further fatwas (in English) stating Sayyid's Sistani's position on egg donation: the use of donor eggs is deemed permissible, without marriage to the egg donor being enjoined. They were, however, silent on the subject of surrogacy arrangements. Scholastic debate aside, then, like Sayyid Fadlallah, Sayyid Sistani finds the use of donor sperm clearly prohibited, but that of donor eggs permissible; however, it seems – if my reading of the correspondence is sound – that Sistani does not insist on marriage to the egg donor in such scenarios. Although widely perceived as a conservative figure, then, his position here is in fact relatively unrestrictive. He is less sure, however, than Khamene'i and Fadlallah that the ascription of maternity should follow genetic lines. To round off the account, the post-mortem use of sperm is prohibited, but a resulting child would be the legitimate child of the man who was the source of the sperm, although it would not inherit from him (Hajj and Jawad 2007: 502).[49]

Hakim

As for Ayatollah Hakim, I visited his branch office in Beirut, where it was felt that the best thing would be for me to send some written questions to the ayatollah himself. These were duly faxed to his office in Najaf, and the staff there emailed back the response, cited here as 'Hakim 2004'. I have also made use of two collections of his fatwas in reply to his followers' questions, one specifically concerning cloning and other medical matters (2001), and the other a source of guidance for Muslims living in the West (2002), as well as my conversations with his son, Sayyid Haidar al-Hakim, his *wakīl* (representative) in Lebanon.[50] Again, I could not claim a wholly comprehensive understanding of Hakim's thought on these complex issues, but as we will see, his comments open up still further dimensions to the debate.

Ayatollah Hakim allows assisted reproduction, AI and IVF, involving husband and wife only, 'as the creation of the embryo does not differ from the usual except in the circumstances' (2004). True, care must be taken concerning the private parts – a problem that could be obviated if the doctor were the husband of the woman (!) – and masturbation for the production of sperm. However, these obstacles can be overcome if the lack of fertility constitutes a severe social impediment (*haraj*). There is no effect on the relation of the child to its parents (on all the preceding see 2001: 37–38, 43–44, 48; 2002: 354–56). As for the involvement of third parties, this does not for Hakim constitute *zinā*, which is 'the natural [*tabī'ī*] sexual act between a man and a woman between whom there is no legal relation' (2004); there is thus no *hadd* punishment (again, one explicitly owed to God – death by stoning or lashes in the case of *zinā*) due for those who undertake such procedures (2004; and see 2001: 48; 2002: 354). As to whether or not such procedures are permitted, this is, it was explained to me, obscure: as such procedures were not present at the time of the Revelation, there is no clear textual evidence. There are two important points to bear in mind: firstly, as we have already noted, wherever there is doubt then the ruling should be permission, and secondly, the result of these procedures is congruent with that of *zinā* in that they lead to the creation of a person from parents whose relationship is illegitimate, which is the rationale for prohibiting *zinā* in some of the religious texts.

Hakim thus chooses to require his followers to exercise caution (*ihtiyāt*) here. In the case of the use of donor eggs, Hakim is asked in one of the collections of fatwas (2002: 352–53) whether one can take an egg from a female 'stranger' (i.e. a woman not married to the man involved), fertilize it with the husband's sperm and place it in the wife's womb, and to whom the child will be related. He replies that obligatory caution (*al-ahwat wujūban*, see above) enjoins not doing so, but if it were done, the child would be related to the husband and the 'stranger', the egg producer, although there is a problem regarding inheritance and one must come to an amicable arrangement regarding that. Sayyid Hakim, then, as we have already observed, holds that parenthood follows genetic lines, or, rather, is to be attributed to the producers of the sperm and egg. As for the relation with the gestational carrier (*al-hādinah*), it is not one of *nasab* as is that with the egg producer, and it is not a milk relation because that depends on specific conditions, notably breastfeeding, that are not here realized (Hakim 2004).

Where fertilization takes place outside the womb, the problem is solely the creation of a person of two illegitimate parents; but where the sperm meets the egg in the womb, as in artificial insemination, there is another problem, as there is good reason to think placing sperm in the womb of a 'stranger' is forbidden (2004). Here Hakim is alluding to the saying of the Prophet Muhammad we encountered above: 'He who will receive the worst tortures on the day of judgement is the man who placed his seed in a womb forbidden to him.'[51] A similar point comes up during discussions of surrogacy, a questioner conceding he knows it is forbidden due to 'mixing of fluids' (*ikhtilāt al-miyāh*) (2001: 40), and Hakim elsewhere replying to the same question by noting that 'discretion obliges not undertaking this procedure and the woman not nurturing an egg fertilised with the sperm of a man not her husband, unless sufficient time has passed for the egg and sperm not to be considered fluid [*mā'*], and rather to be considered in custom as an embryo [*janīn*]' (2002: 353).

If the surrogate is impregnated by artificial insemination, that can be suspected to be prohibited. But if an embryo, no longer 'fluid', is implanted, then 'this procedure is allowed because it does not include a prohibited act' (2004), and the child will be that of the producers of the sperm and egg. As for the surrogate, '[t]he child is not hers, and she does not have the right to ask for it or take custody of it' (2001: 40–41; see also 2002: 353). However, the 'two wives' procedure is legally permitted: if one wanted to rescue oneself from the suspicion of doing what is forbidden regarding surrogacy then one should marry the surrogate mother, in which case the procedure is completely permissible (2004). The criticism that in such cases lineage confusion (*ikhtilāt al-ansāb*) would result is not sound 'because the egg is fertilised with the husband's sperm' (2004): either Hakim is considering *nasab* here in its agnatic aspects alone, or he is stressing that the conditions of the procedure make it clear whose egg and whose sperm are involved, thus making clear the ensuing *nasab* relations.[52]

With regard to this distinction between sperm per se and embryos formed of donor sperm, a Shiite doctor I spoke to made a similar point, although on different grounds: 'There is a cultural aspect to sperm – if a woman is inseminated with sperm, it's contaminating her purity of body,[53] mixing with her fluids. In the case of another man [i.e. not her husband] that's *zinā*. But if you remove the egg from her body, fertilise it with a sperm – just one, by ICSI,[54] so not flooding her with impure fluid, then put an embryo back in the body, then that's not *zinā*. That's my opinion anyway.' If the principle in suspecting surrogacy is the use of fluids, then using the embryo would seem to clear the way for any woman to carry the child. The doctor continued:

> There are surrogacy scenarios where a sister comes with her brother and his wife. The wife cannot carry a child, but has viable eggs; the sister is willing to carry the pregnancy. You do IVF on the eggs and implant them in the sister, so she is not contaminated with her brother's sperm. Or there could be four parties, husband, wife, sister and egg donor, where the wife has no ovarian function or uterus. You have to have the donor because you couldn't inseminate the sister with her brother's sperm. The wife will have nothing to do with it but by law it will be hers because they're married.

Inspired by the doctor's account, no doubt more hypothetical than a matter of common practice, I asked Sayyid Hakim about this scenario and he found no special problem, although one could not of course marry one's sister to remove all doubt of wrongdoing here (2004).[55]

Regarding the use of gametes after death, '[i]f someone dies their link with this life is cut, and there is no marriage tie, save with matters concerning the death, such as washing the corpse, inheritance etc. So both the sperm and egg are those of strangers' (2004). In one of the fatwa collections, Hakim is asked (2001: 50–52) about the status of a will where a childless man instructs that his wife should be fertilized with his preserved sperm after his death. Hakim replies that the will is not binding as the wife leaves her husband's guardianship (*'ismah*) after his death, and it is forbidden to fertilize a woman with sperm other than her husband's; therefore she is obliged to refuse the instruction. The most guarded path would be to consider an ensuing child legitimate, but that circumspection only comes to bear on the matter of inheritance. If the fertilization took place in ignorance of the prohibition, with the participants thinking it permissible, then the child has the same ruling as a child born of sex in doubtful circumstances (*walad al-shubhah*) – for instance, where the marriage contract was, unbeknownst to the couple, not formally correct – being legitimate and inheriting and being inherited from. In any case, the child does not inherit from his father or from anyone who died before the sperm fertilized the egg, but does from those who die thereafter.[56]

So Sayyid Hakim allows procedures involving a husband and wife but finds those involving unmarried third parties problematic and advises his followers not to undertake them. If they do then the resulting children will have full relations with their (biological) parents, except in the matter of inheritance, where care is required. Some of the problems can be obviated by transplanting embryos rather than male sexual substances alone, as there is rather clear textual evidence for prohibiting the latter: by implication then, the way could perhaps seem to be clear for IVF using donor sperm and eggs, and for using donor eggs upon temporarily marrying the egg donor, although again, Hakim is reluctant to give carte blanche here.

Before we bring this section to a close, it might perhaps be worth reflecting on why these authorities are so often so guarded in their rulings. As Sayyid Hakim himself (or whoever was writing on his behalf) told me in his email to me,

> This is common for jurisprudents in situations where they cannot give a decisive fatwa due to the lack of sufficient evidences or their obscurity, and here the jurisprudent is rescued by enjoining caution, to guarantee his guiltlessness before God, praise and exalt Him, due to the danger of giving a fatwa because of its implication of a judgement on God's holy shariah.

In this regard, his son's words to me in explanation of why some eminent jurists choose not to assume the *marja‘*-ship were touching:

> It is dangerous. They like studying, reading books and being close to God. But a *marja‘* has to judge and give fatwas – a great many fatwas! God will ask him on the day of judgement, 'Why did you give this ruling, why did you give that ruling?'

Not just held to account for his own decisions, the *marja‘* is held responsible for all those decisions his followers made in accordance with his guidance, a weighty burden indeed.

Islamic views on assisted reproduction: A summary

Sunnis and Shiites share a vision of an Islamic society, a system of rights and duties, based fundamentally on obligations between kin. Adultery and other confusions of paternity and maternity subvert the roots of Islamic society and are prohibited in the strongest terms. However, there are differences of opinion as to how assisted reproduction should be placed within this system.

All are agreed that procedures involving the husband and wife are permissible and that legitimate children result. Procedures involving third parties may be assimilated to, although not considered equivalent to, illicit sex by Sunni and some Shiite opinion. For the Sunnis I have consulted, the status of the resulting children is thus equivalent to, if not identical with, that of bastards: there is no paternity awarded to the husband in the case of the use of donor sperm, for instance. For all the Shiite authorities I have considered here, even when the procedures are prohibited the resulting children are considered legitimate, although matters of inheritance are the subject of further debate. The permissibility of polygamy in Islamic law raises the possibility of procedures involving two wives, one providing the egg, the other carrying the resulting embryo in her uterus. The Sunnis have, by and large, decided that such procedures are also not to be allowed. These are more readily allowed by Shiites. The institution of temporary marriage in Shiite law allows, under some opinion, the legitimization of egg donation and surrogacy arrangements by contracting temporary marriages between the husband and the donor or the surrogate for the required time period.

Thus almost all opinion prohibits artificial insemination by donor. The exception here is Ayatollah Khamene'i, who holds the most unrestrictive position of all, and allows AID, along with egg donation, surrogacy arrangements and the postmortem use of gametes. IVF procedures using donor sperm (as opposed to direct insemination) may be allowed by some Shiite authorities, who find that it is the insertion of the sperm itself, rather than an embryo constituted from it, that is the problem, but the majority of opinion, Sunni and Shiite, finds such procedures dubious. Again, donor eggs are not allowed by the Sunnis but are permitted by many Shiite authorities, although often with the stipulation of marriage between the donor and the husband of the recipient. The same is broadly true of surrogacy arrangements. In such cases, opinion is divided as to which woman should be awarded maternity: most Sunni and many Shiite authorities find the gestational carrier the mother; a minority of Sunni and, as regards the cases I have considered here, most Shiite authorities follow 'biology', attributing paternity and maternity to the producers of the sperm and egg that were united to produce the embryo. Where Shiite authorities allow the use of donor gametes and stipulate that relatedness follows genetic lines, were their followers to follow the letter of these rulings some interesting patterns of relatedness would result.

Taking all the material together, there seems to be wide scope for variation in opinion and interpretation, a scope fully exploited by the Shiite authorities, supposedly less constrained in this regard than the Sunnis. Theoretical debate is open in both cases, and legal opinion is clearly not static: positions have changed and are still changing. We should not be surprised to find this openness and diversity of opinion reflected when we turn to the practice of assisted reproduction in Lebanon. Equally, we should not be surprised to find the sexual propriety of these procedures a key issue, as it is in the Islamic debates.

Notes

1. With the notable exception of Ayatollah Muhsin al-Hakim (not, note, Muhammad Saʿid al-Hakim, here 'Ayatollah Hakim', whose views we will consider in detail below), who was the most widely followed *marjaʿ* in the world until his death in 1970, and who held artificial insemination to be forbidden and a resulting child to have no *nasab* to the father, the source of the sperm, for a legitimate child must, in his opinion, arise from an act of sexual intercourse (I draw here on the account of renowned Lebanese jurist [d. 1979] Muhammad Jawad Mughniyah [2003: 346], who corresponded with Ayatollah Hakim on this point [see also ʿA. al-K. Fadlallah 2007: 57; M. R. al-Sistani 2004: 95, 412]).

2. As Inhorn has noted (2003: 97, 114; 2004a; 2006a; 2006b).

3. I spoke to Shaykh Muqdad again in 2008 and he confirmed the positions I have related here.

4. He does make the point elsewhere (Khamene'i 2003, part 2: 78–80).

5. I have found *sāhib* hard to translate here. The word has as basic meanings 'associate', 'possessor/master' and 'author/originator of'; while it is a vague word, its referent seems clear enough here, although the principle of relation is perhaps not as explicit as one might like. 'Owner' would be a plausible translation elsewhere, but it is nowhere suggested, as far as I know, that an infertile couple who come to possess donated gametes own

them, and thus they are the *nasab* parents (cf. my note on the 'owner of the milk', Chapter 1). In the case of *sāhibat al-rahim*, 'owner of the womb', i.e. the gestational carrier, clearly 'producer' will be inappropriate.

6. So too Ayatollahs Khu'i (Iraq, d. 1992), Fadlallah (but see below), Ha'iri and Tabrizi (Iran both), according to Shaykh al-Hajj (2006: 33).

7. Shaykh al-Hajj (2006: 31–32), for one, draws the same conclusion regarding Khamene'i's position.

8. The 2002 edition has an extra phrase again referring to the complex ramifications of this position: 'one must take care in the matters of inheritance and extension of sacrosanctity [*nashr al-hurmah*]', the latter referring to the domain of marriage prohibition and hence intimacy – one can be intimate with, i.e. not veil before, those one cannot marry, broadly speaking.

9. In conversation, Sayyid 'Abd al-Karim Fadlallah (introduced below) intimated that there were others who shared this view, although he did not name them. The only other reference I have found is in a volume published in Beirut comparing the opinions of leading authorities on a variety of matters: here Ayatollah Bahjat, based in Qom, Iran, is also cited as finding donor insemination permissible (Mahmudi 2004: 233).

10. As Ayatollah Fadlallah notes elsewhere (1995: 15), a woman fostering could get a lactating sister to breastfeed the child, making her the child's milk aunt: 'this is a legal ruse [*hīlah shar'īyah*], but a true one'.

11. As Iranian Ayatollah Sane'i noted in email correspondence with me (see Clarke 2007a). Shaykh Muqdad makes the same point in a manuscript article on 'Reproduction with donor sperm' (*al-talqīh bi-nutfat al-ajnabī*) that he very kindly made available to me.

12. Although it is by no means certain that this doctor really knows whether these rules are applied within the private sphere, and in any case one would have thought that most children born of such procedures would still be too young for many of the issues to be pressing.

13. According to Ayatollah Sane'i, 'if the owner of the sperm has given up his sperm ownership, for example he has delivered his sperm to the sperm bank to be used by anyone, then he is not considered as the father' (email correspondence with the author [reproduced in full in Clarke 2007a]).

14. A procedure that has provoked considerable controversy in the West, as in the case of Diane Blood in the U.K.: first refused permission to use her dead husband's sperm by the British Human Fertilisation and Embryology Authority, she was later granted permission by an Appeal Court judgement to export the sperm to Belgium and undertake the procedure

there, under her rights as a European citizen (Simpson 2001; Carsten
2004: 1–2). According to Hajj's (2006: 13, 18–19) survey, while all
Shiite authorities, save Ayatollah Muhammad Muhammad Sadiq al-Sadr
(assassinated in Najaf by Saddam Hussein's regime in 1999), allow the
freezing of gametes, most disallow their use after death and divorce (although Ayatollahs Khu'i and Sistani, for instance, allow it within the
'waiting period' ['*iddah*] after a revocable divorce). Sunni clerics have
also discussed the matter, and Rispler-Chaim (1993: 23) cites authorities
allowing and disallowing postmortem gamete use, as does Salamah
(1998: 81–83, 97–98), who is clear that prohibition is the majority view
(so too Ibrahim 1990: 159–62), as in the recent fatwa from al-Azhar
(Hawley 2001).

15. The similarity of names is potentially confusing, but I have taken
pains to refer to Sayyid 'Abd al-Karim Fadlallah by his full name
throughout, as opposed to my use of 'Sayyid Fadlallah' or sometimes
simply 'Fadlallah' to refer to Ayatollah Muhammad Husayn Fadlallah.

16. Iranian Ayatollah Makarim Shirazi (2003: 470–71), asked about the
permissibility of embryo donation, allows it, although it would be better
not to accept payment for the embryo, he feels. He awards parenthood to
the genetic parents, and, asked if they could, despite a prior agreement to
donate the embryo, ask for the child after its birth, even some years later,
he replies that the most cautious path is to rule that they can with the
consent of the woman who carried the child.

17. Sayyid 'Abd al-Karim Fadlallah (2007: 39) gives short shrift to arguments from 'lineage confusion' (*ikhtilāt al-ansāb*), but this term
seems to have a different meaning from that in the Sunni discourse, referring here specifically to what would in English be called 'incestuous'
combinations of gametes.

18. Shaykh Muqdad deals with each of these arguments for prohibition
and rejects each in turn in his manuscript 'Reproduction with donor
sperm'.

19. One knowledgeable source in a rival camp thought the most likely
source of the ruling was the ayatollah's advisors, but also noted that this
opinion belonged to a brief burst of jurisprudential activity immediately
succeeding Khamene'i's elevation to the *marja'īyah*. 'Perhaps he didn't
have much experience at this point', my source suggested, because, according to him, extra conditions were put in place subsequently, stipulat-
ing that the woman be married (i.e. a single woman could not undertake
assisted conception) and that the identity of the sperm donor be known,
for instance (I have found no published record of this). Also, he further
suggested, being the people's political leader perhaps brings one more in
touch with their needs, and with the realities of the modern world, a line

of explanation I have myself followed elsewhere (Clarke 2007a).

20. Also so long as the appropriate precautions are taken regarding looking at and touching the private parts of course, especially if the doctor were a man. Shaykh 'Atwi added: 'One could argue that this could be permitted due to necessity or severe distress [*haraj*]: if her husband would divorce her if she did not get pregnant.'

21. 'Muslim or non-Muslim, non-relative or relative [*muslim aw ghayr muslim, ba'īd aw qarīb*]', as Shaykh 'Atwi put it.

22. For which I must thank Shaykh 'Atwi and the custodians of the sayyid's archives. My compilation, obtained in 2008, numbers fifty petitions dating from 2005 to 2008 and reflects the sayyid's global reach: while most are in Arabic, some are in English, some French, and some are from converts to Islam in the U.S., for example. This would not comprise the entirety of questions sent regarding these matters, as the compilers of the database seek to avoid repetition of content. Each question on the database is numbered, and I have supplied those numbers here as a form of reference.

23. Iranian Ayatollah Shirazi (1998: 427) is posed such a scenario in a collection of his replies to fatwa requests, where the wife divorces her husband, marries another man, uses his sperm to fertilize her egg, remarries her husband and then implants the embryo in her womb: that is allowed in necessity, Shirazi rules, but the child is related to the providers of the gametes. In another petition, a woman recounts her plight, married eight years to an infertile husband: can she use another man's sperm, in a medical clinic of course? She has heard that this is allowed as it helps prevent divorces: it resembles a blood transplant. 'This deed is a sin', Shirazi sternly replies, advising her rather to divorce her husband, and then, after the end of the *'iddah,* marry another man temporarily – for a single day, for example – then take his sperm to the clinic, impregnate yourself with it, and then return to your first husband after the birth of the child (Shirazi 2003: 469–70).

24. One correspondent in my collection of Sayyid Fadlallah's unpublished fatwas (no. 70,324) talks of looking for a 'legal loophole' or 'way out' (*manfadh shar'ī*) of his dilemma: after divorcing his first wife, with whom he had a daughter, he remarried, but suffered from the atrophy of one of his testicles. He married again having travelled abroad, telling his new wife that he could no longer have children, which she accepted. But then they came to Lebanon and 'she began to suffer from the story of her husband not being capable of begetting children and started saying that she couldn't live without offspring'. Donor insemination via divorce and remarriage as above seems to be the solution.

25. An exception here is Ayatollah Shirazi (2003: 468), who holds the child of donor insemination (forbidden) to be the illegitimate child of the sperm donor, and thus denied the right to inherit from him (and see the section on Sistani and Hakim below).

26. His *risālah,* the comprehensive legal treatise that serves to prove one's credentials as a *marja',* or 'source' of religious guidance. His inclusion of these medical innovations in what is a very conventional format is striking.

27. This precedent is cited by both Ayatollahs Khu'i and Sistani, for example (Hajj and Jawad 2007: 461, 501). Such illicit sexual behaviour demands punishment, as Imam Hasan explained: 'The *mahr* [bride price] of the virgin shall be exacted from the married woman because the child would not be delivered without the virgin losing her virginity. Then, the other woman shall be stoned to death because of her marital status. Regarding the pregnant woman, they shall wait until she delivers and the child shall be given to the father, i.e. the person of whose sperm it was born. After this, she shall be flogged' (cited Mughniyah 2003: 342–43). Sayyid Muhammad Rida Sistani (2004: 88–90) considers this tradition in a discussion of whether an unmarried woman could bear a child by artificial insemination, and wonders light-heartedly whether, where the breaking of the maidenhead is deemed the problem, the baby might be delivered by Caesarean section.

28. Ayatollah Fadlallah also notes his opinion in a response to a similar question from another petitioner (Fadlallah 2001, vol. 1: 274). From a transcription of a series of lectures by Shaykh Muhammad Sind explicating and commenting upon Sayyid Khu'i's opinion (Ridawi 2002: 75ff.), it would appear that Khu'i forbade donor insemination, but regarded an ensuing child as the legitimate child of the sperm donor, inheriting from him; surrogacy arrangements were also forbidden, although the use of donor eggs seems to be permitted, with no condition of marriage mentioned (this may be Shaykh Sind's own opinion here, as I have other reason to think Khu'i did enjoin marriage is such cases [see above]).

29. Sayyid 'Abd al-Karim Fadlallah (2007: 66) reports that in conversation with Ayatollah Muhammad Ruhani (since deceased) in Qom, Ayatollah Ruhani took the same position, arguing that *wālidah,* one of the Arabic words for mother, meant, in customary understandings, 'deliverer'. As he himself told me, Sayyid 'Abd al-Karim Fadlallah pointed out in reply that the masculine form (*wālid*) is used for 'father' with no suggestion that fathers deliver babies (2007: 63).

30. Shaykh al-Hajj (2006: 36) cites exactly these three in his own survey. I can add Ayatollah Shirazi (1998: 427; 2003: 469).

31. E.g. Ayatollahs Mirza 'Ali al-Gharawi (assassinated in Iraq by Saddam Hussein's regime in 1998), Muhammad Muhammad Sadiq al-Sadr, Ha'iri and Tabrizi (Hajj 2006: 36–37).

32. Sayyid 'Abd al-Karim Fadlallah (2007: 75 n. 1) recounts how at a conference, a Christian doctor, on learning of these traditions, commented on how clever Imam 'Ali was. Sayyid 'Abd al-Karim Fadlallah replied that this is hardly an instance of cleverness, but rather of revelation.

33. So too Ayatollah Shirazi (1998: 427; 2003: 469), who also finds the husband of the gestational carrier to be prohibited from marriage to the child, as is the husband of the milk mother, the 'owner of the milk' (see note to Chapter 1).

34. Doctors working in one of Iran's most important centres for fertility treatment have been trying to persuade Iranian *marāji'* to elevate the status of the gestational carrier by taking this line of argument even further, in order to render the use of donor eggs less inconvenient for recipients (presumably with reference in particular to Ayatollah Khamene'i's position). They have prepared presentations including video footage of the embryo growing in the womb in order to convince the shaykhs that the carrying mother does indeed 'make the flesh and bone grow', and indeed the foetus is constituted from her body cells, albeit not those carrying genetic information, and thus some legally recognizable form of maternity should be given to her (interviews with doctors at the Royan Institute, Tehran).

35. Again, masturbation, other than performed by parties bound by a marriage contract, is considered by the majority of jurists, including Fadlallah, as forbidden. Fadlallah (2003, vol. 3: 502) thus notes that while telephone sex with one's wife is perfectly acceptable, including to the point of orgasm, a husband's helping himself on the way through self-masturbation is prohibited. We might note here that Fadlallah, very controversially, does not prohibit self-masturbation on the part of women, because he does not see it as equivalent to male masturbation, no 'seed' being ejaculated (Aziz 2001: 210–11). This position was adopted after taking medical advice, and I was fortunate enough to talk to one of the doctors who gave it: 'Fadlallah is a friend, he calls and asks questions. Once he rang about the woman's orgasm. A woman, who had lost her husband, didn't want to commit adultery, had asked if masturbation renders the fast void, like for men. That is, does it produce *janābah* [major ritual pollution] – woman have this in menstruation, but what about vaginal sexual secretion? I told him no, it's like sweating, a transudate, it has no gamete. It's like an erection – otherwise men would have *janābah* all the time!'

36. Also the opinion of Ayatollahs Khu'i, Khamene'i, Gharawi, Muhammad Muhammad Sadiq al-Sadr and Tabrizi (Hajj 2006: 31). Conversely, one could argue that such an arrangement would be easier were the surrogate single, as there would then be no contravention of the rights of her husband ('A. al-K. Fadlallah 2007: 44). Ayatollah Shirazi (1998: 426–27; 2003: 469) allows surrogacy (*al-umm al-nā'ibah*) with or without marriage or indeed payment for it. Given the problems of forbidden looking and touching, it has to be in a case of necessity.

37. As some further examples of similar questions posed by the sayyid's followers, in one published fatwa collection, Fadlallah (2001, vol. 1: 274) is asked if a mother may carry her daughter's child if the daughter is unable. He notes that the mother would be carrying another man's sperm (that of her daughter's husband), which he holds to be problematic, not least because the man is prohibited to her in marriage (*min al-mahārim*). Another petitioner asks about a surrogacy arrangement where a man marries a woman, contracting with her to bear his child, which will then be given to his first wife in return for a sum of money. Fadlallah notes that this is permitted in religious law (after all, it amounts to no more than taking a second wife), but one has to take care of the humane aspects of such a scenario concerning the relation of a mother and her child.

38. As I reported in previous publications (Clarke 2005, 2006a, 2006b). However, the more nuanced account given here should be seen as superseding that in my earlier work.

39. For the website, in English, see http://english.bayynat.org.lb/Issues/ Artificial.htm (consulted 31/03/2007). Inhorn (2006b: 112) has it that before 2003, Fadlallah held that egg donation was not to be allowed at all, but he then issued a fatwa allowing egg donation with marriage.

40. I have examples of queries asking about this specifically. One (fatwa no. 76,679 from my collection) asks about the use of a woman's mother's egg, citing a story on the BBC News website.

41. If the sperm and egg were to have coalesced (*in'aqadat*) before the man's death then the child would inherit (cited Hajj 2006: 57).

42. Shaykh al-Hajj posed a number of specific questions to the sayyid himself, including whether the same ruling applies to a husband who is brain-dead, but kept physically alive through artificial assistance, and to a husband who is missing, presumed dead. The sayyid replied that in the first instance the man is counted as dead, and in the second as alive (Hajj 2006: 56). Shaykh Hajj also asked whether non-Muslims who had frozen their gametes before converting to Islam could then use them, the issue presumably turning on the impermissibility of marriages with non-believers. The sayyid said that indeed they could (Hajj 2006: 58).

43. There are a surprisingly large number of questions about this matter in the sayyid's published fatwa collections (see e.g. Fadlallah 2001, vol. 1: 270ff.). One in particular (2001, vol. 2: 437) has more than enough circumstantial detail to seem to derive from a real dilemma rather than merely a point of theoretical debate: 'A woman is suffering from an illness preventing her from conceiving, and doctors have told her that she will need a period after her treatment before she will be cured and be able to conceive. Her husband preserved some of his sperm in a sperm bank, and then died; and after some time after his death the woman was treated and cured, and became able to conceive. So is it possible for her to conceive from that sperm of her husband's? And what is the ruling of the child? And how about the question of inheritance, knowing that the husband put his sperm in that bank for this purpose?'

44. This last point, regarding intent, is added by Sistani to the opinion of his mentor Khu'i, which he otherwise follows quite closely here, as Hajj and Jawad's (2007: 461, 501) comparative compilation of their fatwas allows us to see.

45. I must admit to having erred previously (Clarke 2005, 2006a, 2006b) in attributing Sayyid Khu'i's opinion that maternity is to be assigned to the gestational carrier to Ayatollah Sistani by reading Sayyid Muhammad Rida Sistani's references to 'the sayyid the teacher' in his work as references to his father; I am now clear that these in fact refer to Sayyid Khu'i (in my defence, this is, as has no doubt become apparent, a complicated field). Muhammad Rida Sistani (2004: 450) himself avowedly finds this the strongest opinion. Nevertheless, as he himself (2004: 428ff.) notes, echoing 'Abd al-Karim Fadlallah's comments cited above, establishing the required, exact meaning of words such as 'bore' (*walada*) used in texts such as the Quranic verse relied upon here (see above), and, what is more, the meaning used in the society of the time of the Revelation, the Arabian society of the seventh century AD, is problematic to say the least. Further problems arise for him due to the supposed infallibility of the Shiite Imams. Many traditions of their sayings reveal a premodern understanding of human reproduction. So, for instance, of the monogenetic 'the child is to the loins and the woman is but a container', he comments: 'The Imam is the gate of the city of knowledge and he could not say something like this unless it were to testify to the presence of the stated delusion' at that time (2004: 430). And he comments on some traditions regarding the inheritance of characteristics that they are 'far from the requirements of modern science, in addition to most of them containing what it is impossible to accept as coming from the Imams, our guides, peace be upon them. In some of them it is said that the flesh and blood and hair of the child is created from the seed of his mother, and his bone and nerves and veins are created from his father's seed!!' (2004: 444).

46. Shaykh al-Hajj (2006: 38) deduces that Sistani, uniquely, holds that neither woman is the mother. That is to say, one imagines, that full motherhood requires both a genetic and gestational tie (see e.g. M. R. Sistani 2004: 424ff.). One could also rule that both are mothers, both ties being deemed sufficient, if not necessary, and Sayyid 'Abd al-Karim Fadlallah told me in conversation that he had himself tended towards this position before shifting recently to thinking the genetic principle the correct one.

47. So too Tabrizi; Fadlallah agrees with Sistani here (Hajj 2006: 39–40).

48. The reply had been sent in Farsi as manuscript and I had had to enlist the help of Sistani's office in London in order to decipher it. The translation arrived with the comment, 'This reply obviously raises some questions.' 'But do not despair', it continued, 'the attached file will throw some light on any unanswered questions you may have' (the attached file being the English language fatwas described below).

49. I have further sent direct to Sayyid Muhammad Rida Sistani in Najaf, through the kind auspices of Ayatollah Sistani's Beirut offices, a detailed and comprehensive questionnaire regarding all these issues, but at the time of writing no reply was yet forthcoming. That is to be expected: Ayatollah Sistani and his immediate circle have rather more pressing business.

50. As has no doubt become apparent, kinship ties are very apparent in the Shiite religious establishment. However, religious authority is not, formally speaking, passed on through succession along kinship lines.

51. See Muhammad Rida Sistani (2004: 55–59) for a discussion of this and similar sayings. Within Judaism similar concerns apply (Kahn 2000: 103–4). Iranian Ayatollah Sane'i uses this point to encourage those who would use donor sperm to do so through IVF arrangements where an embryo is transplanted rather than male sexual fluid (Clarke 2007a).

52. Although again, as noted above, 'lineage confusion' often seems in the Shiite discussions to have a somewhat different meaning from that employed in the Sunni debates, referring more specifically to 'incestuous' combinations of gametes.

53. Semen is one of a limited set of ritually polluting substances, contact with which requires ritual ablution before prayer etc. This polluting aspect of certain bodily fluids is a rather different logic of substance from that which Françoise Héritier imagines, for instance (see Chapter 1). 'Sperm' can of course refer in English to both spermatozoa, male sex cells per se, and semen, the male reproductive fluid in which the spermatozoa are suspended. While the distinction is unimportant in Western debate, it is not here.

54. Intracytoplasmic sperm injection. Individual sperm are injected into ova under a high-powered microscope: one sperm is sufficient.

55. I have a similar query amongst my collection of unpublished fatwas from Sayyid Fadlallah's offices (no. 90,794): 'My sister has been married for eight years and hasn't been blessed with children, due to her husband's infertility. His infertility is beyond scientific assistance – the doctors say they are waiting for a miracle from God for him to be able to have children. My question is, can she take someone's sperm, fertilise the egg of that man's wife with it, transfer it to her womb and then register the child in the name of that man and his wife but bring it up herself???? And if it were permissible, could that person be her brother?????' (question marks as original). This is, the answer comes, not allowed.

56. With regard to all the preceding, it makes no difference whether the fertilization took place before or after the end of the *'iddah*. It is clear that it is the fertilization that must take place within marriage and not the production of the sperm, because Hakim is asked elsewhere (2002: 354) whether a husband and wife can make use of the husband's sperm collected before they were married, and replies that that is permissible.

Chapter 5

MEDICAL PERSPECTIVES

Having come to terms with the Islamic legal debates over fertility treatment, it is helpful to have some idea of how the issues play out beyond the clerical world. Here I draw on the perspectives of medical practitioners in Lebanon, as well as referring to the work of other scholars studying fertility treatment in Lebanon and the wider Middle East. Almost all the doctors I spoke to have worked both inside and outside of Lebanon, and thus had interesting comparative insights. The regulatory situation was one prominent theme, with doctors commonly worrying that the assisted reproductive sector in Lebanon was somewhat anarchic, with little, if any, state-sponsored regulation. In this field, as in many other areas of life in Lebanon, religious precepts have an important role for doctors as well as patients; and indeed the very diversity of religious opinion was a factor commonly cited in explanation of the difficulty in evolving regulatory legislation satisfactory to all.

But beyond the specificities of religious opinion, shared notions of social, and especially sexual, propriety were a constantly stressed motif of my conversations, and an important theme to grasp.[1] For instance there are, to the best of my knowledge, no same-sex couples starting families with recourse to the possibilities of assisted conception in Lebanon, a frequently cited example of the 'immorality' of the West. And, as we saw in Chapter 2, it is taken as axiomatic that 'a single mother can't register a child only in her name: it would be a bastard [*ibn harām*].' One fertility specialist, a Christian man, commented on his experiences working in France and Lebanon: 'A patient came and said: "I have two wives, which do you want?" I said, "the younger". I was shocked – I'd been in France for some years. But when I first went to France I was shocked at couples having children who weren't married. In Europe you have more solutions – the woman can sleep with another man.' Expectations as to female sexual continence are high, and, for some, then, a point of cultural identity and comparison. A female Druze gynaecologist commented to me that: 'I know many women of 40, 45, not married, who haven't found the right man, but want to be mothers. But they're afraid of God. I have met many women in Beirut who say, "Why don't I have sex with this handsome guy, have a child just like in the West". But it's impossible – their family will kill them!'

In addition to the importance of religious frameworks of moral behaviour, and the comparison with the supposed moral norms of 'the West', she alludes to the rhetoric of honour, more or less prevalent and potent in Lebanon according to class, community and locale, but often pointed to by doctors in my conversations with them as an important component of the local ethical landscape for me to grasp. My very first medical contact, in mainly Sunni Muslim Tripoli, hastily told me that were I to work with patients I would have to sign a confidentiality clause, as issues of life and death were involved – 'if the *walī* [a woman's guardian, usually her father] were to find out then there might be honour killings'. That is, a suspicion of sexual deviance – for fertility treatment would seem to constitute such – is enough to ruin the public standing of a woman and by extension her male relatives. One means to redeem the matter is, notionally, to kill the woman concerned. Such crimes do happen in Lebanon. But given the comparative rarity of such occurrences, this was, I think, more rhetoric than reality.[2] I did not talk to patients, and this particular issue did not surface again, but it serves as an indication of not just the vital importance of notions of sexual propriety, but also an almost exaggerated rhetorical concern for privacy, although I visited a large number of clinics, and indeed, most embarrassingly, ran into somebody I knew at one of them. This careful concern for the protection of the boundary between intimate knowledge and public reputation is another core theme to keep in mind.

We should note immediately then that infertility treatment in Lebanon is, or is commonly presented as, an area of great concern for confidentiality, secrecy even, on the part of both the patients and the doctors. As Inhorn (2004b: 2097) comments, reflecting on her studies of infertility treatment in Egypt and Lebanon, 'In the Middle East, infertility and IVF are shrouded in layers of secrecy and social suffering … ethnographic access is shaped – and potentially limited – by powerful feelings of privacy and protectiveness'. Of her experiences of in one fertility clinic in Beirut, she writes (2004b: 2097):

I was told bluntly by one of the nurses during the first week of my
arrival that my study of male infertility in Lebanon would 'never succeed'. She pointed to the ongoing stigma of infertility, especially
among the working-class southern Lebanese Shiite Muslim men who
werè the primary clients of the clinic. She told me how they and their
wives sometimes hid in the private recovery rooms on the upper floor
of the clinic, and would not leave until the 'coast was clear' and other
patients that they might recognize were no longer present.[3]

Infertility is, then, stigmatized (Inhorn 1994, 2003, 2004a): 'They
don't want people to think there's something wrong with them', as
one doctor remarked to me. As another put it: 'The file is secret – because infertility is like a handicap – if the woman (or man) is infertile, they might propose another marriage. People don't want the
neighbour or cousin having treatment for a problem. So although the
centre has had about 700 babies born, the clients say "Please don't
tell" – so publicity is difficult!'

The perceived need for secrecy could, according to some of the
doctors I spoke with, be extended to exclude friends from the circle
of knowledge, sometimes even close family and sometimes even the
spouse, especially where donor gametes are being used (a comparatively rare scenario, one should emphasize). One doctor told me that
'[s]ome patients say they don't want their husbands to find out. We
don't allow this, but some clinics might'. And another said, 'Sometimes I get a man who asks for donor sperm without his wife knowing it. And women asking for eggs.' We should no doubt not make
too much of such asides, but we should certainly note the assumptions that are being made here.

This brings us to a second consideration. Although rather less
prevalent with greater public awareness of what IVF involves, there
remains a strong impression that having any form of infertility treatment will mean that the child 'isn't yours', stereotypically because it
is suspected another man's sperm has been used, tantamount to having had illicit sexual relations, *zinā* (see also Inhorn 2003; 2004a:
174–75 [on Lebanon]; 2004b: 2102 [on Egypt]). This is, as we have
noted on many occasions, a heinous crime in Islamic law. But this
preoccupation with the propriety of sexual relations equally extends
to Christians, for whom *zinā* – 'adultery', 'fornication' – is also repugnant. While the religious discourses of marriage prohibitions and
legitimate sexual relations may vary, the social ethic of male 'honour' – as the doctor cited above put it – and female sexual continence

is shared. Patients themselves might be suspicious, as one doctor told me:

> Sometimes they say, 'I accept you, but you're not in the lab. How do I know about the lab assistant – she doesn't know me, what does she care? Maybe she'll do it...' [i.e. mix up the sperm]. Now, with ICSI [intracytoplasmic sperm injection, a variant of IVF], you explain, we need only five or six sperm, even if you have only one million.[4] You give them confidence. So then they will agree, 'Okay, yes the lab woman has no reason'. Some, very, very rarely, want to see what you are doing in the lab, see the name on the bottle. Then I encourage them to have DNA tests if they have any doubts. I say, 'Look, if you're not convinced you must do the DNA test. Go to the lab.' I don't give them the name of a specific lab, or the patient will be suspicious. If he says, 'No, I have a problem with this,' I say, 'Okay, look, I'll pay – you must do it if you're not sure.'

I followed this up and visited a doctor whose name he mentioned. This doctor had indeed received patients coming for this very purpose, and had given them the requisite information and advice. As Inhorn (2003: 243) puts it with regard to Egypt, 'the already "secret stigma" of infertility, and especially male infertility, is intensified into a "top secret stigma" by virtue of participation in the morally ambivalent, even disreputable world of test-tube baby making'. While secrecy is a concern even in 'normal' IVF, using the spouses' gametes, procedures involving donor gametes – again, comparatively rare – are still more highly secret, for fear of being seen to perform the religiously forbidden, and even to bear a 'bastard'. One doctor talked of patients seeking donor treatments 'looking around them, looking over their shoulders'. These are clearly not trivial worries. Take this doctor's story of a 'donor tourist': 'I had a Kuwaiti woman asking for egg donation – she was very anxious about it, she kept asking if anyone could find out – I said well if there was a genetic test then they could find out. I sent her to Beirut – she was pregnant, became hysterical, and ended up having an abortion because she was so afraid that it might be found out.'

People often seem to travel, even internationally, to increase their chances of protecting their privacy. There is a persistent idea of Lebanon, a country with a population of several millions, being a restrictively small place, where everyone knows each other, like a village: '*Mujtamaʿ ktīr dayyiq, saghīr* [a very narrow, small society]' as one doctor put it. A doctor working in Tripoli estimated that less than 10 per cent of his clients came from the city. Another said that

patients from Beirut would go to Tripoli and vice versa. Doctors also
noted patients from Syria, Jordan, Egypt, Saudi Arabia and the
Gulf.[5] Most Arab countries can now offer advanced fertility treatment, so patients coming to Lebanon are presumably seeking
anonymity (see Inhorn 2006a: 175), or the greater freedom in choice
of techniques that Lebanon's more relaxed regulatory environment
allows, as we will see.[6] So one doctor commented: 'Take Jordan:
they have good clinics, but they don't do donor. They refer the patients to me for donor work. Lebanon is the first place you would go
for that.' 'Not London?' I asked. 'No,' he replied, 'you [English
donors] have blonde hair and blue eyes'. Doctors who had good relations with Egyptian practitioners told me that '[i]n Egypt they send
people to Lebanon for egg donation'. Inhorn (2003: 114–15) notes
the same phenomenon, citing one Egyptian doctor to the effect that
'Sunni patients who come to him sometimes reason that third-party
donation is now a realistic option, given that at least one branch of
Islam has allowed the practice', referring to the relatively unrestrictive opinions of Shiite authorities such as Ayatollah Khamene'i, influential in Lebanon, as we saw in the previous chapter.[7]

As a result of the emphasis on confidentiality, the standard account I was given was that no statistics or other published 'facts' are
available, especially with regard to the more controversial procedures I was particularly interested in:[8] 'There are no statistics on
donor [procedures] – no one would dare – it's not acceptable socially
and religiously', as one doctor told me; another went further, saying,
'There are no statistics at all – and if there were they would be false'.
This was another common trope, the supposed dissimulation of am-
bitious medical practitioners, as attributed to them in gossipy asides
by their rivals at least. There are possibly, as anywhere else, a few
rogues as some doctors alleged, but regardless, it was this widespread pessimism and suspicion that things in Lebanon were not as
they should be, in this respect as in others, that was striking. At any
rate, my account here is thus perforce tentative as to the facts and figures of fertility treatment, and concentrates rather on doctors' impressions of what sense is being made of these new possibilities.

Nevertheless, we should certainly give some idea of the scale of
the phenomenon, at least as of 2003–04, the time of my principal
fieldwork, before the political turmoil following the assassination of
Rafiq Hariri and the 2006 war with Israel, when doctors were optimistic with regard to the commercial side of their operations. That
optimism has since disappeared, along with the patients (Inhorn,

personal comment): Lebanon's political crises have translated into economic disaster. There are, or were, undoubtedly a large number of doctors offering fertility treatment of some sort. However, most of the effective modern infertility treatments such as IVF and ICSI require sophisticated laboratories and are thus beyond the capability of an ordinary gynaecologist. There are nevertheless doctors who have training in infertility treatment but do not work in a centre: they may well have access to one; equally, within a centre there may be more than one 'recruiting doctor'. Most doctors prefer to be their own boss if at all possible; however, the equipment required for advanced fertility treatment is expensive – estimates were of the order of $100–350,000 – and would be a very considerable investment in the currently depressed economic climate in Lebanon.[9] Nevertheless, such facilities do exist and provide the means to practise IVF, ICSI and the use and storage of donated ova and embryos in some cases. The number of competent centres was a point of some debate: estimates ranged from five to twenty-five.[10] Doctors distinguished 'working centres' from those that are 'just on paper'. The large number of centres is 'silly. Thirty cycles a year is not going to give results'.[11] It was felt that there were probably between five and eight centres that were actually undertaking considerable amounts of work. While the majority of centres are to be found in Beirut, other major cities such as Tripoli and Sidon have their own, and doctors who claim the requisite knowledge and access to the required facilities can be found all over the country.

Despite the lack of readily available statistical information, doctors provided me with their own estimates, which serve at least to give a rough idea of the scale of the sector (in 2003–04). One doctor estimated as follows: 'IVF and ICSI and AI are very common: per month, about 2–300 cycles, in a population of 2–3 million. There are five clinics in Beirut, two in Sidon, two in Tripoli, so at least ten in Lebanon. Each clinic is doing 25–30 cycles a month. The biggest centres might be carrying out 40 to 50 cycles a month.' Another guessed that '[a]ll in all there are 3,000–3,500 cases a year in all of Lebanon'. Of those, they estimated, maybe 10 per cent are donor cycles, nowadays mostly egg donation due to the advent of ICSI, which has provided a solution to many instances of male infertility and has thus rendered donor insemination largely obsolete. Doctors were vague as to rates of infertility, but felt they were comparable with the world average. Some felt that male infertility was higher 'due to the war'; others that infertility was lower than in the West as the rate of sexually transmitted disease (STD) was lower; others that it was higher because people did not seek treatment for STDs so readily, or Lebanese men had contracted STDs in Africa, where there are sizeable expatriate communities where 'they hang around Europeans too much', or because levels of stress were now so high given the advent of satellite television and other modern technologies.[12] One point worth noting is that the pressure on married couples to produce children is such as to drive them to seek advice and treatment earlier than in the West, for example, and to persist in such treatment even after prolonged failure, which might produce apparently inflated rates of infertility.

As for the patients, almost invariably doctors reported seeing patients from all religious groups: 'a bouquet', as one put it. Some doctors practising away from Beirut do draw primarily on a local base: thus a doctor in Nabatiyah, a mainly Shiite town in the South of Lebanon, will have mostly Shiite patients. However, doctors commonly suggest that many patients come from further afield, probably, they thought, for reasons of confidentiality. Despite the expense of such treatments, patients range from very rich to very poor, and it is common for the doctor to suggest that his prices vary according to the client's means. It may well be that patients would prefer to see a doctor from the same religious group as themselves, or the same sex – 'women like to go to a doctor who is a woman – that's the first thing', a female doctor told me, although almost all the infertility specialists I came across were men. But these are certainly not necessary conditions. In any case, patients often end up moving from one doctor to another: 'Patients are popping from place to place', as one doctor put it. 'Your aunt or sister would recommend a doctor to you – maybe they're good, maybe you're lucky. Or you just have to keep chasing, until you find a good one. How many cycles you have to go through until then...'

When talking in the most general terms of the differences between their interactions with patients in Lebanon and in the Western settings where many had previously practised, some felt that patients' grasp of what fertility treatment might involve was relatively less sophisticated, which placed greater responsibility on doctors' shoulders; another widely reported theme was the enormous pressure on married couples to have children (see Inhorn 1994, 1996, 2003). As one doctor told me, this pressure comes 'from the family, the father and mother-in-law. I was in Brussels: people here in Lebanon come earlier than in Europe, after six months of marriage'.

People seek treatment very soon after marriage, sometimes after only a couple of months without pregnancy; and many seek advice and tests even before marriage: 'Newlyweds, after eight months without children, they're starting to feel sick.' Or as another doctor put it, 'they want you to have children the next day. And women are getting married at an older age now here in Lebanon, so they have to hurry'. Doctors commonly felt that this atmosphere of urgency and anxiety was deeply unhelpful: 'There is social pressure – you want to prove you're virile or feminine. People are so genital-focused. Patients should be more reasonable. Rushing around just because the neighbour says you're infertile, that's no good.' This pressure and observation comes in the first instance from those closest, as this doctor put it: 'The Middle East is a closed system, you have sisters, cousins, relatives who can see you don't have children.' While the 'closeness' of 'Eastern' society was often valorized by my Lebanese informants of all walks and life and religious affiliations, in contrast, say, with the supposed chill and distance of 'the West's' fragmented and individualistic society, it can also prove claustrophobic (Clarke 2007b).

While some doctors felt that this greater pressure to have children in the Middle East was a regional 'custom' – 'You can't imagine how a couple who can't have children in the Middle East feels' – others associated the situation with religion. While it is in point of fact Christian precepts that most explicitly tie reproduction to the purpose of marriage, Islam is often more emphatically depicted as pronatal. One (Shiite, male) doctor quoted a famous Quranic verse (18:46) to me: '*Al-māl wa-l-banūn zīnat al-hayāt al-dunyā* [wealth and children are the ornament of this life]. He who has money seeks kids. Money without children is not acceptable religiously. If a woman doesn't get kids, it is a religious obligation [*wājib*] to go to the doctor. If you get married, you complete your religion. Reproduction is for respect [*karāmah*]. They should at least try IVF and so on if they don't have children.'

Nevertheless, there is of course a strong current of religious discourse that on the contrary advocates forbearance in the face of God's will, as in cases of infertility, for example. Rather more materially, under Lebanon's confessional legal system, it is the ease of divorce and the possibility of polygamy for Muslims, as opposed to Christians, that renders infertile Muslim women still more vulnerable than Christian ones (see Inhorn 1994, 1996, 2003 [on Egypt]). A lack of children could well lead to the break-up of a marriage.[13] Under the shariah inspired regime of personal status for Muslims, Sunni and Shiite men can both divorce their wives relatively easily. A Sunni need only tell his wife she is divorced; a Shiite can do likewise, albeit under certain conditions and before witnesses. For Maronite Catholic and Greek Orthodox Christians, on the other hand, divorce laws follow the teachings of their churches: marriage is a union for life, only to be dissolved under exceptional circumstances and by indulgence of the relevant authorities. Furthermore, a Muslim man need not even divorce his wife: he can marry another.[14] As one doctor put it: 'Here people choose to solve the problem another way – to marry another woman. If the problem is with the man, on the other hand, the wife will have to accept her destiny.'

And even if a Muslim woman were to divorce her husband – for which she needs to bring a court case – on the grounds of his infertility, which is certainly possible, her subsequent social position and possibilities of remarrying are generally poor. Of course, if it was the husband that was infertile and he married again without issue, he would run the risk of attracting suspicion as to his own incapacity. One doctor summed up:

> In our society, women who can't reproduce are under huge, huge pressure. This applies to all religions, but especially Muslims. A baby is a kind of security to the mother in the marriage. If I don't have a baby, my husband will divorce me, or take another wife. The tie is conditional on having a baby. When they have one, they have more rights to inheritance later. The husband will be more tied. And for Christians, social pressure is very high, from the in-laws, mostly on the woman. It's about being a proper person.

There is thus also considerable gender bias in the perception of infertility that doctors have to take into account:[15] 'The first target of blame is the woman. If there's a male problem, then it has to be more secret. This male issue surprised me [on returning to Lebanon after practising in the U.S.] – no matter what you do, men are always healthy – you can't blame them for infertility, they won't come back!'

The gender bias is also apparent in a preference for male children over female: 'it's a major problem – they only want boys, even if they have no children. They are not satisfied with just any old child.' Many doctors found this hard to take, given the constant battles to have a child at all. 'Even now, people who have been infertile for ten to fifteen years are saying "Can I have a boy?" Don't ask that! Pray to have a baby.' One doctor had this example: 'A woman had an attack on the ultrasound table, because it was twin girls after ten years of infertility. She said, "I've come this far for twin girls!!!"" Patients apparently very commonly ask if sex can be selected, and it is clear that this could be a very lucrative sideline, once the reliable means of so doing is established in Lebanon. Most doctors were clear that the technology for fully reliable sex selection (or 'family balancing' as some doctors prefer) of embryos, by pre-implantation genetic diagnosis (PGD), was not yet available, although it soon would be, no doubt:[16] as one doctor told me, 'Sooner or later we'll have to have a freezing system and PGD, just to keep up, because there'll be a huge demand for sexing. I might go for it in *really* stressful situations – four girls, or where the son would be the only heir'. Another doctor, who did claim such powers, placed similar conditions:

> I have the technique, but I don't offer it because I don't like discrimination. If they ask and have a convincing reason ... If they have nine girls and want a boy. Nine, note, not three! Or those who have social problems – if he's a millionaire and he has only girls, for example. He wants a boy because the girls don't inherit. If he has a brother he could enter into the inheritance. So, Salim al-Hoss, the Sunni ex–prime minister, has two daughters: he changed religion to Shiite so that they could inherit.[17] At that time there was no gender selection. If there had been, I'm sure he would have gone for it!

All these pressures and desires surrounding reproduction lead people to spend very considerable sums on treatment, for even if treatment is relatively cheap by international standards, it is not for the average Lebanese couple, who are living through a protracted economic crisis.[18]

Legislative issues

Many effective techniques, regularly practised in the Western settings where most of these doctors learnt these skills, are highly controversial in Lebanon. Although all doctors were happy to talk about IVF and infertility treatment, sensitivities were aroused by the subject of the use of donor gametes, a topic of especial interest to me. Some insisted on its being 'immoral', even 'illegal', adamant that nothing of the like happened in Lebanon. Others were totally open about their use of donor eggs, but felt that donor sperm was beyond the pale. Surrogacy was another difficult topic. This sensitivity, and the resulting occasional reticence, again makes it hard to claim ac-

cess to all the facts here, although Marcia Inhorn's recent work with
infertility patients in Lebanon (2004a, 2006a) confirms that donor
sperm and eggs are both being used. But we should again stress that
these procedures are exceptional rather than the norm. The topic of
'donors' was something of a litmus test as to how frankly a doctor
was prepared to speak. Take this conversation:

> There's no use of donor sperm in Lebanon. They probably don't
> even do it in Iran.[19] Well, maybe the people at Hospital X, al-
> though they would deny it probably. Actually, most clinics do
> sperm donation but say they don't.
>
> Do you do it?
>
> No.

This reticence on the part of doctors stems from the lack of clarity as
to the legality of many forms of fertility treatment. Many doctors
told me that they would be happy to offer procedures using donor gametes, as they had in the West, were there a clear framework of regulation to secure their position: 'We don't do donor stuff here. Not
because of religion, but because of regulation. There are no laws. I
don't want to get into trouble. If egg donation were legalized, doctors would do it. If sperm donation were better thought of, we could
have a bank.' Or, as another doctor put it: 'We are a bit limited here,
as we don't have a law here to protect us. Religion will interfere. You
couldn't say it's "illegal", but the social structure... It wouldn't be
acceptable.'
    Where religion prohibits the use of donor sperm and donor eggs,
as is the case in Maronite Catholic and Greek Orthodox Christianity,
Sunni Islam and much of Shiite Islam, and where lay opinion is also
highly suspicious of such procedures, doctors feel vulnerable without the protection of civil law. Equally, many of the ethical decisions
a doctor may be faced with are far from simple, and some expressed
a wish for guidance. One commented that whereas in the U.S. he
could refer any difficult ethical decision to the ethical committee of
the hospital, no such thing existed where he worked now in Lebanon.
'I'm on my own. There needs to be a general set of guidelines to
make things easier, for egg and sperm donation for example. There
should be strict criteria.' Given the lack of indigenous guidelines,
many doctors have decided to follow the recommendations of the
medical ethical bodies they worked with before. One doctor who had
practised in the U.K., for instance, yearned for 'something like the
HFEA'.[20]

A point of some contention was whether or not there is any law at all governing these procedures in Lebanon, and what indeed might constitute 'law'.[21] Many doctors would respond to questions about the use of donor sperm with a hasty 'But it's illegal!', although others were less certain. The following comments should give an idea as to the state of confusion prevailing:

> Donor sperm – careful, it's illegal. Well, okay, the law is unclear, but we take a stand. Although these things are happening of course.

> Is it illegal? There's no law about it. There's no civil law for Muslims: the Quran is the law. There is civil law for Christians.

> I don't actually know if there's a law about this. I take a consent form, like in Europe.

> In Lebanon, donor is forbidden in law. How to find out about the law? I honestly don't know. It was issued about ten to fifteen years ago. Well, okay, there was talk about the Lebanese order of physicians making some legislation. That was a year ago.

There are guidelines for medical practice that have a passage referring to artificial insemination, but they date back some decades, well before the advent of IVF, although some doctors suggested to me that they could be stretched to include donor egg procedures. In a recent effort to bring the legal situation up to date, a committee was commissioned by then Prime Minister Hariri (since assassinated) to draft new legislation covering IVF as well. The draft that emerged would have banned the use of third-party procedures and limited access to assisted reproduction to married heterosexual couples.[22]

A doctor heading up the project told me some of the background to the story:

> We, the committee on ethics, were ad hoc appointed by the prime minister to advise on ethical dilemmas. We have submitted one law on informed consent, for example, published in the *Gazette*. We prepared a law on IVF: there were some contentious issues; some ministers said that it might contravene the positions of some of the religious communities, and we would have to get their opinions. Eighteen committees [i.e. one for each of the officially recognized religious communities]! So it's pretty much dead. The Maronite Church would not look favourably at any artificial method. In the draft law we tried to make it palatable, especially to Islam. We ruled out unmarried couples, no single women, no gays and no lesbians. We eliminated foster parenting [surrogacy arrangements presumably] – they couldn't be paid. We had to provide comparative legislation. As it stands, there are no laws here governing who does what. If

> you're a licensed physician you can do IVF. There's no control of the
> quality of services, storage of sperm and so on. I am positive uneth-
> ical activities take place.

Of course, what is and is not 'unethical' is a matter of opinion. He
cited the use of donor eggs, for instance, but a Christian doctor I
spoke with felt that not allowing the use of donor eggs, a technique
of such potential benefit to patients, was in itself unethical: 'Egg donation is forbidden and you do it. That's not corrupt. It's forbidding
it that's corrupt.'

It seemed to me that the proposed law must have fallen foul of the
position of either the Christians, especially the most powerful, and
Catholic, group, the Maronites, who disagree with IVF per se, or that
of some of the Shiites, whose authorities allow the use of donor eggs
and even sperm, in the case of Ayatollah Khamene'i, and who would
thus oppose an attempt to brand such procedures as illegal. I put the
latter point to one of the doctors associated with the proposed law,
citing Khamene'i's fatwa allowing the use of donor sperm and eggs.
'I don't think that's genuine', he said. 'But I have the book', I insisted. 'Anyway', he continued, 'the lawmakers don't care what
Khamene'i says, they go by Fadlallah, and he doesn't allow eggs'.
This last point, besides being politically contentious, caused me
some consternation, given my own understandings of Sayyid Fadlallah's position, which may indeed have been confused (see Chapter
4). 'You must have misunderstood', the doctor told me: 'I am almost
his advisor, so I know.' Given the lack of clarity over the position of
only one Shiite authority – and I make no claims to certainty myself
in this regard – and the highly politically charged question of which
Shiite authority is authoritative as far as the Lebanese Shiite community is concerned, it is perhaps unsurprising that the project was
abandoned when faced with the prospect of securing the agreement
of all eighteen religious communities.

Other doctors tended to confirm my ideas: 'It failed in Parliament,
because some people said that some clerics, for example, allowed
donor insemination. It's politics – it comes from the fact that religion
still controls man in this part of the world.' Another felt that '[t]he
Shia blocked it. One of the ministers of health in Lebanon was Shiite – he told me that they [the Shiites] don't accept it [the use of
donor gametes] – but I said "Oh yes they do!"' I recounted my own
similar experience, and he commented that '[i]t was probably an old
fatwa, things have changed a lot'. It was also suggested to me that
pressure might have been brought to bear by other parties: 'Some

centres lobbied the Parliament members, because they didn't want sperm and egg donation banned', one doctor told me. However, some doctors very plausibly suggested the law might have failed for other reasons, namely lack of money and interest – Lebanon has more important priorities.[23]

Religious precepts

Beyond the rather uncertain legal situation, there are, as we have seen, specific religious guidelines for fertility treatments, and in such areas of moral uncertainty in Lebanon it is, by and large, religion that is the final arbiter. However, relatively few doctors struck me – in my interviews with them in the clinical setting at least – as overtly religious, usually professing a 'scientific' worldview and concentrating on helping people as best they can. Christian doctors, who formed the majority of those I talked to, often felt that they had to work against the strictures of religion. The Catholic Church, of which the Maronite Church, the largest and most powerful Christian community in Lebanon, is part, is deeply conservative in many matters, such as contraception for example, and infertility treatment is no exception. All medical intervention in conception is forbidden, although this prohibition seems to be widely ignored by the laity. As one doctor commented: 'Let the Church accept contraceptive pills and then we'll talk about IVF.' The Greek Orthodox Church also had a dim view of medical assistance in conception, although it seems their leaders have recently been swayed by the pleas of desperate infertile couples and feel procedures using the gametes of husband and wife may be acceptable.[24] For the most part, then, doctors seemed to hold themselves aloof from religious considerations; as we have noted, many preferred to follow the biomedical ethical standards of the Western clinical settings they had previously practised in.

Ethical choices beyond that were seen by many to be the patients' responsibility: 'Many times we don't offer philosophical or ethical dimensions: we offer scientific procedures. They should have thought about what they want. Or if they're our own patients, we're following them with regard to their fertility, then we'll say you need IVF or whatever. The most important factor is religion here in our country. If it's acceptable in their religion then they'll do it.' Similarly, an overtly pious Shiite doctor told me: 'If they come, we don't give them the religious opinions. That's not my work! No, we say what's available, and the people decide.' On this account, one goes to one expert – the doctor – and finds out what the options are, and then consults another – the shaykh or priest – to ask if they are allowed or not: 'first they ask, then they call Fadlallah', as one doctor told me of some of his Shiite patients. Or conversely, as many doctors noted, patients often come to them very well informed as to the religious positions, Muslim patients perhaps even with written fatwas permitting them to undertake one or another course of treatment (see Inhorn 2003: 104; 2006a). These topics are much discussed on television and radio and in magazines, and they are featured in films and soap operas. Several doctors mentioned their recent appearances on television programmes to discuss these matters, perhaps debating the ethics with a shaykh or priest.

Of course, far from all Lebanese take their religion quite so seriously. But doctors, for their part, certainly do not ignore the religious and social conditions in which they work. As one said to me: 'We try to stick to people's religious convictions. We're serving a community, after all. It doesn't serve to mess with that.' But as regards the guardians of morality, the fault lines of moral debate in Lebanon do not necessarily fall in the places one might expect, looking from outside. For example, a secular Christian doctor returning from the U.S. and looking to offer donor egg procedures, which he finds 'ethical' according to international medical standards, would find certain Shiite Ayatollahs his most potent allies here.

Controversial procedures

Now I turn to the practitioners' perspectives on the controversial procedures of especial interest to us here, as giving the most direct insights into the fault lines of kinship thinking. Again, one should stress that these are exceptional cases we are discussing, rather than the norm. First and foremost among the challenging procedures being performed are those using donor gametes. These are clearly extremely difficult for most patients to accept, although certainly not impossible, even for those whose religious laws prohibit it. Despite the churches' conservative positions with regard to assisted reproduction in general, Christians are seen by some doctors as more flexible here, although rather than tying that impression to some spurious 'cultural' explanation, the reasons are once again seen as rooted in Lebanon's legal system of personal status: 'Muslims can divorce, take another wife, but Christians no, it's harder. So they're more likely to go for egg donation, for example, but they need time to make the decision.' But doctors also commonly reported Muslims using these techniques, allowed by some religious authorities, prohibited by others. Some doctors were in fact surprised at the level of patient awareness of these possibilities, across the communitarian spectrum: 'Coming from the U.S., I was initially really surprised that they accept donors so easily. I had patients telling me about donors.' Nevertheless, we should keep this in perspective: overall, these techniques are clearly controversial.

Donor sperm

One has to distinguish sharply between the use of donor eggs and that of semen and sperm, to recall the further distinction that was drawn in previous chapters between the use of spermatozoa in IVF procedures creating an embryo for transplantation into the woman's body, and the introduction of another man's semen through her vagina. To take sperm first, the use of donor sperm is far more problematic 'ethically' and socially. Having another man's semen, especially, put inside one's wife's body seems much more like adultery and being cuckolded. 'Sperm goes in. Anything to do with sperm, they think it's sexual', as one doctor put it. Semen has a distinct cultural significance, being considered the active agent of reproduction and an impure substance in Islamic thought: contact with it requires ritual ablution to render one ritually pure, essential for prayer and other religious duties. As we have seen, all Islamic authorities save Ayatollah Khamene'i prohibit the use of donor sperm, as do the Maronite and Greek Orthodox Churches. Further, in donor insemination the husband is rendered completely functionless, in contrast with donor egg procedures, where the wife will carry the child.[25]

Nevertheless, fertility treatment using donor sperm is available in Lebanon, a boon for those men whose infertility is otherwise untreatable (Inhorn 2006a). The number of such men is considerably lower than in earlier years, given the advent of ICSI:[26] thus, no doubt, many of the comments on sperm donation belong to the past. As one doctor said: 'It's becoming very rare. Now I probably have a case only once every six or seven months, only when they are completely infertile. But even of those very few would accept donor sperm.' Yet despite its ethical problems, in practical terms donor insemination is easy, cheap and effective, and does not involve the complications for a man's wife that ICSI, as a variant of IVF, does. Most sperm comes from anonymous donors, medical students for the most part, who may receive a small consideration from the patient in return for their donation.[27] While the use of donor sperm is morally suspect, the prospect of 'sperm banks' seems to be considered totally unacceptable. This means fresh sperm has to be used, not allowing proper screening for diseases in the opinion of several doctors. According to one such: 'I don't use donor sperm for medical reasons; it doesn't follow the guidelines, because it's fresh not frozen. AIDS and hepatitis take time to incubate, so it should be kept for six months and screened. For this to be possible it has to be supported by law, which it isn't.' But those doctors who did offer this technique were clear that they had a sound pool of donors, 'specific people who we've checked for diseases'.

Given the emphasis on confidentiality, a major concern for patients is, reportedly, how the donor looks. While one strand of local rhetoric would have having 'blonde and blue-eyed' children as an admirable prospect (see Inhorn 2006b: 116), when it comes to concrete practice that ideal rather falls by the wayside. Blonde and blue-eyed children might attract suspicion, as a doctor working in another hospital told me: 'The problem is people asking does the child look like you – the neighbours and relatives. It all has to be so secret. They do ask about race. I say, don't worry, we don't take Sri Lankans [a common source of immigrant labour], just Lebanese, people like you see outside the window.' While some doctors reported patients taking an interest in other of the donors' qualities, most seemed to feel that this was not a major issue. A doctor who had also worked in North America commented: 'In the U.S. you can choose donor characteristics, blonde, clever and so on. People here in Lebanon don't ask, they just want to have a baby.' Given the conflicts of recent Lebanese history, I tentatively wondered if perhaps the religion of the donor might be an issue, but here I was clearly overreading 'sectarianism'. I asked one Shiite doctor with a large Shiite clientele, who had carried out donor insemination, if his patients had insisted that the donor material be from a Shiite. He said no, obviously finding it a stupid question. One doctor told me that he did type the donors by sect, but his experience was that it was the donors – Christian medical students – who worried more than the recipients.[28] However, what was a worry for both doctors and patients was 'what was the background of the man, the sperm donor?' An 'immoral' donor would be unwelcome: they might have sexual diseases. While the dangers of using sperm from a man infected with a sexually transmitted disease are of genuine concern, the problem was expressed in terms of the ubiquitous ideology of sexual morality rather than hygiene alone.[29]

Sometimes, reportedly, a patient would specifically request that a relative's gametes be used. As one doctor informed me: 'Sometimes people come with their father or brother to ask to use their sperm. With the brother I've done it. With the father I didn't, because the sperm is old.'[30] Many doctors were wary of such activities, pointing to the potential for family conflicts. This doctor cited concerns over pitting one brother against another, a clichéd theme of local discourse, but a worry in fact derived, with rather delightful irony, from his previous experience in England:

> Yes, men use their brother. When I was in London, the consultant said that in England people had asked for this. They had told them yes, but they weren't using it in fact, they used a sperm donor without telling them. Because this guy will know it's his child. And they had a lot of problems with this. The brother would come and then want his child. Then they could say no, we didn't use it – get a test. In Lebanon, I personally tell them it's not advisable to use kin gametes. If they're not convinced then I make them sign a consent form to the effect that I've explained the problems and have no responsibility. Sometimes they, the donors, refuse even to have an STD test – so it's a disclaimer of medical responsibility as much as anything else.

Another doctor explicitly linked this bringing of a male relative's sperm to the agnatic ideology of the 'tribe': 'Some families bring the sperm of the brother for example, but I don't accept it – it should be anonymous. This is feudal thinking – the tribe. There are rules about sperm, because of bad experiences. How will the brother be looking at the son? Like a father?' A doctor working in the Shiite suburbs of Beirut told me that the sperm used in sperm donor procedures comes from '[a] relative, not the *arhām*, the first degree, but a cousin [*ibn 'amm*, the father's brother's son]', directly echoing the agnatic emphasis that we picked up in our discussion of patrilateral parallel cousin marriage.

This doctor, and much of her clientele, apparently followed Ayatollah Khamene'i, and this use of a close relative would fit nicely with Khamene'i's representative Shaykh Muqdad's stipulation that it would be better if the identity of the sperm donor were known (see Chapter 4). However, even where the fatwas allow the use of donor gametes, especially sperm, not all believers may be ready to profit

from them: just because something is not forbidden, that does not
mean it is necessarily praiseworthy, or indeed socially acceptable. 'If
you don't accept, that's your choice. These are *al-mubāhāt* [what is
allowed]: just because it's allowed, doesn't mean you have to do it',
the doctor continued. 'The problem is not religion but the people: 90
per cent don't accept it. Maybe 10 per cent would do it, if they were
really desperate. It's all a question of tradition and custom.' As another doctor put it: 'The problem of sperm is a problem of machismo
rather than religion.' Another gynaecologist working in the south of
Lebanon, again with a predominantly Shiite clientele, told me that
she would not even consider counselling people to try sperm donation: she knows they will refuse and it would lower their opinion of
her. I commented that society is more conservative than religion
here. 'Yes', she said, 'many people don't use donor gametes because
of the social pressures. "I can't allow society to destroy my life even
for a baby," they think'. She made the following, perhaps surprising
point in comparison with abortion, religiously prohibited: 'The
question of donors is more sensitive – with an abortion, no one will
know. Using a sperm donor is an open question for the future. So we
don't get so much sperm donor use: here people choose to solve the
problem another way, by marrying another woman [*sic*]. If the problem is with the man, the wife will accept her destiny.'

And where people are using the unrestrictive positions to carry
out procedures involving third parties, it is far from clear that all the
implications of those positions are followed through, especially regarding the assignment of paternity and maternity. As we have seen,
those authorities who allow the use of donor gametes assign maternity and paternity along genetic lines: a resulting child is that of the
genetic parent – the donor – and not the recipient. But I was told on
a number of occasions that all concerned are often in fact considerably happier if the identity of the sperm donor is kept a secret from
everyone except the medical centre, which should check for trans-
missible diseases. According to one doctor, local Shiite religious authorities were happy to let concerns for social harmony take
precedence here: 'Now it is kept secret – even the shaykhs want it
kept secret – so there's no social problems. But the sperm donor
must be known, so there's no possibility of marrying your sister.
There are no sperm or egg banks. In law this is illegal, although they
are trying to get a law through to change that, but it has stalled because of religion. The centre knows the identity of the donor, but the
patients don't. It's so they don't use one infected with hepatitis or

some other disease.' Thus beyond the nominally clearly defined lines of Islamic law lies a much more complicated reality, where diverse ethical and legal positions and the rather more conservative demands of social propriety are all in the balance.

Donor eggs

While sperm donation is ethically difficult, egg donation is seen as much less so by both doctors and patients, although the practical difficulties are of course considerably greater, requiring as it does gruelling courses of hormonal treatments for the donor to stimulate 'superovulation' and a surgical procedure to remove the eggs. As we have already noted, there are many doctors who feel that donor egg procedures in particular should be allowed and safeguarded in law, even if they do not advocate allowing the use of donor sperm. While male infertility is now most frequently treatable with the advent of ICSI, infertility among older women especially is most easily treated with the use of donor eggs.[31] And doctors commonly reported that patients were receptive to the idea: 'I was very surprised: the idea of having a donor is kind of unacceptable. Coming from the U.S. I was under the impression that women wouldn't accept this. Now I'm coming more and more to see that no, that's not the case.' This includes Muslims, although many authorities, notably among the Sunni consensus, find such procedures religiously impermissible, as we have seen. The religiously correct course, then, would be either forbearance, or for the man to take another wife, as in this doctor's account of a consultation with a wealthy Sunni patient: 'I said to him, "Look, your wife is 45 years old, you're a millionaire, get a donor egg." He replied, "No I prefer to take another wife" – in front of her! "Why?" I said. "You love your wife." "Muslim law prevents me from using another egg, but allows me to marry another woman".' However, it seems clear that other Muslim men are willing to explore the possibility of using a donor egg and thus preserve their marriage (Inhorn 2006a).

As we have already noted, obtaining donor eggs is complicated, requiring hormonal treatments and a surgical procedure. Furthermore, young women in Lebanon are very unlikely to consent to undergo such a procedure, as it is carried out by means of the vagina: virginity is vitally important for unmarried young women, who are expected to be *virgo intacta* upon marriage, yet this cohort is precisely the usual providers of donor eggs in many Western countries, for example.[32] Thus there is not the same access to anonymously provided eggs, except where egg donors are brought in from outside Lebanon, from the U.S. for instance, as happens in at least one clinic (Inhorn 2006a). Again, such sources lead to rumours of inappropriately fair children resulting, although a doctor involved was clear: 'Yes, they want non-blonde and non-blue-eyed. So we bring Mediterranean types, Italian-Americans – Mexicans even, but you can't say that because people are a bit snobbish in Lebanon.'

Such sources are relatively rare, however, and eggs are usually obtained through women undergoing fertility treatment themselves: any eggs collected from them surplus to their own requirements can be used to help others, as is also the case for embryos. As one doctor told me: 'They do it in a nice way: "God gave me a child, so why not for someone else".' Patients might also receive a discount on their treatment in return. Another doctor gave me a detailed account of 'egg-sharing': 'This is when a patient does IVF, doesn't have much money, but is young, and stimulates well. She's got lots of eggs. So she takes half, gives half to another couple of ladies. She doesn't pay – the other two ladies pay for the three. This is common. But there are problems with this: you have to synchronize the patients. You don't know in advance if she'll stimulate. So you have a line of patients waiting. It's not synchronized; it lowers your success chances, makes it more stressful for the recipient.'

Due to these considerations, this doctor preferred to use a 'designated donor', that is, one specific donor who will give her eggs to the patient. This might be arranged through the doctor, and the donor might even be unknown to the recipient, as above, but more often she would be a relative or a friend: 'Because of the economic situation in Lebanon, I want to use a known donor – a sister, someone related – someone who's not looking for money, but giving their eggs to a friend. Because a designated donor is very costly, and cost is very important.' Doctors seemed much less reluctant to countenance these transfers of gametes between female relatives than they were in the case of males: 'Eggs, that's different', as one doctor put it. In fact some doctors hinted that the world of female egg-sharing was not one that interested males had access to: 'We use a relative – a sister or cousin – they wouldn't want their husband to know.' Nevertheless, as to the difference between male and female gametes here, one must not forget that where donor eggs are used, the recipient will carry the child, and '[o]f course it's the woman carrying the child who will feel like she is the mother', while in the use of donor sperm the husband is cut out of the process altogether.

A reportedly prolific Shiite practitioner, a follower of Ayatollah Khamene'i, explained to me his Shiite patients' preference for donor eggs over donor sperm, in an interview that brought out the pertinent issues nicely: 'In Lebanon we use the egg – this is the biggest thing, much more than sperm. Because it is better in the shariah and custom. And the transfer of an egg from woman to woman is not *zinā* [fornication, adultery], because it's from woman to woman. And the husband is excluded completely in donor insemination.' He makes the interesting point, not made, it should be noted, by the Islamic authorities, that the use of eggs need not be considered *zinā*, illicit sex, because it does not involve a man. He continued: 'They get eggs from family and friends [*aqribā', asdiqā'*]. They must be known, because of illnesses, and also their behaviour, because they might sleep with lots of people, then they might have diseases like AIDS. And they prefer somebody who looks the same. The sister is best, and should be married – because they must be a virgin before marriage, and the technique goes through the vagina.' Again, moral and hygienic issues are tied together: just like marrying one's cousin, one knows what one is getting in the case of an egg from a relative or friend. Their morals will be acceptable – specifically their sexual morals, for it is the possibility of the transmission of sexually transmitted disease that is seen as of greatest concern. They – and thus the child – will look the same, in the case of a relative or a well-chosen friend, which will minimize gossip; and there is the further observation regarding the 'morality' of the procedure itself.

As we saw in the previous chapter, there has been some feeling among Shiite religious thinkers that egg donation would be more proper were there a marriage contract between the donor and the husband of the recipient,[33] although, as another Shiite doctor told me: 'It could be one's wife in religion rather than in civil law. Marriage isn't a matter of civil law, it is a religious thing.' However, as we also saw, religious opinion has in some cases evolved away from a position where that was mandatory, as another doctor explained: 'That was a long time ago before the *ijtihād* came out that they did this. They even did it *in absentia* – you know the name of the woman donating, some shaykh performed the necessary formalities, you would have witnesses.' This evolution of religious opinion helps: as noted before, the dropping of the requirement has enabled sisters, among other relatives, to donate, since Islam prohibits marriage to two sisters simultaneously. 'Before they accepted the donor egg of a married woman – they would marry the woman for a day, then take an egg. Now any donor is accepted. I have had sisters giving eggs in the case of a sister's premature menopause.'

Again, a key practical issue concerning those Shiite rulings permitting the use of donor gametes is that the child will not then be that of the couple, and again, the very real pressures of social expectation complicate the neat patterns of the Islamic law of the ulama. Before society if not before God, this stipulation may perhaps not be overtly observed. As another Shiite doctor performing donor procedures for Shiite patients told me, 'People definitely don't follow the religious idea of the egg donor being the mother. It's legally registered in the name of the couple. No one knows'.[34] Bureaucratically, then, according to this doctor at least, the child is registered as that of the couple, notwithstanding any religious injunctions, namely those of Ayatollahs Khamene'i and Fadlallah, that should demand otherwise. While under Lebanon's legal regime such rulings should perhaps be taken into consideration, the assumption of the Shiite (and Sunni) Islamic courts, charged with establishing relatedness, would certainly be that the standard procedure is to be followed: in the case of a child of a married woman, *nasab* is awarded to her and her husband, unless a suit is brought to the contrary (see Chapter 1). For many doctors, perhaps not so attuned to the religious debate, this seems like a non-question. I asked one, 'How would you register the child – is it the child of the couple, even if a donor gamete was used?' He replied, 'Yes, all over the world it's like that isn't it?' But a more religiously knowledgeable Shiite doctor responded: 'The law is not important. In Lebanon it tries not to oppose religion.' And another doctor, working within the ambit of Hezbollah and hence knowledgeable of the position of Ayatollah Khamene'i for instance, said of donor insemination: 'Register it as the child of the husband, this is legally fine. No one will know. It's very confidential.' However, there could perhaps be legal consequences subsequently were a case to come before the religious courts, regarding an inheritance, for example. This is an issue for the future. As we have had occasion to observe more than once before, it is clear that the relation between religious prescriptions, the law and everyday life is more complicated than mere perusal of the fatwas would suggest (see Inhorn 2006a: 98–99).

Surrogacy: Social conservatism and religious challenge

There is still another unconventional possibility, namely that the child is carried to term by a woman other than the eventual 'mother' who serves as a gestational surrogate: perhaps the wife has viable eggs but no uterus, or cannot bear a child because she has cardiac problems, or has neither eggs nor uterus. Many doctors stated flatly that this did not happen, or even was impossible in the Lebanese social climate: 'There are no surrogate motherhood arrangements – it's impossible for social reasons.' That is, it is not socially acceptable for unmarried or divorced women to be pregnant, still less for married ones to give their child away.

However, there were several doctors who told me of their experiences in this field, and it seemed clear that such procedures have occasionally been carried out, albeit in the utmost secrecy and, in this case especially, very, very rarely.

> Surrogate mothers? Yes – I have had couples who wanted it. But it's very difficult to get in Lebanon. The male prefers to sleep with the surrogate mother. But he doesn't realize she could just leave. A man came and said, 'I can get a Romanian one, she works in nightclubs. She would be willing for $4,000.' But she's a drinker. So we refused. In a nightclub, she's exposed to a lot of smoke, drink. He brought the girl to the clinic! He said he would put her in a hotel during the pregnancy, but she has to work – it's on her permit. But generally, look, it's no problem: when the surrogate gets pregnant, the wife will go overseas, and then come back. This happens, you know: people go overseas, and come back with a child.

The doctor clearly found this request to use an Eastern European nightclub hostess as a gestational surrogate unacceptable: her lifestyle – certainly stereotypically immoral by local standards – raised hygienic concerns. He is nevertheless clear that such procedures are very occasionally undertaken, as was another doctor who told me that patients 'bring women from the Philippines, Sri Lanka – the housekeeper[35] – because they're not the same colour' and thus their lack of relation to the child will be the clearer.[36] 'It's very, very important this! For the woman it's better – she sees the baby is not related to her.' He continued:

> They pay a maid normally $150, $200 [a month]. So perhaps they give a gift: $1–2,000, it's like three to six months supplementary wages. They're living with the family; they're like one of the family, eating with them. They think like this – if you have a premature baby, they put it in neonatal for two months. So this is like that, only for six to nine months! We have one case of surrogacy every two to five years.
>
> Wouldn't the neighbours notice?

No, probably she won't leave the house, or they go to the mountains.
The wife will put something under her jumper.

Still, let us note again that, as this doctor stressed, this is 'very, very exceptional.'

Here again, then, where religious opinion allows such procedures, it is in advance of that of wider society. Another doctor, a Sunni working in the predominantly Shiite South, told me of two cases he had had of female patients with eggs but no uterus. They came with letters from Sayyid Fadlallah stating that another woman could be used as a gestational carrier if the husband were to marry her. The doctor refused to carry out the procedure in both instances, in accordance with his own ethical position. But a Shiite doctor also working in the South had another story concerning surrogate arrangements that highlights still better some of the tensions here: 'A veiled *sayyidah* [female descendant of the Prophet] came: "I am pregnant, I want ultrasound, but I am carrying another's baby." The egg was from the wife, and the third party was the carrier. "Shame on you", I said. "Don't say that, I've got a fatwa here," she said. I should have read this before, and I did read more afterwards. They gave her money and that's allowed too.' Far from Islamic legal opinion constricting the onward march of challenging and controversial procedures for overcoming infertility, it often facilitates it, to the surprise and indeed initial moral censure of this doctor, more a secularist than a pietist, it should be noted: religious opinion may sometimes confound local moral common sense.

To conclude, real life is then, as one might expect, more complicated than the Islamic law of the shaykhs. Most of the possibilities that the new reproductive technologies offer are available in Lebanon, although many doctors worry as to the lack of clear state-sponsored regulation. Given the strongly pro-natal environment, these techniques are much in demand. This includes, unusually for the wider region, controversial procedures such as those involving donor gametes, our especial interest here, although these are comparatively rare, indeed almost – if not quite – unheard of in the case of surrogacy arrangements. Even where some religious opinion, especially that of some Shiite authorities, may be notably unrestrictive with regard to such opportunities, the opinion of wider society perhaps remains rather more conservative. People of all religious communities share some core principles of sexual propriety and respect for the right to privacy that need to be kept firmly in mind. Further, there is considerable social pressure to conform to those principles.

While, as we noted above, those religious opinions that do allow some of the controversial procedures hold out the prospect of complex and in some senses unprecedented patterns of kinship relatedness, these are not, as yet, the crux of the matter in the Lebanese contexts we have glimpsed here. It is rather these patterns of moral choice and challenge that are the more pressing issue, ones whose lineaments are sometimes surprising, from a 'Western' perspective at least, and that we now attempt to map out somewhat more fully.

Notes

1. Kahn's Israel, with unmarried women and lesbian couples using donor sperm, looks very different, although sexual propriety is equally an important element of the rabbinical debates. Kahn presents, for instance, a tableau of an ultra-orthodox rabbi presiding over the circumcision of the AID child of lesbian parents (2000: 41–42). An unmarried, religious woman wanting a child considered both adoption, a virtuous deed, and AID, where she would be thought a 'whore', and chose the latter (2000: 56). These scenarios are inconceivable in the settings I have experience of. Pertinent perhaps is that in Jewish law, children born to unmarried Jewish women are not illegitimate; only married Jewish women can commit 'adultery' (2000: 74–75).

2. As we have already noted (Chapter 2), such crimes do sometimes occur in Lebanon, but relatively infrequently.

3. Elsewhere, however, Inhorn (2004a: 171) does suggest that something of a normalization of IVF is under way.

4. A fertile quantity would be something over twenty million. In ICSI (intracytoplasmic sperm injection), a recent variant of IVF, individual sperm are injected into ova through 'micro-manipulation' under a high-powered microscope: just one sperm is thus now sufficient for conception, providing a solution to many cases of male infertility. As Inhorn (2003: 231ff.) describes, the advent of ICSI has changed the gender dynamics of infertility treatment in the Islamic Middle East: suddenly many previously infertile men can have recourse to effective treatment. However, their wives may by now be too old to provide fertile eggs for the procedure, putting new pressure on them and raising the possibility of their husband taking another, younger wife.

5. This 'reproductive tourism' is a recognized phenomenon (Inhorn 2003: 2, 114–15, 281 n. 3).

6. Lebanese expatriates also return to the homeland for treatment – perhaps in the summer vacation many spend in Lebanon – as it is considerably cheaper than, for example, the U.S. An IVF cycle – i.e. a round of egg collection, fertilization and transfer – that in the U.S. might cost $15–20,000 plus medication costs could be obtained in Lebanon in 2003–04 for $1,500–3,000. Having said that, I have heard of higher prices.

7. The 1959 al-Azhar fatwa recognizing Shiite (Ja'farite) law as a school alongside the four Sunni schools (see Chapter 2) arguably clears the way officially for such a move.

8. Kahn (2000: 58) also had problems obtaining statistics in Israel: the doctors there want to avoid attracting too much attention, lest religious forces put a stop to some of their more controversial activities.

9. Serour et al. (1991: 51) estimate $400–500,000.

10. Inhorn (2004a: 166) reckons on approximately fifteen.

11. A 'cycle' is one round of egg collection, fertilization and transfer, taking four to six weeks in all. These cycles of treatment are, we should note, physically debilitating, even dangerous, for the woman undergoing them, who has to take large amounts of hormonal drugs to stimulate superovulation, and then undergo surgery to have eggs collected. With the low rates of successful embryo implantation, a woman may well have to go through a number of such cycles before even this stage is successfully completed, let alone carrying a foetus or multiple foetuses to term and delivering them successfully, and in many cases repeated IVF treatment is unsuccessful.

12. Inhorn (2004a) has a much fuller discussion of infertility rates and causes, writing as a medical anthropologist expert on the topic.

13. Some doctors felt that this was putting them under pressure in turn: 'It puts you under pressure – their marriage depends on the success of this procedure. Sometimes you do it almost for free, because you feel this is a social case. I had a case, I was treating a woman, and it wasn't working. She came in; I needed to discuss a further failure with her. The woman said, "He's filed for divorce!"'

14. Up to a maximum of four, legally speaking, although in practice having two wives is rare and having more almost unheard of.

15. Inhorn has explored this theme over a series of publications spanning many years (e.g. 1994, 1996, 2003).

16. This is as opposed to special diets, timetables for intercourse and the Ericsson technique, where sperm is separated into X and Y chromosome–bearing spermatozoa in a centrifuge, none of which are wholly reliable. Sex selection is practised in Egypt, Jordan and Saudi Arabia (Inhorn, personal comment).

17. Sunni inheritance law grants agnates precedence over daughters in the matter of inheritance, although Shiite law does not. As personal status law is determined by religious affiliation, one has to change sect – a bureaucratic procedure – if one wants to be subject to a different regime of inheritance (see Chapter 2).

18. Lebanese per capita GDP was in 2003–04 an estimated $5,000, with 28 per cent of the population living below the poverty line (according to the 2005 online CIA World Factbook), as compared with the commonly quoted figure of $1,500–2,000 for one cycle of IVF.

19. Iran's spiritual leader, Ayatollah Khamene'i, being just about the only authority that allows the use of donor sperm. As we noted in the previous chapter, according to Tremayne (2006, n.d.) donor sperm is used in Iran, but by the roundabout route of a wife divorcing her husband, temporarily marrying the sperm donor and then remarrying her original husband.

20. The British Human Fertilisation and Embryology Authority, a statutory review body established by the Human Fertilisation and Embryology Act of 1990 to maintain a code of practice that will apply to all infertility clinics undertaking activities licensed under the act. It is primarily a licensing body.

21. Inhorn (2003: 99) cites Meirow and Schenker (1997) and Blank (1998) to the effect that in Lebanon, as in all other Muslim countries, sperm donation is strictly prohibited, but also (2006a: 114) notes, as I do here, the lack of regulation and parliamentary law regarding more recent techniques.

22. I am very grateful to one of the doctors most directly involved for giving me a copy of the draft law, translated in Clarke (2005: Appendix 2).

23. I was hoping to interview Marwan Hamade, who, I was told, was minister of health at the time of the discussions over the proposed law. He was, however, badly injured by a car bomb in an assassination attempt during the period of my fieldwork (1 October 2004).

24. As Archbishop George Khudr – who himself opposed such a relaxation of the Church's restrictions – told me. The Greek Orthodox Hospi-

tal in Beirut now has an assisted reproduction centre.

25. One doctor told me that some men would ask him, 'Can you at least mix my fluid with the donor's, so that a bit of me goes into it?'

26. Again, this is because this variant of IVF can use just one spermatozoon, making male infertility far more easily overcome than before its advent. 'ICSI has made men equal', as one doctor says.

27. $50–100, according to one of my informants.

28. Although in a more recent discussion another doctor felt that Druze and Christian patients were now asking more frequently for 'non-Muslim' donors, the Druze (nominally Muslim under the terms of official Lebanese confessional classification, one might note) wanting Druze donors in particular.

29. As a further example of the pattern, couples in Lebanon undertake a medical test before marriage: as I was told in a discussion in the Sunni courts, this is not just to check for genetically transmitted diseases, 'for the children' (*li-l-awlād*), but also to check for sexually transmitted diseases, 'for the morals' (*li-l-akhlāq*).

30. Tremayne (n.d.) reports similar strategies for Iran.

31. As Inhorn (2003: 231ff.) points out, these are often the wives of men whose infertility has latterly been overcome through the advent of ICSI, after the wives' own reproductive powers had waned.

32. In Shaykh Muhammad 'Ali al-Hajj's (2006: 28) account, a Shiite jurisprudential perspective, there is no doubt that it is a woman's right to carry out a procedure that might damage her hymen should she wish; there is no Islamic legal precept that would prevent her. But socially it is refused, and it is thus proper for women not to be careless in this regard. Should an unmarried woman of older years be worried that she might not be able to marry until such a time as her fertility might be diminished, this constitutes an exception. He also notes that it is medically possible, if rare nowadays, to effect the procedure by means of piercing the belly. Shaykh al-Hajj (2006: 55) also put the matter to Sayyid Fadlallah, who stated that whether or not the woman undergoing such a procedure is a virgin is immaterial to its permissibility, but the virgin is advised not to do something that might damage her future.

33. Again, Tremayne (2006, n.d.) reports that in Iran the use of temporary marriages to legitimate egg donation is the norm.

34. In the case of the surrogacy procedures that some fatwas make possi-

ble, the opposite problem obtains. Religiously, the ensuing child is related to the husband and wife commissioning the surrogate, but state bureaucracy would seem to lag behind, as a doctor explained: 'Surrogacy is very difficult here. We don't have legislation. If she's pregnant, and delivers in hospital, it's very difficult to register not in her name.'

35. It is very common in Lebanon for middle- and upper-class families to employ a live-in maidservant from a more impoverished country.

36. Ragoné (2000) describes similar ideas at work in North America.

Part III

CONFRONTATIONS

Our Freud had been the first to reveal the appalling dangers of family
life. The world was full of fathers – was therefore full of misery;
full of mothers – therefore of every kind of perversion from
sadism to chastity; full of brothers, sisters, uncles, aunts –
full of madness and suicide. 'And yet, among the savages of Samoa,
in certain islands off the coast of New Guinea...' The tropical
sunshine lay like warm honey on the naked bodies of children
tumbling promiscuously among the hibiscus blossoms.
Home was in any one of twenty palm-thatched houses. In the
Trobriands conception was the work of ancestral ghosts; nobody had
ever heard of a father. 'Extremes,' said the Controller,
'meet. For the good reason that they were made to meet.'

. . . .

Lenina shook her head. 'Somehow.' She mused, 'I hadn't been feeling
very keen on promiscuity lately. There are times when one doesn't.
Haven't you found that too, Fanny?' Fanny nodded her sympathy
and understanding. 'But one's got to make the effort,' she said
sententiously, 'one's got to play the game. After all, everyone belongs
to everyone else.' 'Yes, everyone belongs to everyone else,' Lenina
repeated slowly and, sighing, was silent for a moment;
then taking Fanny's hand, gave it a little squeeze.
'You're quite right, Fanny. As usual. I'll make the effort.'

Aldous Huxley, *Brave New World*

Chapter 6

BRAVE NEW WORLDS?

Anthropology, Islam and the new morality

We started, in Chapter 1, by setting the 'new kinship studies' of recent anthropology in historical context, as part of a sustained programme of questioning traditional moral categories. We took Britain as our example, from the late nineteenth century onwards, where Parliament debated and legislated a series of changes with regard to kinship specifically, concerning divorce, incest and affinity. Anthropologists were called upon for their own special expertise: knowledge of societies with different modes of social organization from that of Britain, and theories as to what was universal and what not in this regard. It will be helpful in this final chapter to start by reiterating some of those themes, as we come to set the Islamic debates and ethnography of Lebanon in wider context. Sexual propriety was a key theme of those debates and that ethnography; it has also been a key theme within certain strands of anthropology, part of what I very crudely term here the wider 'liberal tradition', to which new 'scientific' understandings of social relations, including kinship, were allied.[1]

While our focus in Chapter 1 was on kinship, interest in moral reform was much wider: anthropologists such as Margaret Mead and Bronislaw Malinowski were intimately involved in the 'first "sexual revolution"' of the 1920s (Martin 1996), as the epigraph above evidences in its allusion to the 'savages of Samoa' and the Trobriand Is-

lands. I quote from Aldous Huxley's (1932) dystopian vision of a
Brave new world of mechanized human reproduction and mandatory
promiscuity. 'Brave new worlds' have ever since been evoked – not
always appositely – in discussions of the new reproductive technologies such as IVF, which were mere science fiction in Huxley's day,
and a brief consideration of what he was satirizing makes a neat
counterpoint to the themes we have been exploring.[2] In the 1920s,
when Huxley was writing, a 'New Morality' was in the air, heralded
for example by Samuel Schmalhausen, an American high-school
teacher turned prophet of the new moral movement, as key to a future 'new civilisation', 'really new in the original sense that it as-
signs a status of reasonable respectability to behaviour branded
throughout the moralistic Christian countries as immoral, disreputable: for example, auto-eroticism, adultery, easy divorce, promiscuity, homosexual affection, casualness in love life' (cited in
Firchow 1984: 51), and strenuously argued for by Dora Russell, wife
of Bertrand, in *The right to be happy* (1927), a direct attack on Christian morality, pleading for the guiltless enjoyment of sex.

World famous philosopher Bertrand Russell himself argued similarly in his wildly popular *Marriage and morals* (1929), which sold
out rapidly on both sides of the Atlantic.[3] Here Russell draws on Malinowski's vision of the matrilineal society where the physiological
basis for paternity is unknown,[4] making it part of an evolutionary
schema moving then to patriarchy, exemplified by 'Abrahamic' society, then to Christian repression of sex, and finally to a call for sexual liberation and nudism. Russell also sets the work of Mead
against the preconceptions of unhealthy 'Victorian morality', noting
that she 'asserts that adolescent disorders are unknown in [Samoa],
and she attributes this fact to the prevalent sexual freedom', with the
aside that 'This sexual freedom, it is true, is being somewhat cur-
tailed by missionary activity' (1929: 219–20). Malinowski and
Mead's work was also held in the highest regard by the most
renowned 'sexologist' of them all, Havelock Ellis (another fan of
nudism), who called Mead's *Coming of age in Samoa* 'fascinating,
valuable, and instructive', adding that 'the great master in these
fields is Professor Bronislaw Malinowski, and I could not pay higher
tribute to Miss Mead than to mention her name in connection with
his' (Howard 1984: 127).[5] Havelock Ellis had the greatest of respect
for Malinowski, the arch-modernist anthropologist (Ardener 2007
[1985]), writing the preface to Malinowski's *Sexual life of savages*,[6]
and for another distinguished anthropologist of the time, Edward

Westermarck, whom he admired for his (scholarly) moral relativism (Grosskurth 1981: 384ff.). And Ellis certainly saw himself as fighting for moral progress. At the end of his years, '[a] not altogether justified sense of moral revolution achieved in his life appeared in Ellis's writing: "I cannot see now a girl walking along the street with her free air, her unswathed limbs, her gay and scanty raiment, without being conscious of a thrill of joy in the presence of a symbol of life that in my youth was unknown"' (Brome 1979: 235).

Anthropology was, then, an acknowledged pillar of this wider questioning and subsequent transformation of 'Victorian morality', especially here sexual morality, but extending to kinship, as we saw at the beginning of this book: by the century's end, it was not just sex outside marriage that was unremarkable, but also being born outside of marriage. This distinction between what was previously termed 'legitimacy' and 'illegitimacy' is, by contrast, a point on which much turns in the Islamic legal debates we have been exploring. There has indeed been a moral revolution in the West in the past century, and anthropology has been a foot soldier in that revolution. Mead was but extending the Boasian programme of freeing Western civilization from its prejudices (Hatch 1983), a programme that, again, can be seen to have continued to run through anthropology right up to the feminist anthropology and 'new kinship' of today, where it has an interest in 'defamiliarizing the "natural"' (see Chapter 1). As Carsten (2004: 25) reminds us: 'In the past it appeared that the myriad examples of how "they do things differently there" might promote new ways of understanding – and even perhaps new ways of doing – in the West' – hence, perhaps, 'the tendency in anthropology … to concentrate on the seemingly exotic and bizarre' (Carsten 1997: 22).

But paradoxically hence also perhaps the present turn to 'anthropology at home', of which the studies of assisted reproduction in Britain and North America, for example, are notable examples. Firchow (1984: 90), in a literary critical commentary on *Brave new world*, comments on Huxley's use of anthropology cited above that Mead and Malinowski's 'savage' examples are supposed to be seen as 'among the new world's models of nonrepressive and sexually liberated groups. The new world state … is moving not so much into the future as into … the savage past.' Let us cast a glance further back still, to the Victorian perspective. Here is J.F. McLennan's (1970 [1865]: 6) nineteenth-century programme for anthropology:

For the features of primitive life, we must look, not to tribes of the Kirghiz type, but to those of Central Africa, the wilds of America, the hills of India, and the islands of the Pacific; with some of whom we find marriage laws unknown, the family system undeveloped, and even the only acknowledged blood-relationship that through mothers. These facts of today are, in a sense, the most ancient history. In the sciences of law and society, old means not old in chronology, but in structure: that is most archaic which lies nearest to the beginning of human progress considered as a development, and that is most modern which is farthest removed from that beginning.[7]

Indeed, 'tribes of the Kirghiz type' have not been central to anthropological discourse, which has, as McLennan predicted, focused largely on Africa, the Americas, India and Melanesia. But, in what he would no doubt find some sort of bizarre evolutionary full circle, the features that McLennan sees as commending the study of 'primitive' regions – the lack of marriage, family and paternal relations – are precisely those that many in the Islamic world, for instance, would see as typifying the modern Western social condition. And as we have seen with regard to the new kinship studies, where Western anthropologists have been able to find the 'unconventional' at home, they have celebrated it; indeed, according to Patterson (2005: 7), such home-grown examples have allowed these new kinship studies of the West to 'have claimed the moral heartland of this renaissance [in kinship studies], policing the boundaries for signs of incursion from the exoticism of the "classic" past.'[8]

Sexual morality and Islamic polemic

Such moral reform and questioning of received moral categories is not confined to Britain or 'the West', which are in themselves far from settled or homogeneous in this regard.[9] As we noted in passing in Chapter 2, the twentieth century saw a global wave of legal reform that included many of the countries of the Middle East, where law codes were introduced instituting radical and progressive changes with regard to the laws of marriage and divorce, for example, while utilizing the language and heritage of the shariah in an attempt to legitimize those changes (Anderson 1976; Mayer 1995): in many Middle Eastern countries, women's power to initiate divorce has been much increased and men's right to polygyny removed or restricted. Nevertheless, these reforms were instituted by political elites widely perceived as lacking in legitimacy, and calls for their repeal or reform have been a common popularist strategy on the part of Islamizing movements and regimes, such as the Muslim Brotherhood in

Egypt or the Islamic Revolution in Iran, for example. Women's rights and sexual freedoms including those of homosexuals, for instance, have become heavily politicized issues of domestic and global politics, most especially in the context of the latest round of tension and conflict between the United States and Europe, on the one hand, and many predominantly Muslim states on the other.

To move to a common strand of popular (especially Muslim) discourse in Lebanon and the wider region, which would no doubt find a sympathetic audience in some quarters of Western opinion too, 'in the West [*bi-l-gharb*], there are no morals [*mā fī akhlāq*]', that is, sexual morality.[10] Girls just have sex as they like. There is, allegedly, freedom in such matters: people do whatever they want without restraint. Were a similar freedom to be instituted 'in the East', the restrictions of morality removed, then people 'would be screwing in the street', as one young male friend put it to me. In the West, once a daughter or sister reaches eighteen then there is nothing that the male relative can say or do to compel her to follow a proper course of sexual conduct: 'She could have sex with her boyfriend in front of you and you could do nothing about it, right?' This lack of sexual morality leads to a lack of concern as to the 'cleanliness' of the bonds of kinship (*nasab*) – a husband has no reason to think his wife faithful, and thus does not know if 'his' children are 'really his', thus does not interest himself much in them, thus the break-up of the family. 'How can you be surprised at the abuses perpetrated by Americans at Abu Ghraib prison – all Americans are bastards,' born out of wedlock that is, and thus lacking in 'morals', I was told at the time of the scandal over the treatment of Iraqi prisoners in Iraq. While the 'Western' and 'Eastern' social systems are seen to be broadly identical, founded on the family, the West has degenerated: the family, and hence society, have broken down, fragmented. When a child turns eighteen in the West, so this discourse proceeds, they will leave home and then never get in touch with their parents again. Lebanese society, by contrast, is notionally one of strong social, and particularly family, relations.

To quote a specifically Islamic source, one from our earlier study of the debates over assisted reproduction, the Syrian Shaykh 'Abd al-Hamid Tuhmaz (1987: 41), for instance, writes that:

> The more a person's faith in God, praise and glorify Him, increases, so are their feelings of fatherhood and motherhood stronger ... Thus it is that we see that the unbelievers are characterized by the harshness of their hearts and the dullness of the feelings of humanity in their souls. No wonder then that we see them cutting the ties of kin-

ship [*yaqta'ān arhām-hum*][11] and abandoning their children and their flesh and blood [*filadhāt akbād-hum*] for the sake of their worldly delights and bodily pleasures. The severing of kinship and dissolution of the family have become the foremost of the traits prominent in their social lives.

This is a key theme of Islamic polemic, with a sharp edge: more than mere competition for self-satisfaction, this intercivilizational moral comparison is a ubiquitous modality of the political struggle that rages over the wider Middle East, that leads conversely, for instance, Hollywood celebrities to clamour for military intervention against 'gender apartheid in Afghanistan' (Hirschkind and Mahmood 2002: 340). And lending this theme a real urgency are the perception that such moral depravity is spreading, via television and Internet pornography, and a strong undercurrent of frustration. 'Marry them young', advised the Prophet, but the financial demands placed upon a man seeking marriage, in the context of a dire economic situation in Lebanon at least, are often too onerous for that. While the Prophet also declared that 'marriage is half of one's religion' and 'there is no monasticism in Islam', a generation of young Muslim men has been forced into chastity by a combination of unemployment and escalating expectations, where they have not wholeheartedly embraced 'the new morality' themselves in Beirut's teeming nightclubs and bars. We might also remember that the kinds of assumptions that are being made about 'morals' here are not just confined to Islamic specialist or lay Muslim discourse. The Christian doctor who yearned for some form of regulation 'like the [British] HFEA' (see Chapter 5) also left Britain for the sake of his young children: 'There's too much drugs and early sex there.' Sexual morality ran as a theme throughout the Islamic legal debates over assisted reproduction, but also throughout the doctors' accounts of the shared assumptions that Lebanese of all religious communities bring to the practice of fertility treatment, even if Lebanon is more 'liberal' in these regards than most countries in the region.

To exploit the more 'exotic' portions of my ethnography here then – the use of donor gametes, for instance – as examples in order to 'defamiliarize the "natural"' in Western kinship thinking, would seem rather to run against the grain of history. Indeed it would be not just analytically problematic but politically perverse: Islamic writers and politicians are, broadly speaking, pitting themselves against the perceived moral 'degeneracy' of the West, where traditional categories have been 'rethought', as anthropological diction would have it, or even abandoned in some cases, and they feel themselves under moralizing intellectual attack in turn, from feminists and advocates of liberal sexual values: contemporary 'liberal' rhetoric frequently tends towards the didactic, not to say authoritarian.

This liberal critique has strong indigenous roots – the liberal reform agenda is not just a tool of Western imperialism, as some of its opponents would claim – and has become part of the terms of Islamic debate. A burgeoning literature has documented the 'alternative modernities' of reformist Islam generally (e.g. al-Azmeh 1993; Salvatore 1997; Adelkhah 1999; Eickelman 2000), and with regard to feminism in particular (e.g. Abu-Lughod 1998; Mahmood 2005). But where Islamic legal specialists do surprise in allowing some of the more controversial possibilities offered by assisted reproduction, they can hardly be assumed to be engaged in the sorts of projects and interests I have sketched out for the 'liberal West' here. What such examples put under the spotlight, then, is more the ready opposition between 'Islamic' and 'liberal' values itself, the moralizing geography – subscribed to by polemicists on both 'sides' – that has 'Islam' and 'the West' camped on the same plain, albeit on different parts of the battlefield. Further, just as 'the West' is hardly homogeneous in its attitudes towards such issues as those we have been discussing here, so the category 'Islam' contains a multiplicity of different currents and tendencies. We need to think through the Islamic legal examples we have encountered here in their own terms.

Islamic activism, contemporaneity and open-mindedness

If we may return, then, to the Islamic legal reactions to the new reproductive technologies, our primary focus, we might recall again that many of those opinions are surprisingly unrestrictive, notably among the Shiite positions and especially those of Ayatollah Khamene'i, who allows donor insemination, surrogacy arrangements and postmortem gamete use; other authorities allow egg donation. Where it is also stipulated that relatedness is to follow genetic lines, new and complex patterns of relation arise where the child will be related to the gamete donor rather than the recipient, although to what extent such authorities have considered the ramifications of these rulings for kinship practice is debatable (as Tremayne [2006] observes). This is not the only area where Islamic authorities surprise. Much was recently made in the global media of the situation of transsexuals in Shiite Iran, where the path for allowing sex-change operations was opened by Ayatollah Khomeini more than

forty years ago, although wider Iranian society seems less accepting
(Tremayne 2006).

Is this then an Islamic 'brave new world' dissolving traditional
moral concepts, or a glimpse of 'liberal Islam' in action? The Muslim religious specialists and their followers I have worked with here
would hardly relish a comparison of their own projects with Huxley's enduring caricature of Western moral failure, a world where
traditional relations, especially the family, have been swept aside in
the name of progress, and where sexual promiscuity is mandatory
while reproduction is mechanized. Quite the contrary, as we have
noted, Islamic discourse, if one may generalize, is rather one of
steadfast resistance in the face of a perceived imperialistic Western
moral and sexual revolution. Nor are 'liberal values' the right prism
through which to view such Islamic legal opinion. Ayatollah
Khamene'i (let alone Ayatollah Khomeini) can hardly be perceived
as having liberal leanings. Even within the terms of Iranian clerical
politics he stands at the head of conservatism rather than with the
'reformists'. And yet as regards assisted reproduction, his stance is
almost uniquely unrestrictive, scandalously so by some lights.

But in any case, no one who takes seriously the notion of a true,
good path through life, demanded by God, revealed to the Prophet
and transmitted through a clerical elite, can be characterized in such
terms. What is at stake is right knowledge of God's standards, and
Islamic legal scholarship must demonstrate its continuing relevance
in an ever-changing world in this regard: religious authorities such
as Khamene'i argue from within their tradition and not for liberation
from its toils. Rather than 'rethinking' traditional categories, Islamic
thinkers have approached these new problems by thinking through
them: assisted reproduction is discussed in terms of *nasab* (filiation),
zinā (illicit sexual intercourse, 'adultery'), legitimate and illegitimate
(*shar'ī* and *ghayr shar'ī*) relations, foundlings, bastards and milk
kinship. The Islamic legal heritage is brought to bear for precedents
regarding assisted reproduction: artificial insemination has its precedents in classical jurisprudence in the case of the wife who inserts
her husband's semen into her vagina, or transfers it to her lesbian
lover (see Chapters 3 and 4); cloning can be thought through in
terms of the precedents of Jesus, born without a father just as the
clone of a woman would be (Hakim 2001: 19; Sistani 2004: 421), or
Eve, created from Adam's rib (Sistani 2004: 417).

Rather than 'liberal', then, a shaykh sympathetic to the travails of
the faithful and accommodating of their needs might be more read-

ily characterized as 'understanding' (*fahmān*) or 'open-minded' (*munfattih*). A shaykh who is open to the real-life issues facing Muslims in the contemporary world, rather than one who lives in the seminary through texts alone, can 'keep up with the times' (*yuwākib al-'asr*), rather than being 'stuck in the past' (*mutamassik bi-l-mādī*).[12] If I may focus on Shiite jurisprudence a little longer, as we discussed in Chapter 2, Shiites take great pride in the adaptability of their religion: as it is commonly phrased, Shiite authorities 'have *ijtihād*', the power of independent legal reasoning allegedly more restricted in the case of Sunni jurisprudence, although one Sunni judge remarked to me that '[w]e are much-maligned in this respect', and there are similarly progressive elements within Sunnism.[13] As a doctor working in the mainly Shiite south of Lebanon put it:

> There is a religious atmosphere here in the South. And religion enters clearly into matters of gynaecology and sex. But the door of independent reason [*ijtihād*] is open for the Shia. I've lived in France: I can see that the Shia are really open-minded regarding sex. Take temporary marriage for example. If a woman is a widow or divorced,[14] she can make a contract, just like a boyfriend or girlfriend in France, and just agree to have sex. Contraception, the coil for example, is allowed. Abortion: there are a number of fatwas that say at seven weeks you get a heartbeat, before then some say it's allowed. Human cloning for us is allowed, by Sayyid Fadlallah for example. In South Lebanon most people follow the shaykhs: they want to have a fatwa. Okay, there are people who aren't concerned with fatwas: they're the ones who don't accept donor insemination. After all even in France it's known that there can be psychological problems with donor insemination. Here there's no psychological problem because the man depends on the fatwa. If God says okay then that's it.

Freedom, here from anxiety, comes through following rules rather than abandoning them, 'escaping every bond' (Fadlallah cited in Hamiyah 2004: 105); what is at stake is whether or not the rules can 'keep up with the times'. The doctor cites the distinctively Shiite institution of temporary marriage, a contract permitting sexual relations during a defined time period, with fewer rights and obligations than permanent marriage. As Shahla Haeri (1989: 160) reports in her account of temporary marriage in Iran, Iranian Revolutionary clerics promoted the institution as a means of allowing the young, especially students, to overcome the distractions of sexual frustration without falling into sin. Ironically, as Haeri describes, they cited as evidence of the excellence of the institution and thus Islam itself the very work of Bertrand Russell that we alluded to earlier. In *Marriage and morals*, Russell (1929: 125) meditates on the new sexual freedom of the youth of his day, especially prominent in America 'owing, I think, to Prohibition and automobiles', and quotes with approval one Judge Ben B. Lindsey's proposal of a new institution of 'companionate marriage' for impoverished youths, under the terms of which the couple agree to defer having children, and are therefore given the best possible contraceptive advice, and divorce is possible by mutual consent and alimony not due (1929: 129ff.). This would, Russell notes, be particularly useful for students, who would benefit from freedom from 'the Dionysiac characteristics of their present sex relations' (1929: 130).[15] For the high-ranking Iranian officials Haeri interviewed, Russell had discovered this Islamic institution, transmitted it as a remedy for Western ills, and thus acknowledged the superiority of Islam. But the genealogies of rectitude have become somewhat confused here, for Russell was more a prophet of 'permissiveness' than piety, as we have seen.

The doctor singles out Ayatollah Fadlallah, here for his famously ready enthusiasm for research into human cloning (see Chapter 2). Another doctor, also working in the Shiite South, told me, in an interview in English, that:

> Independent people follow Fadlallah because he's more liberal [*sic*], not because he's Lebanese. He's good – I consider myself an atheist but I can use Fadlallah's opinion to help my patients. For example, a girl gets engaged [by signing an Islamic marriage contract, *'katab al-kitāb'*; customarily, marriage requires further celebrations], has sex with the boy and becomes a woman. Then he leaves her before they are married. Virginity is very important, but Fadlallah allows an operation to repair the hymen. So I have something to use in my consultations with such patients. I can talk to them armed with his opinion, because many people accept it. I can say, look he's a good man, a knowledgeable man, a respectable man.

Indeed, Sayyid Fadlallah does find hymen repair in such circumstances permissible. The notional problem here is that such an operation constitutes concealing or falsifying the truth to a new husband: one is affecting to be a virgin when one is not.[16] But, as a doctor noted in addressing the sayyid in the course of a celebrated lecture to the Middle East Hospital, Beirut, in some circumstances a doctor is forced to be guarded with the truth and repair the hymen, on account of the potentially mortal dangers the honour ethic poses for a woman in such difficulties. The sayyid agreed, noting the dangers that arise from what he terms 'the backward mentality that the woman bears responsibility for the honour of the family and the man does not', and assured the doctors assembled that they might carry out such operations with a calm heart (Fadlallah 1995: 6). Similar considerations apply with regard to abortion, which the sayyid also deems permissible in some such circumstances, where an illicit pregnancy constitutes a threat to the life of the mother (1995: 12–14).[17]

Fadlallah, who, as we have seen, is more cautious than Khamene'i in the matter of the use of donor sperm, forbidding it, is the one who has been more the focus of criticism within some Shiite circles for his lack of restriction in other areas. As I was told, unlike many authorities he does not prohibit all music or iconography and allows the use of playing cards without gambling, shaving where office regulations insist upon it and 'shaking hands with a Christian with wet hands', as one non-specialist put it to me – the putative danger being one of ritual pollution.[18] In fact, this latter insistence on the 'purity of the human being' irrespective of religious identity is considered by many, especially his followers in the West, to be his most progressive ruling of all, and it is linked to his broader concern with breaking down sectarian differences, much appreciated in Lebanon, although not by the wider Shiite clerical establishment (see Aziz 2001: 211). Clearly the boundaries fall in different places from those a 'Western' audience might expect, although the controversy that arose over Fadlallah's refusal to forbid female masturbation (see Chapter 4) is perhaps more easily assimilated to polemics against 'sexual permissiveness'. Sayyid Fadlallah's legal rulings regarding the status and freedom of women more generally are strikingly progressive, granting women the right to political participation and leadership, to sexual satisfaction within marriage and control over their own bodies with regard to birth control and pregnancy, and to work outside the marital home with or without their husbands' permission (Aziz 2001: 208–11; Hamiyah 2004: 73–169; Fadlallah 2005a).

Fadlallah, like the Iranian Islamic revolutionaries, espouses an activist, politically conscious vision of Islam, an 'Islamic liberation theology' that addresses the social injustice faced by the Lebanese Shiite community, Muslims more widely and the world's oppressed generally (Sankari 2005). As a functionary in the sayyid's offices noted in conversation with me: 'The Quran says that Islam is for every time and place [*li-kull 'asr wa makān*]. Keeping up with the times is a religious obligation [*wājib*]; that is why you have got movement in *ijtihād*. This is activist, conscious Islam [*al-islām al-harakī al-wā'ī*], not the Sufi Islam, which is withdrawn from the world, nor the tyrannical [*zālim*] Islam that says only we are right, and we will kill everyone else.' This engagement with the world and its contemporary problems and issues necessitates a willingness to use Shiite jurists' relative freedom to exercise their own independent reasoning (*ijtihād*) to the maximum.

The Lebanese Hezbollah, much influenced by Fadlallah as well as Iranian Islamist clerics and intellectuals, espouses similar attitudes, seeing the appropriation of 'techno-economic knowledge and scientific developments, which acquire legal justification in Shi'i society through the process of *ijtihād* ... as essential to revolutionary progress' (Abisaab 2006: 233), part of what Deeb (2006 *passim*) calls the 'enchanted modern' of the pious Shiite communities of Beirut's southern suburbs. Hezbollah's seminaries, according to Abisaab (2006: 249), place still greater emphasis on the 'rationalist' approach to Islamic jurisprudence than those of Iraq and Iran, and I have commonly heard it suggested that Lebanon's particularity, its diversity of religious communities and history of openness to the West, has led to an especially 'open-minded' perspective. Sayyid Fadlallah is most insistent on the importance of dialogue with 'the Other', vital in the context of Lebanon's confessional politics and the current global political crisis between 'the West' and 'Islam' (see e.g. Fadlallah 2005b; 2007: 35–47). This, then, is a particular type of Islam, although as we have seen, in the domain of medical ethics Islamic authorities more generally have been keen to react to these new possibilities and have certainly not ruled them out reflexively: almost all authorities, Sunni and Shiite, allow the use of techniques such as artificial insemination and in vitro fertilization, for example. And although Sayyid Sistani, for instance, is widely perceived as a more 'traditional' figure than Khamene'i or Fadlallah, he is by no means obviously much more restrictive in these matters.

Of course, one might nevertheless question how 'understanding' or 'open-minded' positions are when they allow fertility treatment so long as the woman's private parts are only seen and touched by her husband, or allow the use of donor gametes but not the claiming of parenthood to a resulting child. Much still remains to be negotiated: the extent to which a procedure is 'necessary', for example. Let us not forget, then, that process of negotiation, the flexibility and contextuality of Islamic legal opinion that we discussed earlier (Chapter 2): beyond the public pronouncements, the shaykhs well appreciate that particular circumstances dictate particular solutions. And such adaptation of 'rule' to circumstance is manifest in other Islamic legal modalities beyond 'activist Islam' – witness the tradition of 'legal ruses' (*hiyal shar'īyah*), here paralleled by the use of temporary marriage to validate egg donation, or milk kinship to render domestic relations more convenient by creating kinship-like relations between members of the same household. This is not 'new kinship' but a long-standing strategy, as shown by Haeri's (1989) work on temporary marriage in Iran, used to simplify travelling arrangements or neighbourly relations for groups of unrelated persons of mixed sex by creating kinship relationships between them, or Altorki's (1980) account of the similar uses made of milk kinship in Saudi Arabia (see Chapter 1, and see Khatib-Chahidi 1992 on Iran). These relations are chosen, 'elective', but not in contradistinction to those that are not. We are dealing, obviously enough, with very different patterns and ideologies of freedom and constraint from those envisaged by the liberal reformers of 'Victorian values' cited above, and thus, according to the genealogy I have laid out at least, from those assumed by the new kinship studies.

Substance and propriety

These patterns give nuance to the nominally 'scientific' kinship notions of modernity. Schneider (1980: 23) wrote of 'American kinship' that kinship is 'whatever the biogenetic relationship is', so that '[i]f science discovers new facts about biogenetic relationship, then that is what kinship is'. And the new kinship studies, one might note, are much concerned with this notional interest in 'biogenetics' found in the contemporary West. Strathern (1999b [1993]: 177) has an interesting comment with regard to her collaborators' ethnography of the sense British people are making of assisted reproduction: 'in thinking through the relational consequences of certain procreative possibilities, people may position the parties involved as though donors and recipients of gametes were instead partners to a sexual act. What seems at issue is less the propriety of the partners' actions than the consequences for the combination of substances' – that is, whether or not they are hazardously 'incestuous', according to the 'biological' vision whose genealogy Wolfram (1987) has described, as we saw in Chapter 1. Vice versa, in Islamic legal thought it is precisely the propriety of the actions that is most at issue, rather than the combination of substances.[19] First and foremost, for the Islamic legal specialists, kinship must formally be whatever God says it is, in the Quran and through the Prophet, although of course scientific advance offers challenges and opportunities here.[20] And in this tradition, sexual propriety is a material consideration with regard to kinship relation: *nasab* (filiation, 'consanguinity') is, in terms of classical Islamic law, legitimate relatedness specifically, dependent on being conceived and born within wedlock, not mere 'biogenetic' relatedness.

Given the vagaries of human life, *nasab* might sometimes be awarded by default to a child who is not the biological child: if a husband does not challenge the legitimacy of his wife's pregnancy, so long as it is delivered within certain credible time periods, then the child is his and cannot subsequently be denied.[21] But more importantly, as we have seen (Chapters 1 and 2), not all biological children are legitimate children: in classical Islamic law, the bastard is denied paternal relations by the Sunni schools, and both paternal and maternal relations in Shiite jurisprudence (Coulson 1971: 173; Kohlberg 1985: 245, 251–52); legitimacy is a material component of filiation. As Muslim intellectual Munawar Anees (1984: 116) has it, directly addressing the distinction between biological and social relatedness central to the 'new kinship' discussions: 'Islam, therefore, does not endorse parenthood as two distinct entities: biological and social – Muslim parenthood is biosocial.' With regard to assisted reproduction, then, while the realm of practice may be more complex again, on the ideological level there is a very pronounced concern for the movements and admixture of certain substances, specifically sperm and ova. But the problem at hand is whether the use of gametes from a man and a woman who are not married is like *zinā* or not: again, not a question of substance, but rather one of propriety.[22]

So in a way, the most radical move of all in the Islamic debates over assisted reproduction, it seems to me, is not so much that of authorities who allow some controversial procedures as that of those authorities, predominantly Shiite (see Chapter 4), who argue that whether or not donor procedures are permissible, subsequent children are legitimate and are the children of the gamete providers. Thus, whether or not their biological parents are married, they acquire *nasab* to both of them. It is only *zinā* proper that does not give rise to full *nasab* relations. In a case of donor insemination, *nasab* will be awarded to the biological and not the 'social' father (I apostrophize because there is no such term in the Islamic discourse). Still more strikingly, Ayatollah Sistani – again, who is usually considered a more 'traditional' figure than Khamene'i or Fadlallah, say, and who is not so sure that kinship relation follows 'biogenetic' lines in cases of egg donation or surrogacy arrangements – holds that:

Nasab has two types:

1. Legitimate [*shar'ī*], which results other than from *zinā*, whether the sex were permissible in itself or prohibited circumstantially, such as sex during the menstrual period, the act of worship or ritual purity for the Hajj, or otherwise, such as in ambiguous circumstances [*shubhah*], or through one of the methods other than sexual intercourse of fertilizing the woman with the man's semen.

2. Illegitimate [*ghayr shar'ī*], from *zinā* or *sifāh* [fornication].

Marriage prohibitions, like the rest of the rulings under the heading of *nasab* – except inheritance – include both types. (Sistani 2002, vol. 3: 38)

This is, to my mind, surprising, for the generally recognized Shiite position in the secondary literature is that there is no *nasab* relation at all established with a child of *zinā*, neither with the mother or father (see references cited above), even if classical opinion, Sunni and Shiite did not, by and large, view marriage with one's illegitimate daughter as permissible (Kohlberg 1985: 245–6; Salamah 1998: 170 ff.).[23] Sistani's son Sayyid Muhammad Rida Sistani (2004: 416) notes that that indeed is the most celebrated opinion, the consensus even: in his own comprehensive reading, he did not find a classical authority who differed, only some of the modern ones. Besides his father, he gives the example of Ayatollah Khu'i (d. 1992), whom, one might remember, Ayatollah Sistani is commonly considered to have 'succeeded'. Ayatollah Fadlallah, also a disciple of Khu'i, holds similar views: '*Nasab* is established by *zinā* just as it is established by legitimate filiation, and all the obligations of *nasab* are established by it: marriage prohibition, the right of guardianship and custody, the obligation of maintenance by the able party of the incapable, the tie of compassion [*silat al-rahim*], and the rest except inheritance' (2003, vol. 3: 522).[24] This is a relatively recent move, according to Muhammad Rida Sistani's account. Here, then, if anywhere, perhaps we do see an implied 'biologization' of kinship, or at least of the term *nasab* itself.

But we also get a sense of what that biologization would involve: not so much the suzerainty of scientific and medical notions as a downplaying of the consequences, for one's relationship to one's children, of the circumstances in which they were conceived. On this reading, what distinguishes the modern British approach, for example, is perhaps not so much the privileging of 'biogenetic' relatedness as the diminished salience of the quality of the social relation from which it issues. Legitimacy, the propriety or impropriety of the circumstances of one's birth, no longer has the same crucial importance as it once had, certainly in terms of the assumptions of wider society but also, gradually, in law: in the British case, it is not so much the scientific revolution that explains this as the sexual one.[25] One might further observe that the geneticization of identity allows a more profound separation between identity predicated upon the social relationship of birth – as in the Lebanese case, where one's state identity card stipulates one's parents' identity and, until recently, the quality of their social relationship in terms of the legitimacy or illegitimacy of one's birth (see Chapter 2) – and identity established between individual and state alone, characterized by full realization of individuality on the one hand, but also nakedness before the state on the other, requiring a stripping away of such intermediate relationships and institutions. Again, should this process reach its fullest fruition in Britain, scientific advance will have made it possible, but it will be a change in political culture that will have brought it about.

Paternity testing

These Shiite authorities are also ready to recognize medical paternity tests. In the cases of Ayatollahs Sistani and Fadlallah's legal compendia, such tests find their place as an addendum to the older methods of the legal tradition they are preserving and renewing. So Fadlallah (2003, vol. 3: 524–26) addresses the difficult question of assigning paternity where a woman has had sex with more than one man in recent times: in a case of divorce and remarriage, then one can look to the timing of the delivery of the child to see whom it would most plausibly be related to; if both men could be the father then they must draw lots. On the other hand, if she is under the guardianship of her husband and has committed *zinā*, then lots are not to be drawn. Rather, the child is related to the husband because it is born in his 'marriage bed', following, one assumes, the Prophetic saying 'the child is to the marriage bed, and to the adulterer the stone' (*al-walad li-l-firāsh wa-li-l-'āhir al-hajr*, see Chapters 1 and 3).[26] If she does not have a husband then lots are drawn, as they are also if the children of two wives became mixed up: 'All of the above is where there is no other easy and decisive way to remove the problem and doubt. So if it is correct what scientists say, that there are exact medical tests that can bring certainty regarding the filiation of the child to the father, it is obligatory to use them, go by their results and abandon the previously stated ways. And were the child related to a man relying on one of those latter, and then a test revealed it were not his child, then one should follow the medical test' (2003, vol. 3: 526). Also, a husband cannot deny his wife's child *nasab* if it is established that the child is his through a medical test (2003, vol. 3: 520).[27]

Let us note, however, that the circumstances Fadlallah is addressing in the latter case are exceptional: ordinarily a positive genetic test will not be sufficient to establish full *nasab*, as that will require proof of marriage.[28] Generally speaking, full legitimate kinship relation cannot be awarded or denied by genetic test alone. This would seem to be the majority Islamic legal position. The fatwa-issuing council of the Mecca-based (Sunni) Muslim World League, for example, issued a resolution that although genetic fingerprinting is acknowledged to be almost infallible and is undoubtedly of use in criminal investigations, it cannot be relied upon in matters of *nasab*, either to prove the soundness of claims of relatedness or their falsehood, for there what is at stake is 'protection of people's honour and care for their kinship relations' (al-Majma' al-Fiqhi al-Islami 2007b [2002]: 343–44). The classical criteria must still be applied: a child born to a married couple is that of the husband and wife, unless the husband repudiates wife and child (Eich 2005: 104ff.).[29] Islamic thinkers know that you cannot reduce kinship to genes. Such a reduction would seem to be the radical conclusion of 'the West', or at least the West of much anthropological analysis.

Nevertheless, throughout the region, as in Europe and North America, there is an impetus on the part of the civil legal establishment towards legal reform in these matters that takes scientific advance into account. Eich (2005: 107) cites the example of Tunisia, where despite a lack of support from the National Fatwa Institution, laws were passed in 1992 and 2003 stating that paternity can be proved through genetic testing and the father would then be liable for maintenance. Lebanese civil courts have also accepted the use of genetic testing as a way of establishing paternity, following a precedent set in French law for recognizing the child of *concubinage* (*musākinah* in Arabic translation) by means of such a device, as documented for example in a case in the journal of the Lebanese Bar Association (Ghassoub 2000). The commentator notes that '[t]he tie of blood must give rise to a legal tie', any other choice or intention notwithstanding (2000: 550), and quotes a French authority to the effect that the day that there is a definite scientific proof of paternity, then most of the legislation previously put in place will lose its utility: the law must be reformed.[30] But 'biological' (2000: 551) 'children of *concubinage*' have no place in the explicitly Islamic contexts I have experience of, except as an embarrassment. Such medical tests for relatedness are available in Lebanon: officially, mandated by court orders, and unofficially, for private purposes, as I will describe shortly. Nevertheless, the Islamic judges, Sunni and Shiite, whom I spoke to in Lebanon concerning this matter were most reluctant to admit a decisive role for this new evidentiary resource. One Sunni judge told me that

> If we get a case of establishing relation [*ithbāt al-nasab*], we just look for proof of marriage and the timing of the delivery.[31] 'The child to the marriage bed' [*al-walad li-l-firāsh*, see above] – this opposes the DNA test. We always look to the interests of the child and not the parents. There has to be another father. There's no textual evidence that could be used for the DNA tests. In any case, DNA isn't 100 per cent accurate, right? We just judge here and now. That doesn't mean the matter is over – it's in the hereafter.

This is borne out by examples in a compilation of cases recorded in the Sunni courts (Homsi 2003).[32] In one instance (Homsi 2003: 116–18), from the court of Tyre in 1994, a woman sued to establish the *nasab* relation of her child to a man: medical tests confirmed that the child was his, but it was clear that the child had been conceived outside of wedlock, and the case was rejected. A distinguished Shiite jurist, adviser to the Shiite high court, told me of a similar scenario where a woman had brought a case against a man, claiming that he was the father of her child, now grown to a young man, but she had no proof that they had been married. My informant had been struck by the astonishing resemblance between the youth and his alleged father, and had suggested they have recourse to a DNA test, but his colleagues refused on the grounds that such a test cannot be absolutely certain, despite the rulings of some of the distinguished Shiite authorities cited above.

Another Sunni judge told me about a case of adoption, nominally prohibited under Islamic law as we have seen (Chapter 2), which sums up what is at stake: 'A man took in a girl and registered her in his name. Then he wanted to marry her. "I lied, she's not my daughter," he told me. No way! In such cases, we go for what's on the surface [*al-zāhir*], not what's behind it [*al-bātin*]. She stays his daughter.'[33] As we are reminded by the reference to people's 'honour' (there, *'ird*) in the Muslim World League's resolution cited above, what mere 'biogenetic' readings of kinship would strip away is not just the consideration of the propriety of a child's origins, but also the assumption of their propriety, the consideration of privacy privileged in the Lebanese contexts we discussed with regard to fertility treatment. Nowadays, however, technology allows one to see much more of what might have once stayed hidden, and which, for this judge at least, would better stay hidden. Paternity testing – the crudest expression of a reduction of kinship to biology – threatens an entire realm of privacy and never knowing about the secrets of sexual and social life. As renowned Sunni jurist Shaykh Yusuf al-Qaradawi (cited Khushn 2007: 282) has it, were such tests to be allowed, they could only be used by wives to prove their innocence and not by husbands to accuse their wives of infidelity: the classical Islamic legal institution of 'repudiation' (*li'ān*) allows for the latter, while also giving the wife and her child the 'veil' or 'cover' (*satr*) of her being able to swear her innocence, even as she is formally parted from her husband.

So in another case from the Sunni appeals court of Lebanon in 1999 (Homsi 2003: 120–21), where a man asked leave to test his genetic relation to his daughter on the grounds that, as a result of his wife's behaviour, he had come to have doubts in this respect and wanted to put them to rest, the court was firm in its refusal. Such tests are not considered grounds for either establishing or refuting the ascription of *nasab*, 'as has been the reasoning [*ijtihād*] of this high court in many similar cases', and 'supposition [*zinn*] in such a topic does not safeguard the dignity [*karāmah*], future and reputation [*sum'ah*] of the young girl, as the appellant claims, but rather does her wrong and harm [*yusī' ilay-hā wa-yajnī 'alay-hā*], especially as her *nasab* from him and her mother is established by sound, legal contract' (2003: 121). Conversely, in another case (in Tripoli in 1989), the plaintiffs, who were siblings, sought to establish their relation to a man they claimed was their father by establishing his marriage to their mother some thirty years ago, for 'establishing marriage is a means to establish *nasab* ... even a legal ruse [*hīlah*] for doing so when the child is of unknown provenance, due to the bearing of the matter on the humanity of the person and his dignity and respect'. For this the witness of those that had heard the couple were married at the time was deemed sufficient, 'as kinship and marriage are not such as many can see with their own eyes that they obtain, and repute [*shuhrah*] substitutes for eye-witness' here; 'on this

were resolved our venerable forefathers since the dawn of Islam until our own days, and the practice [*'urf*] has endured' (2003: 112). In
another, similar case (in Beirut in 1988), the judges note that for
marriage to be justly assumed, it is enough to see a man go inside
with a woman and hear from people that she is his wife, or see a man
and a woman living together in the same house and enjoying one another's company (2003: 111). One assumes the best, not the worst.

Nevertheless, medical paternity testing is, as we have noted, available in Lebanon, and I spoke to Lebanon's leading practitioner of genetic testing, a relatively recent phenomenon, as well as another
doctor who had long experience of HLA (Human Leukocyte Antigens) testing.[34] Both the doctors had apparently been called upon by
the courts, both civil and religious, including Islamic courts despite
the reservations cited above, and both also reported being approached by private individuals asking for their services.[35] In the vast
majority of cases, as I was told, people were not necessarily seeking
out these tests to establish someone's social identity: it seemed the
tests most readily suggested a litmus test of sexual morality, to prove
or disprove infidelity, with all the unpleasant and indeed potentially
violent consequences that this might entail.[36] The doctor carrying out
genetic tests told me: 'I stopped doing it because it's a headache in
Lebanon – there's no proper recourse after. You don't know what this
guy's going to do to his wife and kids.' The HLA tester also was
against letting this genie out of the bottle:

> I was amazed by the number of tests. Before, I was doing it in
> Canada, where morals are supposedly 'loose', you have common
> wives and so on. You would expect a higher rate of requests of pater
> nity tests. No way: it's much more here. The social array is a macro
> array – you have super-rich, middle classes, and poor. People from
> all religions were involved, Christians and Muslims. But we don't
> do it because of the issues involved: 'I don't want to use it against
> my wife', the husband says, but you know he might. It would jeop
> ardize the family structure. The usual pattern in these requests is: 'I
> just want to confirm things. I'm not sure. I don't doubt my wife to
> tally, but I just want to make sure...' Usually, in 85–90 per cent of
> cases, it's a moral thing – i.e. adultery. The husband makes a claim.
> So, for example, the husband says he has no sperm. 'So it can't be
> mine', he argues. I had such a case – the man brought a paper to prove
> he's infertile. In one case, the husband wouldn't give a sample – he
> was just accusing his wife. The wife went for the court order to prove
> it was his child. The husband said, 'No, she committed adultery' –
> he didn't want to take the consequences of his allegation.

This use of the test as some kind of 'morality' indicator clearly irritated the doctor who had specialized in genetic testing: 'Are these "moral" questions? I hardly think it's moral – it's about getting revenge. 80–90 per cent of husbands who accused their wives were wrong anyway.' Conversely, women can use it to prove their own virtue:

> I had another case: a woman came and said, 'I want a paternity test. This is my husband.' He was so blasé about it. It's very difficult because you can't ask too many questions. 'I want to do this for this child and for every subsequent child,' the wife said. 'Do you really want this test', I asked, 'do you know what it's for?' 'Yes, I want to show him that it's his child.' He came six months later and said, 'We confused you I know, let me explain.' He had really annoyed her, made some remarks about not trusting her, and she wanted to get back at him.

More than being about relationships between parents and children, it seems here, matters of biological relatedness are about relationships between men and women, the trust between them, and their claims to being genuinely moral persons.[37] To grant the possibility of testing those claims 'scientifically' is, as those judges and religious bodies who were wary of doing so suggested, a mixed blessing.

Conclusion: What the neighbours say

We have covered a good deal of ground, from anthropological reactions to new reproductive technologies and anthropological interest in moral renewal and revolution more broadly, through notions of kinship in the Middle East, the Lebanese legal system and the place of adoption within it, and on to Islamic legal debates over assisted reproduction and the geneticization of relatedness, their place in Lebanese medical practice and the political projects within which some of these religious thinkers are working. But some key points have, I hope, become clear.

First of all, Islamic legal specialists have thoroughly debated the possibilities and ramifications of the new reproductive technologies such as in vitro fertilization. The consensus is that such techniques are to be welcomed as a boon for those suffering from infertility. Where the procedures involved take place within certain boundaries, namely that they involve husband and wife alone and that the otherwise problematic exposing of the private parts required is warranted by the necessity of such a procedure to overcome the real distress of childlessness, then nearly all are agreed that they are permissible. Controversy arises over procedures involving parties other than a husband and a wife, as in the use of donor sperm and eggs and surrogacy arrangements. Specifically, can these be assimilated to illicit sexual relations? And what is the status of resulting children? Here opinion is divided, and the consensus among Sunni authorities, who are the majority in global terms, is that such procedures should not be allowed and resulting children may be seen as illegitimate. Some Shiite authorities do allow some procedures, especially those involving two women, as in egg donation and surrogacy arrangements, where it is commonly stipulated that the husband be married to both women, Islamic law allowing polygyny. Such a marriage with an egg donor, for example, could be temporary, as Shiite law allows such unions for a defined period of time. Shiite authorities frequently find children resulting from all such procedures as legitimate: only sexual intercourse proper outside of marriage results in the status of bastardy, which has its own peculiar concomitant rulings, most importantly the denial of rights of inheritance.

These are arguments as to sexual propriety, and consideration of medical accounts of the practice of assisted reproduction in Lebanon shows that such propriety is a very real concern for patients from all religious communities. Confidentiality, or respect for privacy and the intimate sphere, is also of vital importance. This respect for the distinction between public image and private life and for the propriety of actions according to religious and other precepts, taken together with the importance of legitimacy of birth in the Islamic legal notions of kinship we have considered, makes for an informative contrast with central themes of the 'new kinship studies' within recent anthropology that were the initial stimulus for this research. These studies take up a perceived tension within 'Euro-American' kinship thinking between the supposed fixity of 'natural' kinship relations, now construed as 'biogenetic relatedness', and the role of 'culture' or, latterly, 'choice', and have sought to document instances of challenge of the former and privileging of the latter. I have taken this approach as a part of the broader 'liberal' tradition of challenge of received moral wisdom that has helped transform attitudes to sexuality and kinship in many Western countries and beyond. 'Legitimacy' has here faded from relevance, which might, I hazard, in itself help explain the prominence of the biogenetic.

This liberal stance of questioning traditional moral categories, which has some sway in Lebanon, is seen as a direct challenge by Islamic legal authorities, many of whom nevertheless seek to preserve their own tradition while 'keeping up with the times', a project that some commentators have seen as an 'alternative modernity' to that of the liberal West.[38] Faced with new challenges such as these, Islamic thinkers, especially those in the vanguard of reformist Islam, search for new ways to preserve rectitude. Where Islamic legal rulings are perhaps surprisingly unrestrictive, then, this lack of restriction needs to be understood within that broader context, and not according to liberal precepts, as 'liberal Islam', for instance. Nevertheless, these religious rulings may – just like the cutting edge of 'liberal' opinion – be in advance of the notions of society at large. Where their solutions have testing implications for their followers, as in those Shiite positions that allow the use of donor gametes on the condition that a novel, socially problematic set of relationships is honoured, then, as a pious Shiite doctor affiliated to Hezbollah remarked to me, 'religion doesn't concern itself with what the neighbours say'. The audience that matters is God. What is right is right whatever anyone else might think: 'and here is the fatwa to prove it', as the surrogate mother, descendant of the Prophet, told the shocked doctor we heard from in the previous chapter.

But in practice more generally, as far as the Lebanese accounts I have related here are concerned at any rate, even where one has religious permission to undertake such controversial procedures, one may prefer not to advertise that fact, and that wish for privacy is more or less respected. We saw something of what might be at stake in the discussions surrounding paternity testing above. This is not just the difference between doctrine and practice: while, formally speaking, Islam is an explicitly moralizing tradition – it is incumbent on a Muslim to 'command right and forbid wrong' upon his or her fellow Muslims – there are equally elements of that tradition that enjoin the respect of the right of others to an intimate, private space, as well as a public face.[39] As soon as a wrong becomes explicit and inevitable, it must be censured: until then, God knows best. The shaykhs, as we have seen, well know that life does not always correspond to the ideal, but one does not lightly seek openly to overturn the public face of things, and that circumspection includes matters of kinship. Here again, then, one might note, is reason not to seize upon such examples as demonstrating how the 'given' in kinship is not so given after all: such cases are often, according to local notions of privacy, best left well alone. Should the sympathetic writer cover up the whole matter, as do his or her informants? But this would be not only to obliterate an entire realm of ethnography, but also to lose sight of the core principle in which the problem is rooted: the distinction between the public, surface world and the hidden world of private concerns and domestic intimacy – although that distinction is, in the field of kinship as in others, sorely challenged by the sheer perspicacity of the modern medical gaze, as we have seen.

The liberal tradition has, historically, had a similar interest in preserving such private spaces, although, in an age of public confession and reality television, they seem to have become significantly eroded, or at the very least fundamentally reconstructed. Russell and Ellis sought to sweep away the 'hypocrisy' of 'Victorian morality', but while the content of generally received moral wisdom and political rectitude may indeed have changed, the appetite of some for prurience, moralizing and censure has hardly diminished, and the capabilities for observation, 'outing' and ruin at the disposal of the 'unwanted gaze' (Rosen 2000) of the media and the state have become nigh irresistible.[40] The liberality of the contemporary 'liberal West' in such respects frequently seems questionable.

Differences aside, then, both the refractions of the liberal tradition and those of Islamic discourse that I have been working with here may give cover for individuals seeking to pursue courses of action that challenge social convention. However, in practice people in Lebanon, whether pious or liberal one would hazard, value the room to manoeuvre that is afforded by respect for – or a certain generosity regarding – a realm of private concerns away from public image, rather than a collapse of the distinction between the two. This is, I would suggest, no less the case in 'liberal', British contexts, for instance, although that private space cannot be taken for granted, indeed is under threat. With regard to our interest in kinship studies specifically, we have finished by moving beyond 'defamiliarizing the "natural"' to perceiving and interrogating the very particularity of collapsing intellectual and moral debates over kinship into a dialectic between 'biology' and 'choice', no less specific than their collapse into one of propriety versus impropriety. It is in these wider patterns and ideologies of freedom and constraint, I suggest, that the crucial comparative issues lie. So, for instance, one, 'liberal' constellation (that which I have presented here as underpinning the assumptions and interests of the 'new kinship studies') holds that freedom lies in seeing the possibility of transcending physically determined identity and the moral constraints it is supposed to entail, and embracing others through exercise of the will alone; another, 'pious' complex (the liberation theology of Sayyid Fadlallah and sections of the Lebanese Shiite population affiliated with Hezbollah) sees it in the possibility of transcending the mundane (social injustice, but also 'the neighbours') through the embrace of an ever-renewed moral legislation that ensures both one's propriety and one's salvation. They draw on shared historical contexts and currents, address similar issues and turn on similar problems; they also share a certain impatience with the great social hinterland of private compromise, even if their revolutionary sallies against it take very different forms. They are related, although it is for their respective advocates to choose whether to see what lies between them as kinship, alliance or estrangement.

Notes

1. Clearly the liberal tradition is manifold and deeply contested: liberal economic policy, liberal political modalities and sexual liberty, for instance, need hardly come altogether or simultaneously. Britain, the U.S. and France, to take just three examples, have very different histories in this regard. But these elements have been historically interrelated, even if each was fiercely fought over. Further, that history is ongoing: I do not, for instance, imagine the liberal thought of Bertrand Russell and that on which I see the new kinship studies as premised to be identical, even if I classify them together genealogically. Here is not the place to explore these issues in full; my argument should nevertheless be clear enough.

2. For pertinent anthropological examples see e.g. Carsten (2004: 7), Simpson (2004c) and Inhorn (2005).

3. The controversy Russell raised with this and subsequent attacks on traditional morality drove him from his chair in philosophy at the City College New York, with the Bishop of New York declaring him a 'recognised propagandist against both religion and morality', and a man who 'specifically defends adultery', and a hounding lawyer branding his works 'lecherous, lustful, venerous, erotomaniac, aphrodisiac, irreverent, narrow-minded, untruthful and bereft of moral fibre' and their author a nudist who 'winks at homosexualism' (Moorehead 1992: 431–32).

4. 'Three books especially – *Sex and repression in savage society*, *The father in primitive psychology,* and *The sexual life of savages in North-Western Melanesia* are quite indispensable' (Russell 1929: 20).

5. Mead's publisher was of course delighted to receive endorsement from such distinguished figures, writing to her that '[i]t was great good luck to receive, on the same day, the wonderful letters from Havelock Ellis and Dr. Malinowski. We almost staged a celebration when we read them. We got out a bright red band to put around the book with part of Havelock Ellis's comment on the front. That stunt helped the sales materially' (Howard 1984: 127).

6. The respect was reciprocated: Malinowski wrote that he 'always admired and revered' the work of Havelock Ellis, and considered himself his 'pupil and follower' (Malinowski 1929b: xxiii, 1927: viii; and see also Malinowski 1929a). 'We may note that the primitive, for the *moderne,* was seen as unhypocritical, in touch with the natural, and at home with the erotic. It is no surprise therefore that ... *The Sexual Life of Savages* was the work by which Malinowski became most widely known among the lay adherents of the *moderne*' (Ardener 2007 [1985]: 203).

7. It was Paul Dresch who brought this quote, and much else, to my attention.

8. But compare, for instance, Carsten's (2000a, 2004) cross-cultural comparative project.

9. It is perhaps worth recalling that, in the 1920s, the new morality seemed to have reached its apogee in Soviet Russia: Huxley, for instance, remarked of what he called 'moral flat racing' that '[t]he flattest racing in the world, at any rate in the sphere of sexual relationships, is modern Russian racing' (cited in Firchow 1984: 50, 98). Atheist communism has also been one of the enduring targets of Islamist polemic.

10. Geert van Gelder has commented to me that this use of *akhlāq* appears unusual to him as a scholar of classical Islam: *akhlāq* would more commonly refer in such a setting to 'good character', or virtuous dispositions. Compare MacIntyre's (1981: 38–39) analysis of the evolution of the English 'moral' from a Latin translation of Greek *ethikos*, 'pertaining to character', through a series of transformations ending up with a primary reference to sexual behaviour.

11. Literally 'they cut their wombs': this cutting of the womb, or severing of the ties of kinship, is strongly disapproved of in Islamic thought.

12. I must thank Nadim Ladki for this way of seeing the terms of the debate. Some in Shiite jurisprudential circles have suggested to me that this interest in 'contemporaneity' perhaps explains Khamene'i's approach: as Supreme Leader of the Iranian Republic, just like Khomeini, he is far more immersed in the realities of contemporary life and people's problems than the ulama of the great seminaries. Indeed, his previous political experience was presented as reason for his elevation to the highest

office over scholarly candidates (Clarke 2007a).

13. Shaykh Yusuf al-Qaradawi being, by some criteria, one such example.

14. This restriction is one of custom and not Shiite law. Muhammad Rida Sistani (2004: 54) comments: '[W]e see that custom finds repugnant some things allowed in the shariah, such as someone marrying off his daughter or sister in a temporary marriage especially if she were a virgin and especially with consummation of the marriage.'

15. 'Bootlegged sex is in fact as inferior to what it might be as bootlegged alcohol' (Russell 1929: 126). One cannot resist quoting further, for Russell indeed still speaks to contemporary concerns in much of the world I have been exploring: 'To this extent the moralists have been successful. They have not prevented fornication; on the contrary, if anything, their opposition, by making it spicy, has made it more common. But they have succeeded in making it almost as undesirable as they say it is ... They have compelled young people to take sex neat, divorced from daily companionship, from a common work, and from all psychological intimacy ... A graver matter, while official morality remains what it is, is the risk of occasional disaster ... since it is almost impossible for young people in America to acquire a sound knowledge of birth-control methods, unintended pregnancies are not infrequent ... When young people get into a difficulty, they cannot speak of it to their parents without producing an explosion' (Russell 1929: 127–28). Russell, characteristically, goes on to cite Malinowski's *Sexual life of savages* with approval: 'How much more civilized are the Trobriand Islands, where a father will say to his daughter's lover: "You sleep with my child: very well, marry her."'

16. As a member of Fadlallah's fatwa-issuing department pointed out to me, other authorities do allow such an operation, but only for health reasons: Sayyid Fadlallah sees the very damaging social consequences as constituting sufficient impairment.

17. Although the arguments are rather more complex here, with much turning, as in Western debates, on when the foetus is deemed to have become a full person, or in Islamic terms, when 'ensoulment' has taken place.

18. See Fadlallah (2001, vol. 1: 34–37, 193–200, vol. 2: 340–47; 2003, vol. 1: 46).

19. 'Incest', in its English usage, does occupy some portion of Islamic thought here, but in comparison not a very considerable one. *Zinā* in its broad sense, encompassing fornication, adultery and incest, is what is at issue. In his comprehensive Islamic legal analysis of assisted reproduction, Muhammad Rida Sistani (2004) always takes the trouble to devote a separate small section on the use of gametes from relatives forbidden in

marriage (*mahārim*), but it is always subsumed under the larger heading. The substance that really raises problems is the personal wealth that may or may not be transferred through inheritance, an important consideration in Islamic discussions of donor procedures, as we have seen.

20. Compare the Church of England debates regarding incest in modern times, which I cited in Chapter 1, where arguments from religious texts have indeed been more and more supplanted by 'scientific' arguments (Church of England 1940, 1980; and see Wolfram 1987).

21. In this regard, lest the reader be left with the impression of undue exoticism, Dalton (2000: 197–99) reports that California state law follows much the same principle, which judges have made use of to attribute paternity to nonbiologically related would-be fathers (and see Cannell 1990: 673 on the Warnock Report). The minimum and maximum periods of feasible pregnancy have provoked debate within the Islamic tradition, especially the maximum, extending to up to seven years in the case of the North African Maliki school of Sunni Islamic law. Such extended maximum periods, in the light of the advances in medical science and its prestige in the modern era, have come to seem ridiculous, as has, for instance, the parallel customary notion of the 'sleeping child' (*rāqid*), a foetus that stops its development for some time and then subsequently 'wakes up' again, once widespread in North Africa. These notions in some ways shielded and empowered women (Mir-Hosseini 1993: 143ff.), entitling them to extended protection and maintenance from an unwilling husband, for instance, but have been the subject of reform in modern national law codes and much Islamic scholarship.

22. Notions of propriety again trump those of substance in some Islamic legal discussions of milk kinship. Muhammad Rida Sistani (2004: 480–81) notes that 'the reason for the prohibition [of marriage] between nurse and nursling is not the building of the flesh and strengthening of the bone from her milk, otherwise why is a condition of the obtaining of the prohibition that the milk of the nurse results from a legitimate birth, and were her milk to flow without her bearing child or from *zinā*, then it would not give rise to the prohibition?'

23. I am conscious here that I am basing my account of classical opinion on my reading of secondary sources, which may not have similar concerns in mind. My own expertise is too meagre to do otherwise. But Muhammad Rida Sistani's account, cited below, is surely significant.

24. In a fatwa collection Fadlallah is asked: 'Is the child of *zinā* considered a *natural child* [*walad tabī'ī*], so that all the obligations are arranged such as relation to him, maintenance, guardianship, etc., or not?' Fadlallah replies: 'It is evident that he is a child in all of the effects except inheritance' (2001, vol. 1: 278, my emphasis).

25. Although it should be noted that that process is not wholly complete in British law: the procedure for registering the paternity of a child born outside of wedlock remains more complicated than that of a child born to a married couple. And unmarried fathers of children born before 1 December 2003, that is, before the changes instituted by the Adoption and Children Act 2002 came into force, do not automatically have the same rights as married fathers.

26. Certainly, among these Shiites this principle – which would make their more explicitly biological principle of filiation difficult – is not so often quoted, although Muhammad Rida Sistani (2004: 519ff.) makes clear that it is a tradition they have no doubt in accepting as a legitimate saying of the Prophet, and devotes an entire appendix to discussing its implications. He finds the idea that the child should be related to the husband even were it not his biological child hard to accept: '[The proposed meaning] is that the child relates to the owner of the marital bed whether it was created from their semen or not ... How can one rule that the child created from the semen of one person be a child of another person solely because he is husband of the woman who bore it?!' (2004: 524–25). Sistani finds rather that the principle is intended to apply only in cases where there is doubt as to which the father is, the husband or an adulterer. In this case, the benefit of the doubt is given to the husband. However, Sistani is reluctant to deny the adulterer, where there is no doubt as to his paternity of a resulting child, any relation at all to the child; such denial is what some take the implication of 'and to the adulterer the stone' to be, and is what he finds is the position of the Sunnis. Rather, as in the quotation from his father Ayatollah Sistani's legal handbook above, there is a relation between the two, but it falls short of the *nasab* between legitimate parents, most especially in the matter of inheritance, which there is a clear textual indication for denying.

27. Ayatollah Sistani (2002, vol. 3: 114–15, 370) holds a similar position.

28. Nor need this imply that *nasab* can now be considered as equivalent to genetic relationship. The writer who has gone most deeply into this issue, as far as I have found, Muhammad Rida Sistani (2004: 111–12), feels that it is not genes that are the foundation but the gametes that carry them. In the course of a discussion of IVF procedures where the egg of one woman is implanted in the womb of another, he comments: '[T]here is no principle of inherited characteristics in the topic of *nasab*, neither in custom or the shariah, and were it possible to remove some of the genes from the egg and exchange them with other genes, those of another person or an animal for example, before transplanting it in the womb, that would not detract from the soundness of relating the foetus to the egg

and womb owner.' And in the course of a discussion of testicle transplantation, he reviews the objection that 'the testicle carries the man's characteristic and those of his family and his stock [*'irq*] to his children', and likewise the ovary. He replies: 'Perhaps this is the medical standard of fatherhood and motherhood, and it would require that were it possible to remove some of the genes from the sperm and exchange them with the genes of a sperm from another man then the embryo made from it would be shared between the two males ... But this is not the customary standard of fatherhood and motherhood, as there is no precept of genetic identity in the realisation of *nasab* or lack of it in custom. The child constituted from someone's sperm is counted as a child of that person, even if some of the genes were exchanged for those of another' (2004: 131).

29. I must thank Judith Scheele for translating the relevant sections of Eich's (2005) book on Islamic bioethics for me here. This is not the only approach within Sunni Islam by any means: see Abu Zayd (1996) for an attempt to argue for the integration of biological readings of kinship and paternity testing into the Islamic legal tradition.

30. Although one might note that Christian religious law in Lebanon does admit the concept of the 'natural child', and that the couple in the case in question were Christian.

31. That is, that the child was delivered following a period after the marriage was contracted such that it could have been conceived legitimately.

32. I am very grateful to the author, Dr 'Ali al-Homsi, for his kind gift to me of a copy of this volume.

33. A similar case recorded in the compilation cited above (Homsi 2003: 118–19), from Beirut in 1997, finds a man seeking to have his relation to his daughter revoked: he had laid claim (*iqrār*, see Chapter 2) to be related to her, in order, so he claimed, to grant her Lebanese nationality; one surmises that she was perhaps a Palestinian, who would otherwise have been denied it (see Chapter 2); on other occasions, he seems to have depicted this as an illicit 'adoption' (*tabannī*) on the part of him and his wife. The case was rejected.

34. This blood test, usually used to determine compatibility in the case of an organ transplant, can also be used as a crude paternity test. The doctor concerned worked in one of Lebanon's leading organ transplant centres; paternity testing was a sideline of the laboratory.

35. The HLA tester told me that he had fifty court orders a year, and 200–250 requests from private individuals.

36. Even in cases more complex than a simple question of establishing infidelity, matters of reputation were paramount, as in this example given

to me by the HLA tester: 'I saw a case following a man's death. Ten years afterwards, his wife and children – very prominent, super-rich people – came, saying that someone was claiming that the husband had married someone in secret and had a child, who was now claiming to be part of the family. This is not just inheritance; it's reputation, social embarrassment. They wanted to disprove it. But they couldn't do it: they would have had to exhume the body. We couldn't get a sample otherwise. Getting an order to exhume the body would have been even more embarrassing.'

37. In this regard, a (Sunni) lawyer described a case he was handling where a marriage broke down after the husband's discovery that his wife had had an affair. The husband insisted on a divorce, and also on obtaining a DNA test to establish whether or not their newly born child was his; it was, and he was awarded custody, while the wife was denied it. As the lawyer put it to me: 'In our culture, if the wife commits adultery, she shouldn't have custody because she's not good. The woman has lost credibility as a guardian. I have many copies of laws from the States that say that adultery doesn't affect custody. But *al-amānah* – integrity – is vital in Islamic culture.' (Whether similar considerations would apply in the case of a husband committing adultery is another matter: one rather suspects not.) But of course notions of integrity, including ones centring on sexual morality, are equally vital to parts of 'Western culture', as even the briefest consideration of recent British or U.S. politics would attest – it is not that 'there are no morals', but that they are differently constituted.

38. See above and Deeb (2006: 14ff.). I have admittedly steered clear here of the question as to whether these thinkers see themselves as engaged in a project of 'modernity' per se – perhaps not.

39. Cook (2000) provides a richly documented resource concerning this duty (in Arabic, *al-amr bi-l-ma'rūf wa-l-nahy min al-munkar*). Of course in reality that right to privacy may not be respected, especially as far as explicitly 'Islamic' states are concerned.

40. Rosen's phrase ('the unwanted gaze') is taken from Jewish law, which finds windows onto shared courtyards, for instance, an unacceptable intrusion into privacy (J. Rosen 2000: 18–19). Islamic law recognizes similar concerns (see e.g. Cook 2000; L. Rosen 1989).

GLOSSARY OF ARABIC TERMS

ajnabī (f. *ajnabīyah*): a 'stranger', i.e. not a spouse or family member, 'marriageable'. Also used of a sperm or egg 'donor'.

akhlāq (pl. of *khulq*): 'morals', 'character', in contemporary discourse often referring to sexual morality in particular.

al-ḥamdu lillah: 'praise be to God!', 'thank God!'

al-māl wa-l-banūn zīnat al-ḥayāt al-dunyā: 'wealth and children are the ornament of this life' (Quran 18:46).

al-talqīḥ al-ṣinā'ī / iṣṭinā'ī: 'artificial reproduction', i.e. artificial insemination, but also used of in vitro fertilization and assisted conception generally.

al-walad li-l-firāsh wa-li-l-'āhir al-ḥajar: 'the child to the [marriage] bed, and to the adulterer the stone', a saying attributed to the Prophet Muhammad, often interpreted as meaning that paternity should, by default, be assigned to the husband of a married woman.

'amm: paternal uncle, father's brother.

bint al-'amm: agnatic cousin (female), father's brother's daughter.

ibn al-'amm: agnatic cousin (male), the father's brother's son.

aṭfāl al-anābīb (sing. *ṭifl al-unbūb*): lit. 'test-tube babies', and thus 'in vitro fertilization'.

'awrah: the private parts that should be concealed, widely considered in Islamic law as in the case of the man extending from the navel to the knee and in the case of the woman – before male non-relatives – including all of the body except the face, hands and feet, but in all cases absolutely including the genitals and anus.

ayatollah (*āyat allāh*): 'miraculous sign of God', title of respect for high-ranking members of the Shiite clerical elite.

buwayḍah: ovum, 'egg'.

ḍarūrah: 'necessity', considered a valid justification in Islamic law for permitting an otherwise forbidden act (e.g. eating pork rather than starving to death).

dayyūth: cuckold, pimp.

fatwa: an opinion on Islamic law, issued for the guidance of a non-specialist.

faqīh (pl. *fuqahā'*): Islamic legal specialist, jurisprudent.

fiqh: the Islamic science of jurisprudence, 'Islamic law'.

gharīb: 'strange', 'foreign', 'a stranger', non-relative (see *ajnabī*).

ghayr shar'ī: illegitimate ('non-*shar'ī*', q.v.).

ḥadd: a punishment owed to God, stipulated in the religious texts, as for adultery or theft, for example.

ḥadīth: saying attributed to the Prophet Muhammad.

ḥaqīqī (f. *ḥaqīqīyah*): true, real. As in: *ab ḥaqīqī*, 'real father'; *umm ḥaqīqīyah*, 'true mother'.

ḥaqq (pl. *ḥuqūq*): truth, right. As in: *ḥuqūq al-insān*, 'human rights'.

ḥarām: prohibited, forbidden. As in: *ibn ḥarām*, 'son of sin', illegitimate child.

ḥarām 'alayk: 'shame on you!'

ḥaraj: severe difficulty or inconvenience, providing a justification in (Shiite) Islamic law for otherwise forbidden action (cf. *ḍarūrah*).

hijab (*ḥijāb*): 'the veil', modest apparel.

ḥīlah (pl. *ḥiyal*) *shar'īyah*: legal ruse.

'iddah: the waiting period before remarrying enjoined in Islamic law on a widow or divorcee, of approximately three months, i.e. several menstrual periods, or the full term of pregnancy in the case of a pregnant woman.

iḥtiyāṭ: 'caution', an important principle of Shiite jurisprudence.

ijtihād: independent reasoning exercised by an Islamic jurisprudent.

ikhtilāṭ: 'mixing', 'confounding', e.g. of the sexes. As in: *ikhtilāṭ al-ansāb*, 'confounding of lineages'.

iqrār: claim of a child as one's own.

istinsākh: cloning.

Ja'farite: 'Shiite', in the context of the schools of Islamic jurisprudence, after the sixth Imam of the Shia, Ja'far al-Sadiq (d. AD 765).

kafālah: 'fostering', a near synonym of *takafful*. As in: *kafālat al-yatīm*, 'fostering of orphans'.

karāmah: 'nobility', 'self-respect', 'dignity'. As in: *karāmat al-nasab*, 'nobility of lineage'.

laqīṭ (f. *laqīṭah*): a foundling, with no known parentage.

li'ān: repudiation by a man of his wife on suspicion of adultery.

mahr: bride price, paid by the groom to his bride.

maḥram (pl. *maḥārim*): relative prohibited in marriage.

marja' (pl. *marāji'*), *marja' al-taqlīd*: a Shiite religious authority, lit. a 'source (of emulation)'.

mufti: a 'jurisconsult', an Islamic legal specialist who is competent to is-sue fatwas.

mujtahid: an Islamic legal specialist capable of exercising his own inde-pendent reasoning (*ijtihād*, q.v.) with regard to the religious law.

mukhtār: 'sherrif', responsible for state bureaucratic functions pertaining to identity and residency within a locality.

muṣāharah: relations of marriage, alliance, affinity.

nasab (pl. *ansāb*): ties of filiation, 'consanguinity', lineage.

nuṭfah: 'seed', used of sperm and sometimes ova.

qāḍī: judge, especially an Islamic judge.

qarābah: 'closeness', kinship.

qarīb (pl. *aqribā'*): 'close', a relative.

rabīb (f. *rabībah*): ward, stepson/daughter.

raḍā'ah: breastfeeding, suckling.

raḥim (pl. *arḥām*): 'womb'. As in: *raḥim musta'jarah*, 'hired womb', i.e. surrogate mother; *ṣilat al-raḥim*, 'the womb-tie', kinship, compassion; and hence *qaṭ' al-raḥim*, 'cutting the ties of kin-ship', and pl. *arḥām*, 'relatives'.

riḍa': 'milk kinship', kinship-like relations instituted by breastfeeding.

risālah ['amalīyah]: Islamic legal 'epistle' or treatise written by a *marja'* (q.v.) for the benefit of their followers.

riwāyāt: traditions concerning the Prophet and (for Shiites) the Imams.

ṣāḥib (f. *ṣāḥibah*): 'owner', 'originator', 'possessor'. As in: *ṣāḥib al-la-ban*, 'the owner/originator of the milk'; *ṣāḥib al-nuṭfah*, 'the originator of the sperm'; *ṣāḥibat al-buwayḍah*, 'the originator of the egg'; *ṣāḥibat al-raḥim*, 'the owner of the womb'.

sayyid: 'sir', used of descendants of the Prophet Muhammad, especially among the Shia.

shar'ī: 'legitimate' (see also *ghayr shar'ī*, 'illegitimate').

shariah (*sharī'ah*): the right path through life according to divine standards, 'Islamic law'.

shaykh: 'elder', a common term of respect, widely used of religious specialists.

tabannī: adoption.

ṭabī'ī: 'natural'. As in: *al-qānūn al-ṭabī'ī*, 'natural law', 'the law of nature'; *walad ṭabī'ī*, 'natural child'.

ṭā'ifah (pl. *ṭawā'if*): 'sect', confessional community.

takafful: fosterage.

wakīl: representative, agent.

wasṭa (coll., from classical *wāsiṭah*): go-between, intermediary, 'connections'.

yatīm (f. *yatīmah*): orphan.

zinā: all forms of illegitimate sex, i.e., in Islamic law, sexual relations between those between whom there is no valid marriage contract, and thus including fornication, adultery and incest. As in: *ibn / walad al-zinā*, 'child of *zinā*', illegitimate child, bastard.

BIBLIOGRAPHY

'Abd al-Hadi, Abu Sari' Muhammad. 1994/1415. *Atfāl al-anābīb: Ma'
bayān hukm al-talqīh al-sinā'ī wa-l-nasab wa-l-laqīt wa-l-ta-
bannī wa-tahdīd naw' al-janīn*. Cairo: al-Dar al-Dhahabiyah.

Abisaab, R. 2006. 'The cleric as organic intellectual: Revolutionary
Shi'ism in the Lebanese *hawzas*'. In H. Chehabi (ed.), *Distant
relations: Iran and Lebanon in the last 500 years*. London:
Centre for Lebanese Studies in association with I.B. Tauris, pp.
231–58.

Abou Nasr, M. 2004. 'Government fails to embrace orphans'. *Daily Star*,
Beirut. 31 August.

Abu-Lughod, L. 1998. *Remaking women: Feminism and modernity in the
Middle East*. Princeton, NJ: Princeton University Press.

Abu Zayd, Muhammad Muhammad. 1996/1417. '*Dawr al-taqaddum al-
bīolojī fī ithbāt al-nasab*'. *Majallat al-Buhūth* 20 (1):
223–318.

Adelkhah, F. 1999. *Being modern in Iran*. Trans. J. Derrick. London:
Hurst and Co.

Ajami, F. 1986. *The vanished Imam: Musa al-Sadr and the Shia of
Lebanon*. London: I.B. Tauris.

Al-Azmeh, A. 1993. *Islams and modernities*. London: Verso.

Al-Gazali, L. I., A. Bener, Y. M. Abdulrazzaq, R. Micallef, A. I. Al-
Khayat and T. Gaber. 1997. 'Consanguineous marriages in the
United Arab Emirates'. *Journal of Biosocial Science* 29 (4):
491–97.

Altorki, S. 1980. 'Milk-kinship in Arab society: An unexplored problem
in the ethnography of marriage'. *Ethnology* 19 (2): 233–44.

'. . . and a foundling in Sidon'. 1987. *Al-Nahar*, Beirut. 1 August.

Anderson, J. 1976. *Law reform in the Muslim world*. London: Athlone
Press.

Anees, M. 1984. 'Islamic values and Western science: A case study of reproductive biology'. In Z. Sardar (ed.), *The touch of Midas:
Science, values and environment in Islam and the West*. Man-

chester: Manchester University Press, pp. 91–120.

———. 1989. *Islam and biological futures: Ethics, gender and technology*. London: Mansell.

'Appeal from Dar al-Aytam al-Islamiyah to the parents of a foundling girl'. 1987. *Al-Nahar*, Beirut. 30 July.

Ardener, E. 2007 [1985]. 'Social anthropology and the decline of modernism'. In M. Chapman (ed.), *The voice of prophecy and other essays*. Oxford: Berghahn, pp. 191–210.

Aziz, T. 2001. 'Fadlallah and the remaking of the Marja'iya'. In L. Walbridge (ed.), *The most learned of the Shi'a: The institution of the marja'i taqlid*. Oxford: Oxford University Press, pp. 205–215.

'Baby trading'. 2004. *Al-Nahar*, Beirut. 17 August.

Bargach, J. 2002. *Orphans of Islam: Family, abandonment, and secret adoption in Morocco*. Oxford: Rowman and Littlefield.

Barnes, J. A. 1962. 'African models in the New Guinea Highlands'. *Man* 62 (1): 5–9.

Bearman, P., R. Peters and F. Vogel (eds). 2005. *The Islamic school of law: Evolution, devolution, and progress*. Cambridge, MA: Harvard University Press.

Benkheira, M. 2001a. 'Donner le sein, c'est *comme* donner le jour: La doctrine de l'allaitement dans le sunnisme médiéval'. *Studia Islamica* 92 (1): 5–52.

———. 2001b. 'Review of Giladi, *Infants, parents and wet nurses*'. *Revue de l'Histoire des Religions* 218 (3): 413–17.

Blank, R. 1998. 'Regulation of donor insemination'. In K. Daniels and E. Haimes (eds), *Donor insemination: Social science perspectives*. Cambridge: Cambridge University Press, pp. 131–50.

Bodenhorn, B. 2000. '"He used to be my relative": Exploring the bases of relatedness among the Iñupiat of northern Alaska'. In J. Carsten (ed.), *Cultures of relatedness: New approaches to the study of kinship*. Cambridge: Cambridge University Press, pp. 128–48.

Bonte, P. 1994. 'Manière de dire ou manière de faire: Peut-on parler d'un mariage "arabe"?' In P. Bonte (ed.), *Épouser au plus proche: Inceste, prohibitions et stratégies matrimoniales autour de la Méditerranée*. Paris: Éditions de l'École des Hautes Études en Sciences Sociales, pp. 371–98.

Bonte, P. and É. Conte. 1991. 'La Tribu arabe: Approches anthropologiques et orientalistes'. In P. Bonte, É. Conte, C. Hamès and A.W. Ould Cheikh (eds), *Al-Ansâb: La quête des origines: anthropologie historique de la société tribale arabe*. Paris: Éditions de la Maison des Sciences de l'Homme, pp. 13–48.

Bonte, P., É. Conte and P. Dresch (eds). 2001. *Émirs et présidents: Figures de la parenté et du politique dans le monde arabe*. Paris: CNRS Éditions.

Boswell, J. 1988. *Kindness of strangers: The abandonment of children in Western Europe from late antiquity to the Renaissance*. London: Allen Lane.

Bourdieu, P. 1966. 'The sentiment of honour in Kabyle society'. In J.G. Peristiany (ed.), *Honour and shame: The values of Mediterranean society*. Chicago: University of Chicago Press, pp. 193–241.

———. 1977. *Outline of a theory of practice*. Cambridge: Cambridge University Press.

Brome, V. 1979. *Havelock Ellis, philosopher of sex: A biography*. London: Routledge and Kegan Paul.

Buti, Muhammad Saʻid Ramadan al-. 1998/1419. *Maʻ al-nās: Mashūrāt wa-fatāwā* (vol. 1). Damascus: Dar al-Fikr.

———. 2001/1422. *Mashūrāt ijtimāʻīyah*. Damascus: Dar al-Fikr.

———. 2002/1423. *Maʻ al-nās: Mashūrāt wa-fatāwā* (vol. 2). Damascus: Dar al-Fikr.

Cannell, F. 1990. 'Concepts of parenthood: The Warnock Report, the Gillick debate, and modern myths'. *American Ethnologist* 17 (4): 667-86.

Carsten, J. 1995. 'The substance of kinship and the heat of the hearth: Feeding, personhood and relatedness among Malays of Pulau Langkawi'. *American Ethnologist* 22 (2): 223–41.

———. 1997. *The heat of the hearth: The process of kinship in a Malay fishing community*. Oxford: Clarendon Press.

———. 2000a. 'Introduction'. In J. Carsten (ed.), *Cultures of relatedness: New approaches to the study of kinship*. Cambridge: Cambridge University Press, pp. 1–36.

———. 2000b. '"Knowing where you've come from": Ruptures and continuities of time and kinship in narratives of adoption reunions'. *Journal of the Royal Anthropological Institute* 6 (4): 687–703.

———. 2004. *After kinship*. Cambridge: Cambridge University Press.

Chahine, J. 2004a. 'An evolving culture of adoption in Lebanon?' *Daily Star*, Beirut. 8 September.

———. 2004b. 'For some, being a single parent makes perfect sense'. *Daily Star*, Beirut. 20 April.

———. 2004c. 'Laws in Arab world remain lenient on honor crimes'. *Daily Star*, Beirut. 9 September.

Church of England. 1940. *Kindred and affinity as impediments to marriage: Being the report of a commission appointed by his grace the Archbishop of Canterbury*. London: Society for Promoting

Christian Knowledge.

———. 1980. *No just cause. The law of affinity in England and Wales: Some suggestions for change*. London: CIO Publishing.

Clarke, M. 2005. 'Islam and "new kinship": An anthropological study of new reproductive technologies in Lebanon'. D.Phil. Diss.: University of Oxford.

———. 2006a. 'Shiite perspectives on kinship and new reproductive technologies'. *ISIM Review* (17): 26–27.

———. 2006b. 'Islam, kinship and new reproductive technology'. *Anthropology Today* 22 (5): 17–20.

———. 2007a. 'Children of the revolution: Ayatollah Khamene'i's "liberal" views on *in vitro* fertilisation'. *British Journal of Middle Eastern Studies* 34 (3): 287–303.

———. 2007b. 'Closeness in the age of mechanical reproduction: Debating kinship and biomedicine in Lebanon and the Middle East'. *Anthropological Quarterly* 80 (2): 379–402.

———. 2007c. 'Kinship, propriety and assisted reproduction in the Middle East'. *Anthropology of the Middle East* 2 (1): 70-88.

———. 2007d. 'The modernity of milk kinship'. *Social Anthropology* 15 (3): 1–18.

———. 2008. 'New kinship, Islam and the liberal tradition: Sexual morality and new reproductive technology in Lebanon'. *Journal of the Royal Anthropological Institute* 14 (1): 153–69.

Cole, J. 1983. 'Imami jurisprudence and the role of the ulama: Mortaza Ansari on emulating the supreme exemplar'. In N. Keddie (ed.), *Religion and politics in Iran*. New Haven, CT: Yale University Press, pp. 33–46.

Collier, J. and S. Yanagisako (eds). 1987a. *Gender and kinship: Essays toward a unified analysis*. Stanford, CA: Stanford University Press.

———. 1987b. 'Introduction'. In J. Collier and S. Yanagisako (eds), *Gender and kinship: Towards a unified analysis*. Stanford, CA: Stanford University Press, pp. 1–13.

Conte, É. 1987. 'Alliance et parenté élective en Arabie ancienne: Eléments d'une problématique'. *L'Homme* (102): 119–38.

———. 1991. 'Entrer dans le sang: Perceptions arabes des origines'. In P. Bonte, É. Conte, C. Hamès and A.W. Ould Cheikh (eds), *Al-Ansâb, la quête des origines: Anthropologie historique de la société tribale arabe*. Paris: Éditions de la Maison des Sciences de l'Homme, pp. 55–100.

———. 1994a. 'Choisir ses parents dans la société arabe: La situation à l'avènement de l'islam'. In P. Bonte (ed.), *Épouser au plus proche: Inceste, prohibitions et stratégies matrimoniales autour de la Méditerranée*. Paris: Éditions de l'École des Hautes Études en Sciences Sociales, pp. 165–87.

———. 1994b. 'Le pacte, la parenté et le Prophète: Reflexions sur la proximité parentale dans la tradition arabe'. In F. Héritier-Augé and E. Copet-Rougier (eds), *Les complexités de l'alliance, volume IV: Économie, politique et fondements symboliques*. Paris: Éditions des Archives Contemporaines, pp. 143–85.

———. 2000a. 'Énigmes persanes, traditions arabes: Les interdictions matrimoniales dérivées de l'allaitement selon l'ayatollah Khomeyni'. In J.-L. Jamard, E. Terray and M. Xanthakou (eds), *En substances: Textes pour Françoise Héritier*. Paris: Fayard, pp. 157–81.

———. 2000b. 'Mariages arabes: La part du féminin'. *L'Homme* (154/155): 279–307.

———. 2003. 'Agnatic illusions: The element of choice in Arab kinship'. In F. Abdul-Jabar and H. Dawod (eds), *Tribes and power: Nationalism and ethnicity in the Middle East*. London: Saqi, pp. 15–49.

Cook, M. 2000. *Commanding right and forbidding wrong in Islamic thought*. Cambridge: Cambridge University Press.

Copet-Rougier, E. 1994. 'Le mariage "arabe": Une approche théorique'. In P. Bonte (ed.), *Épouser au plus proche: Inceste, prohibitions et stratégies matrimoniales autour de la Méditerranée*. Paris: Éditions de l'École des Hautes Études en Sciences Sociales, pp. 453–73.

Coulson, N. 1971. *Succession in the Muslim family*. Cambridge: Cambridge University Press.

———. 1979. 'Regulation of sexual behavior under traditional Islamic law'. In A.L. al-Sayyid-Marsot (ed.), *Society and the sexes in medieval Islam*. Malibu, CA: Undena Publications, pp. 63–68.

Crowe, C. 1990. 'Whose mind over whose matter? Women, *in vitro* fertilisation and the development of scientific knowledge'. In M. McNeil, I. Varcoe and S. Yearley (eds), *The new reproductive technologies*. New York: St. Martin's Press, pp. 27–57.

Dalton, S. 2000. 'Nonbiological mothers and the legal boundaries of motherhood: An analysis of California law'. In H. Ragoné and F.W. Twine (eds), *Ideologies and technologies of motherhood: Race, class, sexuality, nationalism*. New York: Routledge, pp. 191–232.

Dawood, N. J. 1990. *The Koran*. London: Penguin.

Deeb, L. 2006. *An enchanted modern: Gender and public piety in Shi'i Lebanon*. Princeton, NJ: Princeton University Press.

Delaney, C. 1991. *The seed and the soil: Gender and cosmology in Turkish village society*. Berkeley: University of California Press.

Dolgin, J. 1997. *Defining the family: Law, technology, and reproduction in an uneasy age*. New York: New York University Press.

Dousset, L. 2005. 'Structure and substance: Combining "classic" and "modern" kinship studies in the Australian Western desert'. *Australian Journal of Anthropology* 16 (1): 18–30.

Dresch, P. 1998. 'Mutual deception: Totality, exchange and Islam in the Middle East'. In W. James and N.J. Allen (eds), *Marcel Mauss: A centenary tribute*. Oxford: Berghahn, pp. 111–133.

———. 2005. 'Debates on marriage and nationality in the United Arab Emirates'. In P. Dresch and J. Piscatori (eds), *Monarchies and nations: Globalisation and identity in the Arab state of the Gulf*. London: I. B. Tauris, pp. 136–57.

Edwards, J. 1999 [1993]. 'Explicit connections: Ethnographic enquiry in north-west England'. In J. Edwards, S. Franklin, E. Hirsch, F. Price and M. Strathern (eds), *Technologies of procreation: Kinship in the age of assisted conception* . London: Routledge, pp. 60–85.

———. 2000. *Born and bred: Idioms of kinship and new reproductive technologies in England*. Oxford: Oxford University Press.

Edwards, J., S. Franklin, E. Hirsch, F. Price and M. Strathern. 1999 [1993]. *Technologies of procreation: Kinship in the age of assisted conception*. London: Routledge.

Eich, T. 2005. *Islam und Bioethik: Eine kritische Analyse der modernen Diskussion im islamischen Recht*. Heidelberg: Reichert.

Eickelman, D. 1976. *Moroccan Islam: Tradition and society in a pilgrimage center*. Austin: University of Texas Press.

———. 2000. Islam and the languages of modernity. *Daedalus* 129 (1): 119–35.

El-Cheikh, N. 2000. 'The 1998 proposed civil marriage law in Lebanon: The reaction of the Muslim communities'. In E. Cotran (ed.), *Yearbook of Islamic and Middle Eastern law, volume 5 (1998–1999)*. London: Kluwer Law International, pp. 147–61.

El-Gemayel, A. (ed.) 1985. *The Lebanese legal system*. Washington, D.C.: International Law Institute.

El-Ghoul, A. 2004. 'Delivering in the toughest of times'. *Daily Star*, Beirut. 25 October.

Fadlallah, 'Abd al-Karim. 2007/1428. *Tifl al-unbūb wa-l-istinsākh*. Beirut: Kalimat.

Fadlallah, Muhammad Husayn. 1995. *Al-tibb wa-l-dīn*. Unpublished manuscript of lecture given at the Sharq al-Awsat Hospital Beirut, 9 September.

———. 1999. *"Indamā naktashif asrār al-kawn… naktashif sirr 'izmat allāh*'. In Markaz al-Dirasat wa-l-Abhath al-Islamiyah-al-Masi-

hiyah (ed.), *Al-instinsākh: Bayna-l-islām wa-l-masīhīyah*.
Beirut: Dar al-Fikr al-Lubnani, pp. 289–90.
———. 2001/1422. *Al-masā'il al-fiqhīyah* (2 vols.). Beirut: Dar al-
Malak.
———. 2002a/1422. *Al-akhlāqīyāt al-tibbīyah wa-akhlāqīyāt al-hayāt*.
Beirut: Al-Markaz al-Islami al-Thaqafi.
———. 2002b. Unpublished manuscript of lecture given at St. Joseph
University Beirut, 1 March.
———. 2003/1424. *Fiqh al-sharī'ah* (3 vols.). Beirut: Dar al-Malak.
———. 2005a/1425. *Dunyā al-mar'ah*. Beirut: Dar al-Malak.
———. 2005b/1426. *Fī āfāq al-hiwār al-islāmīyah al-masīhiyah*. Beirut:
Dar al-Malak.
——— (in conversation with Mona Sukariyah). 2007. *'An sanawāt wa-
mawāqif wa-shakhsīyāt: Hākadhā tahaddath... hākadhā qāl*.
Beirut: Dar al-Nahar.
Fageeh, W., H. Razza, H. Jabbad and A. Marzouki. 2002. 'Transplanta-
tion of the human uterus'. *International Journal of Gynaecology
and Obstetrics* 76 (3): 245–51.
Fargues, P. 2000. *Générations arabes: L'alchimie du nombre*. Paris: Fa-
yard.
Firchow, P. 1984. *The end of utopia: A study of Aldous Huxley's Brave
New World*. Lewisburg, PA: Bucknell University Press.
'First test-tube baby born in Lebanon'. 1989. *Al-Nahar*, Beirut. 17 Oct.
Fortes, M. 1953. 'The structure of unilineal descent groups'. *American
Anthropologist* 55 (1): 17–41.
Fortier, C. 2001. 'Le lait, le sperme, le dos. Et le sang? Représentations
physiologiques de la filiation et de la parenté de lait en islam
malékite et dans la societé maure'. *Cahiers d'Études Africaines*
161 (1): 97–138.
Franklin, S. 1990. 'Deconstructing "desperateness": The social construction of infertility in popular representations of new reproductive
technologies'. In M. McNeil, I. Varcoe and S. Yearley (eds), *The
new reproductive technologies*. New York: St. Martin's Press,
pp. 200–29.
———. 1997. *Embodied progress: A cultural account of assisted conception*. London: Routledge.
———. 1999 [1993]. 'Making representations: The parliamentary debate
on the Human Fertilisation and Embryology Act'. In J. Edwards, S. Franklin, E. Hirsch, F. Price and M. Strathern (eds),
*Technologies of procreation: Kinship in the age of assisted con-
ception*. London: Routledge, pp. 127–65.
Franklin, S. and S. McKinnon. 2001a. 'Introduction'. In S. Franklin and
S. McKinnon (eds), *Relative values: Reconfiguring kinship*

studies. Durham, NC: Duke University Press, pp. 1–25.

——— (eds). 2001b. *Relative values: Reconfiguring kinship studies*. Durham, NC: Duke University Press.

Franklin, S. and H. Ragoné (eds). 1998. *Reproducing reproduction: Kinship, power, and technological innovation*. Philadelphia: University of Pennsylvania Press.

Gaonkar, D. (ed.). 2001. *Alternative modernities*. Durham, NC: Duke University Press.

Ghassoub, A. 2000. 'Commentary on ruling no. 78/2000, on 13/4/2000, concerning a case of establishment of paternity'. *Al-'Adl* 2000: 541–52.

Ghusn, Z. 2001. '*Al-Sayyid Muhammad Husayn Fadl Allāh yashrah fatwā tahlīlihi li-l-istinsākh*'. *Al-Safīr*, Beirut. 28 August.

Giladi, A. 1999. *Infants, parents and wet nurses: Medieval Islamic views on breastfeeding and their social implications*. Leiden: Brill.

Gran, P. 1979. 'Medical pluralism in Arab and Egyptian history: An overview of class structures and philosophies of the main phases'. *Social Science and Medicine* 13B (4): 339–48.

Grosskurth, P. 1981. *Havelock Ellis: A biography*. London: Quartet Books.

Haeri, S. 1989. *Law of desire: Temporary marriage in Iran*. London: I.B. Tauris.

Hajj, Muhammad 'Ali al-. 2006/1427. *Al-hukm al-shar'ī li-l-tajmīd al-haywānāt al-manawīyah wa-l-buwaydāt: Al-ahkām al-shar'īyah al-muta'alliqah bi-"bank al-manī" wa "bank al-buwaydāt" wa mā yatafarra' min-hā*. Beirut: Dar al-Manhal al-Lubnani.

Hajj, Muhammad 'Ali al- and As'ad Jawad. 2007/1428. *Al-masā'il al-muntakhabah, al-'ibādāt wa-l-mu'āmilāt: Tibqa fatāwā Āyat Allāh al-'Uzmā al-Sayyid Abu-l-Qāsim al-Khū'ī wa-Āyat Allāh al-'Uzmā al-Sayyid 'Alī al-Husaynī al-Sīstānī*. Beirut: Dar al-Safwah.

Hakim, Muhammad Sa'id al-Tabataba'i al-. 2001/1422. *Fiqh al-istinsākh al-basharī*. Beirut: al-Murshid.

———. 2002/1422. *Murshid al-mughtarib*. Beirut: al-Murshid.

———. 2004. Email response to questions from the author.

Hallaq, W. 1984. 'Was the gate of ijtihad closed?' *International Journal of Middle East Studies* 16 (1): 3–41.

———. 1996. 'Ifta' and ijtihad in Sunni legal theory: A developmental approach'. In M. K. Masud, B. Messick and D. Powers (eds), *Islamic legal interpretation: Muftis and their fatwas*. Cambridge, MA: Harvard University Press, pp. 33–43.

———. 1997. *A history of Islamic legal theories: An introduction to*

Sunnī usūl al-fiqh. Cambridge: Cambridge University Press.

Hamid, Fawzi Muhammad. 1999/1420. *Al-istinsākh al-bashrī: Bayna-l-tahlīl wa-l-tahrīm*. Damascus: Dar al-Safadi.

Hamiyah, Siham. 2004/1425. *Al-mar'ah fī-l-fikr al-falsafī al-ijtimā'ī al-islāmī: Dirāsah fī fikr al-Sayyid Muhammad Husayn Fadl Allāh*. Beirut: Dar al-Malak.

Handler, R. (ed.). 1995. *Schneider on Schneider: The conversion of the Jews and other stories. David Schneider as told to Richard Handler*. Durham, NC: Duke University Press.

Hatch, E. 1983. *Culture and morality: The relativity of values in anthropology*. New York: Columbia University Press.

Hathout, H. 1991. 'Islamic concepts and bioethics'. In B.A. Lustig (ed.), *Theological developments in bioethics 1988/1990*. London: Kluwer Academic, pp. 103–17.

Hatoum, L. 2004. 'Nonprofit Islamic groups prepare to help needy'. *Daily Star*, Beirut. 15 October.

Hawley, C. 2001. 'Egypt clerics ban surrogate mothers'. *BBC News* (news.bbc.co.uk/1/hi/world/middle_east/1255577.stm; accessed 28/3/2007).

Hayden, C. 1995. 'Gender, genetics and generation: Reformulating biology in lesbian kinship'. *Cultural Anthropology* 10 (1): 41–63.

Héritier, F. 1994. 'Identité de substance et parenté de lait dans le monde arabe'. In P. Bonte (ed.), *Épouser au plus proche: Inceste, prohibitions et stratégies matrimoniales autour de la Méditerranée*. Paris: Éditions de l'École des Hautes Études en Sciences Sociales, pp. 149–64.

———. 1999. *Two sisters and their mother: The anthropology of incest*. Trans. J. Herman. New York: Zone Books.

Hirschkind, C. and S. Mahmood. 2002. 'Feminism, the Taliban, and politics of counter-insurgency'. *Anthropology Quarterly* 75 (2): 339–54.

Hocart, A. M. 1937. 'Kinship systems'. *Anthropos* 32 (3–4): 545–51.

Holy, L. 1989. *Kinship, honour and solidarity: Cousin marriage in the Middle East*. Manchester: Manchester University Press.

———. 1996. *Anthropological perspectives on kinship*. London: Pluto Press.

Homsi, 'Ali al-. 2003/1423. *Majmū'at al-mabādi' wa-l-qawā'id al-shar'īyah wa-l-qānūnīyah allatī tabbaqat-hā al-mahākim al-shar'īyah al-sunnīyah*. Beirut: Manshurat al-Halabi al-Huquqiyah.

Hoodbhoy, P. 1991. *Islam and science: Religious orthodoxy and the battle for rationality*. London: Zed Books.

Hosri, N. al-. 1987. 'The orphaned Lebanese age: Families throw away their children'. *Al-Safir*, Beirut. 8 July.

Howard, J. 1984. *Margaret Mead: A life*. London: Harvill Press.

Howell, S. 2006. *The kinning of foreigners: Transnational adoption in a global perspective*. Oxford: Berghahn.

Hunter, E. 2003. 'Are orphanages the only answer for poor families?' *Daily Star*, Beirut. 8 April.

Huxley, A. 1932. *Brave new world: A novel*. London: Chatto and Windus.

Ibrahim, Muhammad Bin. 1990/1411. *Al-ijtihād wa-qadāyā al-'asr*. Tunis: Dar al-Turki li-l-Nashr.

Inhorn, M. 1994. *Quest for conception: Gender, infertility, and Egyptian medical traditions*. Philadelphia: University of Pennsylvania Press.

———. 1996. *Infertility and patriarchy: The cultural politics of gender and family life in Egypt*. Philadelphia: University of Pennsylvania Press.

———. 2003. *Local babies, global science: Gender, religion, and in vitro fertilization in Egypt*. New York: Routledge.

———. 2004a. 'Middle Eastern masculinities in the age of new reproductive technologies: Male infertility and stigma in Egypt and Lebanon'. *Medical Anthropology Quarterly* 18 (2): 162–82.

———. 2004b. 'Privacy, privatization, and the politics of patronage: Ethnographic challenges to penetrating the secret world of Middle Eastern, hospital-based in vitro fertilization'. *Social Science and Medicine* 59 (10): 2095–108.

———. 2005. 'Religion and reproductive technologies: IVF and gamete donation in the Muslim world'. *Anthropology News* 46 (2): 14.

———. 2006a. '"He won't be my son": Middle Eastern Muslim men's discourses of adoption and gamete donation'. *Medical Anthropology Quarterly* 20 (1): 94–120.

———. 2006b. 'Making Muslim babies: IVF and gamete donation in Sunni versus Shi'a Islam'. *Culture, Medicine and Psychiatry* 30 (4): 427–50.

Jad al-Haqq, 'Ali Jad al-Haqq. 1997/1418 [1980]. '*Al-talqīh al-sinā'ī fī-l-islām*'. In Ministry of Religious Endowments (ed.), *Al-fatāwā al-islāmīyah*, vol. 9, 2nd ed. Cairo: Dar al-Ifta' al-Misriyah, pp. 3213–28.

Joseph, S. 1994. 'Brother/sister relationships: Connectivity, love, and power in the reproduction of patriarchy in Lebanon'. *American Ethnologist* 21 (1): 50–73.

Kahn, S. 2000. *Reproducing Jews: A cultural account of assisted conception in Israel*. Durham, NC: Duke University Press.

Kandela, P. 2000. 'Uterine transplantation failure causes Saudi Arabian government clampdown'. *Lancet* 356 (9232): 838.

Khalaji, M. 2006. *The last marja': Sistani and the end of traditional religious authority in Shiism* (Policy focus no. 59). Washington, D.C.: Washington Institute for Near East Policy.

Khamene'i, 'Ali al-Husayni al-. 2003/1424. *Ajwibat al-istiftā'āt*. Beirut: al-Dar al-Islamiyah.

Khatib-Chahidi, J. 1992. 'Milk-kinship in Shi'ite Islamic Iran'. In V. Maher (ed.), *The anthropology of breast-feeding: Natural law or social construct*. Oxford: Berg, pp. 109–32.

Khlat, M. 1988. 'Consanguineous marriage and reproduction in Beirut, Lebanon'. *American Journal of Human Genetics* 43 (2): 188–96.

Khushn, Husayn al-. 2007/1428. *Fiqh al-qadā': Taqrīran li-bahth Samāhat Āyat Allāh al-'Uzmā al-Sayyid Muhammad Husayn Fadl Allāh* (vol. 2). Beirut: Dar al-Malak.

Kilani, Z. and L. Haj Hassan. 2001. 'Sex selection and preimplantation genetic diagnosis at the Farah Hospital'. *Reproductive BioMedicine* 4 (1): 68–70.

Knauft, B. (ed.). 2002. *Critically modern: Alternatives, alterities, anthropologies*. Bloomington: Indiana University Press.

Kohlberg, E. 1985. 'The position of the walad zinā in Imāmī Shī'ism'. *Bulletin of the School of Oriental and African Studies* 48 (2): 237–66.

Konrad, M. 2005. *Nameless relations: Anonymity, Melanesia and reproductive gift exchange between British ova donors and recipients*. Oxford: Berghahn.

Kuper, A. 2002. 'Incest, cousin marriage and the origin of the human sciences in nineteenth century England'. *Past and Present* 174 (1): 158–83.

Lambert, H. 2000. 'Sentiment and substance in North Indian forms of relatedness'. In J. Carsten (ed.), *Cultures of relatedness: New approaches to the study of kinship*. Cambridge: Cambridge University Press, pp. 73–89.

Lamphere, L. 2001. 'Whatever happened to kinship studies? Reflections of a feminist anthropologist'. In L. Stone (ed.), *New directions in anthropological kinship*. Oxford: Rowman and Littlefield, pp. 21–47.

Landau-Tasseron, E. 2003. 'Adoption, acknowledgement of paternity and false genealogical claims in Arabian and Islamic societies'. *Bulletin of the School of Oriental and African Studies* 66 (2): 169–92.

'Laws concerning children without families: Adoption and fostering to attain their rights'. 1983. *Al-Nahar*, Beirut. 13 April.

Leach, E. 1961. *Rethinking anthropology*. London: Athlone Press.

Lévi-Strauss, C. 1949. *Les structures élémentaires de la parenté*. Paris: Presses Universitaires de France.

Lindholm, C. 1996. *The Islamic Middle East: An historical anthropology*. Oxford: Blackwell.

MacIntyre, A. 1981. *After virtue: A study in moral theory*. London: Duckworth.

Mahmood, S. 2005. *Politics of piety: The Islamic revival and the feminist subject*. Princeton, NJ: Princeton University Press.

Mahmud, 'Abd al-Halim. 1981–1982. 'Fī talqīh atfāl al-anābīb'. In 'A.-H. Mahmud, *Fatāwā al-Imām 'Abd al-Halīm Mahmūd*, vol. 2. Cairo: Dar al-Ma'arif, pp. 245–46.

Mahmudi, Muhsin. 2004/1424. *Ahdāth al-fatāwā*. Beirut: al-Dar al-Islamiyah.

Majma' al-Fiqhi al-Islami al-. 2007a [1985]. *Al-qirār al-thānī: Bi-sha'n al-talqīh al-istinā'ī wa-atfāl al-anābīb*. Websource: http://www.themwl.org/Fatwa (accessed 28 March 2007).

———. 2007b [2002]. *Al-qirār al-sābi': Bi-sha'n al-basmah al-wirāthīyah wa majālāt al-istifādah min-hā*. Websource: http://www.themwl.org/Fatwa (accessed 28 March 2007).

Makdisi, U. 2000. *The culture of sectarianism: Community, history, and violence in nineteenth-century Ottoman Lebanon*. Berkeley: University of California Press.

Maktabah al-Buliyah al- (various authors). 2006. *Akhlāqīyāt tibb al-hayāt*. Jounieh: al-Maktabah al-Buliyah.

Malinowski, B. 1927. *Sex and repression in savage society*. London: Kegan Paul.

———. 1929a. 'Havelock Ellis: As a great personality'. In J. Ishill (ed.), *Havelock Ellis, in appreciation*. Berkeley Heights, NJ: Oriole Press, pp. 279–84.

———. 1929b. *The sexual life of savages in northwestern Melanesia: An ethnographic account of courtship, marriage, and family life among the natives of the Trobriand islands, British New Guinea*. London: Routledge and Sons.

Markaz al-dirasat wa-l-abhath al-islamiyah-al-masihiyah. 1999. *Al-instinsākh: Bayna-l-islām wa-l-masīhīyah*. Beirut: Dar al-Fikr al-Lubnani.

Martin, J. 1996. 'Structuring the sexual revolution'. *Theory and Society* 25 (1): 105–51.

Masud, M. K., B. Messick and D. Powers. 1996. 'Muftis, fatwas and Islamic legal interpretation'. In M. K. Masud, B. Messick and D. Powers (eds), *Islamic legal interpretation: Muftis and their fatwas*. Cambridge, MA: Harvard University Press, pp. 3–32.

Mayer, A. 1995. 'Reform of personal status laws in North Africa: a problem of Islamic or Mediterranean laws?' *Middle East Journal* 49 (3): 432-446.

McLennan, J. F. 1970 [1865]. *Primitive marriage: An inquiry into the origin of the form of capture in marriage ceremonies.* Chicago: University of Chicago Press.

McNeil, M. 1990. 'Reproductive technologies: A new terrain for the sociology of technology'. In M. McNeil, I. Varcoe and S. Yearley (eds), *The new reproductive technologies.* New York: St. Martin's Press, pp. 1–26.

Meirow, D. and J. Schenker. 1997. 'The current status of sperm donation in assisted reproduction technology'. *Journal of Assisted Reproduction and Genetics* 14 (3): 133–38.

Messick, B. 1993. *The calligraphic state: Textual domination and history in a Muslim society.* Berkeley: University of California Press.

———. 1996. 'Media muftis: Radio fatwas in Yemen'. In M. K. Masud, B. Messick and D. Powers (eds), *Islamic legal interpretation: Muftis and their fatwas.* Cambridge, MA: Harvard University Press, pp. 310–20.

Mir-Hosseini, Z. 1993. *Marriage on trial: A study of Islamic family law.* London: I.B. Tauris.

Misbah, 'Abd al-Hadi. 1997/1418. *Al-istinsākh: Bayna-l-'ilm wa-l-dīn.* Cairo: al-Dar al-Misriyah al-Lubnaniyah.

Modell, J. 1994. *Kinship with strangers: Adoption and interpretations of kinship in American culture.* Berkeley: University of California Press.

Moorehead, C. 1992. *Bertrand Russell: A life.* London: Sinclair Stevenson.

Mottahedeh, R. 1987. *The mantle of the prophet: Religion and politics in Iran.* Middlesex: Penguin.

Mughniyah, Muhammad Jawad. 2003/1424. *The five schools of Islamic law: Al-Hanafi, al-Hanbali, al-Ja'fari, al-Maliki, al-Shafi'i (trans. of Al-fiqh 'ala al-madhāhib al-khamsah).* Qom: Ansariyan Publications.

Mundy, M. 1995. *Domestic government: Kinship, community and polity in North Yemen.* London: I.B. Tauris.

Murphy, R. and L. Kasdan. 1959. 'The structure of parallel cousin marriage'. *American Anthropologist* 61 (1): 17–29.

Musallam, B. 1983. *Sex and society in Islam: Birth control before the nineteenth century.* Cambridge: Cambridge University Press.

Needham, R. 1962. *Structure and sentiment: A test case in social anthropology.* Chicago: University of Chicago Press.

———. 1971. 'Remarks on the analysis of kinship and marriage'. In R. Needham (ed.), *Rethinking kinship and marriage.* London:

Tavistock, pp. 1–34.

Norton, A. 2007. *Hezbollah: A short history*. Princeton, NJ: Princeton University Press.

Omran, A. 1992. *Family planning in the legacy of Islam*. London: Routledge.

Parkes, P. 2005. 'Milk kinship in Islam: Substance, structure, history'. *Social Anthropology* 13 (3): 307–29.

Parkin, R. 1997. *Kinship: An introduction to the basic concepts*. Oxford: Blackwell Publishers Ltd.

Parkin, R. and L. Stone. 2004. 'General introduction'. In R. Parkin and L. Stone (eds), *Kinship and family: An anthropological reader*. Oxford: Blackwell Publishing, pp. 1–23.

Patterson, M. 2005. 'Introduction: Reclaiming paradigms lost'. *Australian Journal of Anthropology* 16 (1): 1–17.

Peters, E. 1990. *The Bedouin of Cyrenaica: Studies in personal and corporate power*. Cambridge: Cambridge University Press.

Pfeffer, N. 1987. 'Artificial insemination, in vitro fertilisation and the stigma of infertility'. In M. Stanworth (ed.), *Reproductive technologies: Gender, motherhood and medicine*. Cambridge: Polity Press, pp. 81–97.

Picard, E. 2002. *Lebanon, a shattered country: Myths and realities of the wars in Lebanon*. Trans. F. Philip. New York: Holmes and Meier.

Qaradawi, Yusuf al-. 1990/1410. '*Shatl al-janīn*'. In Y. Qaradawi, *Hady al-islām: Fatāwā mu'āsirah*, 5th ed. Kuwait: Dar al-Qalam, pp. 562–63.

———. 1993/1413. *Al-halāl wa-l-harām fī-l-islām*. Beirut: Dar al-Ta'aruf li-l-Matbu'at.

———. 1994. *The lawful and the prohibited in Islam (Al-halāl wa-l-harām fī-l-islām)*. Trans. M. El-Helbawy, M. Siddiqui and S. Shukry. Plainfield, IN: American Trust Publications.

Rabbath, E. 1986. *La formation historique du Liban politique et constitutionnel: Essai de synthèse*. Beirut: Librairie Orientale.

Ragoné, H. 1994. *Surrogate motherhood: Conception in the heart*. Boulder, CO: Westview Press.

———. 1998. 'Incontestable motivations'. In S. Franklin and H. Ragoné (eds), *Reproducing reproduction: Kinship, power, and technological innovation*. Philadelphia: University of Pennsylvania Press, pp. 118–31.

———. 2000. 'Of likeness and difference: How race is being transfigured by gestational surrogacy'. In H. Ragoné and F. W. Twine (eds), *Ideologies and technologies of motherhood: Race, class, sexuality, nationalism*. New York: Routledge, pp. 56–75.

Ragoné, H. and F. W. Twine (eds). 2000. *Ideologies and technologies of motherhood: Race, class, sexuality, nationalism.* New York: Routledge.

Ridawi, Muhammad Hasan al-. 2002/1423. *Fiqh al-tibb wa-l-tadakhkhum al-naqdī.* Beirut: Mu'asassat Umm al-Qura li-l-Haqiq wa-l-Nashr.

Rispler-Chaim, V. 1993. *Islamic medical ethics in the twentieth century.* Leiden: Brill.

Rivière, P. 1985. 'Unscrambling parenthood: The Warnock Report'. *Anthropology Today* 1 (4): 2–7.

Rosen, J. 2000. *The unwanted gaze: The destruction of privacy in America.* New York: Random House.

Rosen, L. 1989. *The anthropology of justice: Law as culture in Islamic society.* New York: Cambridge University Press.

Rougier, B. 2007. *Everyday jihad: The rise of militant Islam among Palestinians in Lebanon.* Cambridge, MA: Harvard University Press.

Rugh, A. 1995. 'Orphanages in Egypt: Contradiction or affirmation in a family-oriented society'. In E.W. Fernea (ed.), *Children in the Muslim Middle East.* Austin: University of Texas Press, pp. 121–41.

Russell, B. 1929. *Marriage and morals.* London: George Allen and Unwin Ltd.

Russell, D. 1927. *The right to be happy.* London: G. Routledge and Sons.

Sa'di, Dawud Salman al-. 2002/1423. *Al-istinsākh: Bayna-l-'ilm wa-l-fiqh.* Beirut: Dar al-Harf al-'Arabi.

Sa'id, Layla 'Abdallah. 1984. *'Huqūq al-tifl fī muhīt al-usrah'. Majallat al-Huqūq* 8 (3): 207–45.

Salamah, Ziyad Ahmed. 1998/1419. *Atfāl al-anābīb: Bayna-l-'ilm wa-l-sharī'ah.* Amman: Al-Dar al-'Arabiyah li-l-'Ulum.

Salvatore, A. 1997. *Islam and the political discourse of modernity.* Reading: Ithaca.

Sankari, J. 2005. *Fadlallah: The making of a radical Shi'ite leader.* London: Saqi.

Scheffler, H. 1991. 'Sexism and naturalism in the study of kinship'. In M. di Leonardo (ed.), *Gender at the crossroads of knowledge: Feminist anthropology in the postmodern era.* Berkeley: University of California Press, pp. 361–82.

Schneider, D. 1965. 'Some muddles in the models: Or, how the system really works'. In M. Banton (ed.), *The relevance of models for social anthropology.* London: Tavistock, pp. 25–86.

———. 1972. 'What is kinship all about?' In P. Reining (ed.), *Kinship studies in the Morgan centennial year*. Washington, DC: Anthropological Society of Washington, pp. 32–63.

———. 1980 [1968]. *American kinship: A cultural account*. Chicago: University of Chicago Press.

———. 1984. *A critique of the study of kinship*. Ann Arbor: University of Michigan Press.

Serour, G. 1993. 'Bioethics in artificial reproduction in the Muslim world'. *Bioethics* 7 (2–3): 207–17.

———. 1998. 'Reproductive choice: A Muslim perspective'. In J. Harris and S. Holm (eds), *The future of human reproduction: Ethics, choice and regulation*. Oxford: Clarendon Press, pp. 191–202.

Serour, G., M. El Ghar and R. T. Mansour. 1991. 'In vitro fertilization and embryo transfer in Egypt'. *International Journal of Gynaecology and Obstetrics* 36 (1): 49–53.

Shah, S. 1995. 'Surrogate parenting: Its legal and moral implications in the Islamic law'. *Hamdard Islamicus* 18: 109–20.

Shaltut, Mahmud. 1965. *Al-fatāwā: Dirāsah li-mushkilāt al-muslim al-muʿāsir fī-l-hayāt al-yawmīyah wa-l-ʿāmmah*. Cairo: Dar al-Qalam.

Shirazi, Makarim al-. 1998/1377–1419. *Al-fatāwā al-jadīdah* (vol. 1). Qom: Madrasat al-Imam ʿAli bin Abi Talib.

———. 2003/1424. *Al-fatāwā al-jadīdah* (vol. 2). Qom: Madrasat al-Imam ʿAli bin Abi Talib.

Simpson, R. 1994. 'Bringing the "unclear" family into focus: Divorce and re-marriage in contemporary Britain'. *Man* (n.s.) 29 (4): 831–51.

———. 2001. 'Making "bad" deaths "good": The kinship consequences of posthumous conception'. *Journal of the Royal Anthropological Institute* 7 (1): 1–18.

———. 2004a. 'Gays, paternity and polyandry: Making sense of new family forms in contemporary Sri Lanka'. In R. Chopra, C. Osella and F. Osella (eds), *South Asian masculinities: context of change, sites of continuity*. New Delhi: Women Unlimited, an associate of Kali for Women, pp. 160–74.

———. 2004b. 'Impossible gifts: Bodies, Buddhism and bioethics in contemporary Sri Lanka'. *Journal of the Royal Anthropological Institute* 10 (4): 839–59.

———. 2004c. 'Localising a Brave New World: New reproductive technologies and the politics of fertility in contemporary Sri Lanka'. In M. Unnithan-Kumar (ed.), *Human reproduction, medical technologies and health*. Oxford: Berghahn, pp. 43–57.

———. 2006. 'Scrambling parenthood: English kinship and the prohibited degrees of affinity'. *Anthropology Today* 22 (3): 3–6.

Sistani, 'Ali al-Husayni al-. 2000/1420. *Al-fiqh li-l-mughtaribīn*. Beirut: Dar al-Mu'arrikh al-'Arabi.

——. 2002/1423. *Minhāj al-sālihīn* (3 vols.). Qom: Maktabat Fadak.

Sistani, Muhammad Rida al-. 2004/1425. *Wasā'il al-injāb al-sinā'īyah*. Beirut: Dar al-Mu'arrikh al-'Arabi.

Skovgaard-Petersen, J. 1997. *Defining Islam for the Egyptian state*. Leiden: Brill.

Smith, W. R. 1885. *Kinship and marriage in early Arabia*. Cambridge: Cambridge University Press.

Sonbol, A. 1995. 'Adoption in Islamic society: A historical survey'. In E.W. Fernea (ed.), *Children in the Muslim Middle East*. Austin: University of Texas Press, pp. 45–67.

Stenberg, L. 1996. *The Islamization of science: Four Muslim positions developing an Islamic modernity*. Stockholm: Almqvist and Wiksell International.

Stone, L. 1997. *Kinship and gender: An introduction*. Boulder, CO: Westview Press.

——. 2001. 'Introduction: Theoretical implications of new directions in anthropological kinship'. In L. Stone (ed.), *New directions in anthropological kinship*. Oxford: Rowman and Littlefield, pp. 1–20.

——. 2004a. 'Contemporary directions in kinship: Introduction'. In R. Parkin and L. Stone (eds), *Kinship and family: An anthropological reader*. Oxford: Blackwell Publishing, pp. 331–41.

——. 2004b. 'Has the world turned? Kinship and family in the contemporary American soap opera'. In R. Parkin and L. Stone (eds), *Kinship and family: An anthropological reader*. Oxford: Blackwell Publishing, pp. 395–407.

Strathern, M. 1992a. *After nature: English kinship in the late twentieth century*. Cambridge: Cambridge University Press.

——. 1992b. *Reproducing the future: Anthropology, kinship, and the new reproductive technologies*. New York: Routledge.

——. 1993. 'Review of K. Weston, *Families we choose: lesbians, gays, kinship*'. *Man* (n.s.) 28 (1): 195–96.

——. 1999a [1993]. 'Introduction to the first edition'. In J. Edwards, S. Franklin, E. Hirsch, F. Price and M. Strathern (eds), *Technologies of procreation: Kinship in the age of assisted conception*. London: Routledge, pp. 9–28.

——. 1999b [1993]. 'Regulation, substitution and possibility'. In J. Edwards, S. Franklin, E. Hirsch, F. Price and M. Strathern (eds), *Technologies of procreation: Kinship in the age of assisted conception*. London: Routledge, pp. 171–202.

——. 2005. *Kinship, law and the unexpected: Relatives are always a surprise*. Cambridge: Cambridge University Press.

Taha, ʻAli Hasan. 2000/1421. *Al-istinsākh al-jīnī: Bayna-l-ʻilm wa-l-dīn*. Beirut: Dar al-Nada.

'The Islamic orphanage: 17 foundlings received by the orphanage in 3 months'. 1987. *Al-Nahar*, Beirut. 7 July.

Traboulsi, Ibrahim. 2000. *Al-zawāj wa-mafāʻīl-hu lada-l-tawāʼif al-mashmūlah fī qānūn 2 nīsān 1951*. Beirut: Al-Manshurat al-Huquqiyah.

Tremayne, S. 2006. 'Not all Muslims are Luddites'. *Anthropology Today* 22 (3): 1–2.

———. 2009. 'Law, ethics, and donor technologies in Shia Iran'. In M. Inhorn and D. Birenbaum-Carmeli (eds), *Assisting reproduction, testing genes: Global encounters with the new biotechnologies*. Oxford: Berghahn (in press).

Tuhmaz, ʻAbd al-Hamid bin Mahmud. 1987/1408. *Al-awlād wa-l-ansāb: Dirāsah li-mawqif al-sharīʻah al-islāmīyah min al-talqīh al-sināʻī wa-mā bi-atfāl al-anābīb*. Beirut: Dar al-ʻUlum.

ʻUlwani, ʻAbd al-Wahid (ed.). 1997. *Al-istinsākh: Jadal al-ʻilm wa-l-dīn wa-l-akhlāq*. Beirut: Dar al-Fikr al-Muʻasir.

van Gelder, G. 2005. *Close relationships: Incest and inbreeding in classical Arabic literature*. London: I.B. Tauris.

Walbridge, L. 2001a. 'Introduction: Shiʻism and authority'. In L. Walbridge (ed.), *The most learned of the Shiʻa: The institution of the marjaʻi taqlid*. Oxford: Oxford University Press, pp. 3–13.

———. 2001b. 'The counterreformation: Becoming a *marjaʻ* in the modern world'. In L. Walbridge (ed.), *The most learned of the Shiʻa: The institution of the marjaʻi taqlid*. Oxford: Oxford University Press, pp. 230–46.

Weston, K. 1991. *Families we choose: Lesbians, gays, kinship*. New York: Columbia University Press.

Wolfram, S. 1987. *Inlaws and outlaws: Kinship and marriage in England*. London: Croom Helm.

Yacoub, A. 2001. *The fiqh of medicine: Responses in Islamic jurisprudence to developments in medical science*. London: TaHa Publishers Ltd.

Yanagisako, S. and C. Delaney. 1995. *Naturalizing power: Essays in feminist cultural analysis*. New York: Routledge.

Yasin, ʻAbd al-Latif. 2000/1421. *Al-istinsākh: Bayna-l-dīn wa-l-ʻilm*. Damascus: Union of Arab Writers.

Yoxen, E. 1990. 'Conflicting concerns: The political context of recent embryo research policy in Britain'. In M. McNeil, I. Varcoe and S. Yearley (eds), *The new reproductive technologies*. New York: St. Martin's Press, pp. 173–99.

Zuhayli, Wahbah al-. 2002/1422. *Al-fiqh al-islāmī wa-adillat-hu* (11 vols.). Damascus: Dar al-Fikr.

———. 2003/1424. *Fatāwā mu'āsirah*. Damascus: Dar al-Fikr.

INDEX

'Abd al-Basit, Shaykh, 114n41,
115n45
'Abd al-Hadi, Dr Abu Sari', 113n29
abortion, 33, 50n12, 155, 1700
 Islamic legal opinions on, 70, 71,
 86n28, 108n2, 193, 195
adoption
 Adoption and Children Act (Britain,
 2002), 213n25
 as theme of the new kinship studies,
 30
 example from Syria of, 21–24
 Hague Convention on (1993), 86n30
 in Egypt, 86n31, 89n50
 in Lebanon, 72–82, 88n40, 202,
 214n33
 in pre-Islamic Arabia, 45–46, 54n49
 Islamic precepts, 23, 24, 46, 72–74,
 80–81, 86n31, 122
 'simple' vs. 'strong', 86n30
 See also fostering, *kafālah, tabannī,*
 takafful
adultery, 41, 101, 103, 113n29, 120,
 124, 141, 147n35, 154, 167,
 177n1, 186, 204, 209n3,
 215n37. *See also zinā*
al-ahwat wujūban. See caution
ajnabī (-yah), 52n24, 100–101,
 111n19, 118, 120, 122, 143n11.
 See also gharīb
Anees, Munawar, 17n3, 109n9, 198
animals (in Islamic discussions of
 kinship and ART), 95–96, 102,
 109n7, 112n24, 115n46, 213n28
anonymity, 11, 12, 156. *See also*

confidentiality, identity, privacy,
 secrecy
artificial insemination, 21, 31–32, 35,
 37, 50n10, 192, 196
 by donor (AID), 21, 31–32, 98, 99,
 104–5, 109n9, 112n25, 120,
 127, 135, 141, 143n9, 145n24,
 146n25, 146n28, 157, 167–68,
 173–74, 191, 193, 198
 by husband (AIH), 98, 101
 Christian opinions on, 112n27
 in Lebanese medical practice, 157,
 163–64, 167–68
 Islamic opinions on, 93, 98–105,
 108, 111n18, 111n20, 120, 122,
 128, 138, 141, 142n1, 146n27,
 192, 196
 using frozen semen after the donor's
 death. *See* postmortem use of
 gametes
assisted reproduction. *See* artificial
 insemination, ICSI, IVF,
 postmortem use of gametes,
 surrogacy
astronomy (used to determine dates of
 the Islamic calendar), 85n21
'Atwi, Shaykh Muhsin, viii, 9–10,
 125–27, 130–31, 132, 133,
 145nn20–22
'awrah, 131. *See also* private parts
Azhar University, al-, 17n3, 37, 64, 98,
 113n31, 114n43, 115n47,
 115n49, 144n14, 178n7
 Shaykhs of, 83n5, 86n31, 89n44, 95,
 100, 102, 109n5, 109n12

www.ingramcontent.com/pod-product-compliance
Lightning Source LLC
Chambersburg PA
CBHW072100020426
42334CB00017B/1582